BIGGER THAN US

BIGGER THAN US

Fearne Cotton

HAPPY BOOKS PLACE

1

Published in 2022 by Ebury Press an imprint of Ebury Publishing
20 Vauxhall Bridge Road,
London SW1V 2SA

Ebury Press is part of the Penguin Random House group of companies
whose addresses can be found at global.penguinrandomhouse.com

First published by Ebury Press in 2022

www.penguin.co.uk

A CIP catalogue record for this book is available from the British Library

ISBN 978 1 52910 866 8

Typeset in Sabon Next and Hello Branch
Title font set in Sud Typeface © VJ Type
Typeset by seagulls.net
Printed and bound in Great Britain by Clays Ltd, Elcograf S.p.A.

The authorised representative in the EEA is Penguin Random House
Ireland, Morrison Chambers, 32 Nassau Street, Dublin D02 YH68.

Penguin Random House is committed to a
sustainable future for our business, our readers
and our planet. This book is made from Forest
Stewardship Council® certified paper.

For Lyndell Mansfield,

love you Pinky.

CONTENTS

Introduction 1

PART 1: LOVE

Shamans 17

Meditation and Yoga 45

The Law of Attraction 73

PART 2: AWARENESS

Energy 105

Enneagrams 131

Astrology and
Planetary Movement 153

PART 3: COMMUNICATION

Prayer 183

Signs 205

Ritual and Ceremony 225

Mediums and Intuition 249

PART 4: SOMETHING BIGGER EVERY DAY

Connection 275

Going Deeper: Further reading
and information 289

Thank yous 294

INTRODUCTION

Writing this book has changed my life. I've gulped down knowledge with an unrivalled thirst and made willing changes to my life in the name of finding a deeper connection and hopefully to write a book that will be meaningful to you. Yet I had no idea of the impact it would have on me. I had no clue that so much would change in such a short space of time. I'm confident it'll have a similar effect on you. All I'm asking is that you have an open mind and then just sit back and enjoy learning from a host of wise minds I'm going to introduce you to.

I'm at a pivotal point in life where I feel that the lurking fog, which crept in like a November morning in my early thirties, is lifting. This book has marked the start of a process of shedding I didn't even know I needed, with old layers of life peeling away, falling off in great swaths to reveal new perspectives and a much welcomed lightness. Are you up for it? Do you want to dig deeper with me? Let me put some lexical oomph behind this life pivot and explain what we are about to do.

By now we all have a rough idea of how to look after our bodies and minds. We know that eating a balanced diet, doing a bit of exercise and remembering that cigarettes look cool in films but suck for our lungs will help our bodies out. We know that having decent relationships with others, doing things we love and refraining from bingeing social media will give us a healthier mind. But what about the other bit? The … what-do-you-wanna-call-it bit? The soul? Spirit? Awareness? Energy? I don't mind what you call it as I'm not sure what name to pin on it myself, but I know it's there. I personally believe – wait, sod it, I want to be pretty definite about this – I KNOW that I am not just a body and a mind. There is some other inexplicable part of me which I think gets forgotten about far too regularly; the part of me that feels a deep instant connection with certain strangers I've met over the years; the part of me that is pure intuition and knows the answer even though I'm tempted to google the question; the part of me that felt and saw a celestial rainbow of colours during childbirth; the part of me that has felt pure bliss when tripping out looking at the sky; the part of me that could burst into a million tiny pieces when hearing a song that just gets me. How am I looking after that part of me? We'll get to that later as we romp through this complex, deep and hopefully nurturing journey together.

As well as nurturing that part of ourselves that gets massively overshadowed by our bodies and minds, I want to explore the concept of everything else outside of us too – again, call it what you like: God, a higher power, the universe – and how we connect and perhaps even communicate with it. Not to complicate matters too much early on but this exterior energy, or higher power, is recognised by many spiritual leaders as something that is within us, not outside of us as we may believe; but, again, we'll get to all of this later down the line.

Reconnecting with Life

I believe that we need to look at this part of ourselves and find new ways to expand our thinking now more than ever before. En masse we've never been in more trouble and we know it. We can't always pinpoint why but the jittery feeling of discontentment is never far away. There probably hasn't been a time in history when we have been so stressed, anxious, depressed, confused and at times disheartened. We are more technologically advanced than ever before, can video-call someone on the other side of the planet, order shoes that arrive on the same day, send satellites into space to aid/support us navigate our route to work and have modern medicine to help us in physical crises, yet we're usually dissatisfied and feel we are lacking. We have more than any other generation, yet that feeling of lacking is growing by the minute. I think all of these uncomfortable feelings are rooted in our total subliminal disconnect. It's something I've talked about at length to my dear friend Sarah Wilson (activist, writer and all-round amazing egg). We are all in 'disconnect'. We know we are abusing our planet, we know we aren't always genuinely connecting with other humans heart to heart, we know we are driven more by fear and less by love and are floundering around wondering why we feel so off-centre. We cannot fix this feeling with a new workout, by changing our diets or with mindfulness alone. Something much bigger, more expansive and more powerful is needed. Connection.

Connection isn't calling up your mate once a week to check in (lovely as that is). True connection is remembering we are all one – not just as individual humans (which we seemingly forget on a daily basis with our road rage, divisive attitudes and war), but also with nature. There is no separation or distinction. That might not ring true to you immediately but it is something I'm going to explore in this book as we work out how to nurture our souls and get back to total connection.

The Hugeness of Life

The title of this book, *Bigger Than Us*, is supposed to be relieving, evoking an en masse collective 'phew' that maybe there is something larger at play. This is not to diminish the human experience, my life or yours, it's simply a way of thinking that allows us to take the heat out of the small annoyances and problems in life so we can remember how huge all of this is. If we remember that we are on a ball spinning in space, and the ONLY ball we know of with life on it – with our own sun and moon and other planets beautifully dancing with synchronicity and precision nearby, all held in place due to energy that we can't see – then maybe it won't matter so much that we messed up at work or said something stupid we regret. Looking at energy allows us to get out of our heads and marvel at the magic that is constantly unfolding all around us. Life is bloody HUGE.

My head is already bursting with thoughts and questions, but hey, that's the mind just trying to steal the limelight again.

More Magic

I would have been petrified to write a book like this five years ago. I would have typed trepidatiously while second-guessing what every cynical person out there might say. I have always felt inferior to cynical people. I've labelled them 'cool', 'edgy' perhaps even more 'intellectual' than me but, honestly, at this point in my life I'm so over that. I love exploring spirituality and what else lies within us and outside of us. The magic, the connection, the inexplicable. I LOVE IT! I'm an out-and-out spiritual junkie and there is no stopping me. So, in short, if you are extremely cynical about this sort of thing, that's cool, welcome along. My job with this book is not to convince you otherwise; it's to hopefully give you some other options and tools that might help you find more meaning, magic and purpose in life.

We often think purpose comes from having power or opportunity but that's not the sort of purpose I'm talking about. I'm talking about purpose and meaning from within. An inner knowing that propels you towards a deeper experience of life. This book is about getting under the itchy clothes of life. Getting beneath the thoughts, rumination and constant noise of the modern world. It's connecting the dots and making sense of the nonsensical. This process throughout the book is not going to be wishy-washy or surface. This book isn't exclusively about burning incense and partaking in gong baths while wearing smocks (although they may feature if there is reason to); it's about getting curious and cultivating the willingness to see life in its full-coloured, bold, ever-changing beauty. I heard a term coined recently that made sense of the commodification of spirituality in recent years: 'spirituality lite', nodding to the vast interest in spiritual rituals without the deeper exploration or openness underpinning them. For example (and please remember I'm not judging anyone here as I'm on this learning curve with you all), many out there may partake in yoga waiting for a six-pack to emerge without experiencing the deep connection from the breath work and mental stillness of the practice. Many will burn sage in their homes hoping that negative energy will magically disappear from their lives without any willingness to look at why they might be attracting negative energy into their lives in the first place. For us to go on this journey together, you will not need to purchase a rose quartz toilet seat or go anywhere near a wind chime. You need nothing more than an open mind and a little curiosity.

The Speed of Life

I'm also deeply fascinated with finding out if it is entirely possible to live a DAILY spiritual life in the velocity of the modern world. I know that minutes after coming out of a meditative state I can shoot to pure rage that my next-day delivery hasn't turned up. The irony! One minute purely IN the moment, the next using time as a weapon against myself. If I'm honest, my spiritual awareness is mostly only rearing its head in those moments I actively carve out time for it. But what about the messy bits of modern life: a bulging inbox, kids screaming and demanding to watch YouTube even when you've said no, a traffic jam and you're half an hour late for work, a friend accusing you of neglect. How can we tap into spirituality in those moments? I'm at a juncture in life where I know that following a spiritual path makes me feel good and now it's time to really commit to it. Spirituality is often seen as an add-on, the extra bit on the side, but more recently I've started to see that it IS life. It's not the side dish to the main course of life. It is the WHOLE meal – starter, main and dessert – the rest is merely seasoning.

I want more peace, a deeper connection, a trust in life, faith instead of worry, more meaningful moments, acceptance in the messy bits, even MEANING in the messy bits. I know the only way for me to do this is to take an even deeper dive into theories, methodologies and practices that have been around way, WAY longer than the internet and modern science.

Making the Ordinary Extraordinary

This isn't a new way of thinking for me, thanks to dear Lin Cotton. The mothership and I have talked about spirituality more than any other subject over my lifetime. Mum is on a constant mission for meaning and mostly magic. She often wants the magical answer or explanation to help soothe worry and fear rather than a statistic or something purely practical. I've watched her zoom in on orbs in photographs to find minuscule, hidden images that may inspire or guide her. She has found many blurry outlines of her late dog Wilf trapped in floating orbs caught on camera in a snapshot moment, which may sound very out of the box to you but, again, if these moments bring peace and connection to the individual, why question it or judge? She always actively encouraged me to look outside of everyday thinking to find the extraordinary and I'm eternally grateful for that. At a young age, I was inadvertently introduced by Mum, to meditation even though I had no clue what it was. She had a cassette (for anyone under twenty-five reading this, you can indeed have sympathy for my generation having to rely on cassettes and their often-tangled tape) which she would often pop on for us both to listen to. We would lie on the '80s dusty-pink floral sofa and zone out while listening to an audio experience that to this day is still crystal clear in my mind. The narrator, using hushed tones, would usher you through a wooden door at the end of a long mosaic-tiled corridor and there you would find yourself in a house with many rooms. Each room we were guided into held a different colour from the last. The first room was red with many red objects within, which you could pick up and examine. The next room was yellow in hue and contained many sunshine-coloured objects of interest. I adored letting my mind wander through this imaginary house and eventually on to a shoreline on a beach umbrellaed with stars. I can so vividly remember the images my imagination threw up in those childhood moments, perhaps more vividly than the real-life occurrences that I experienced. What I didn't realise was that this imagined house was emulating the chakras and their colours and purpose. As an eight-year-old I merely found it a relaxing and super-fun experience but really it was a beautiful, gentle introduction to how we can relax our minds into a meditative state. This experience also subliminally taught me to look outside the box. To reach for the seemingly impossible, to seek the magic and to make the ordinary extraordinary.

Pinner Daze

I grew up in a suburban town on the outskirts of London in a mock Tudor semi-detached house with a hard-working mum who held down four different jobs and a dad who honed his craft as a sign writer for his whole working life (bar a brief stint as a milkman before I was born). Nothing out of the ordinary there. A classic '80s/'90s suburban childhood full of school-packed lunches, chats on house phones and the odd camping holiday thrown into the mix. Yet Mum was always up for the extraordinary, often desperately seeking it out. On Pinner High Street above a small shop that sold crystals and wind chimes there was a therapy room. I just had to call my mum to reacquaint myself with the name of this shop as the decades have made the memory fade to sepia tones and she tells me, with absolute clarity, the shop was called Dreamcatcher, which is no surprise to any of us. You could get many treatments, from reiki to energy healing and past life regression, all while, below the treatment-room window, the good people of Pinner bought their weekly shop in the giant Tesco over the road. My first experience of Pinner's very own spiritual portal was around the age of sixteen. Mum had been before and said I might have fun booking in for a past life regression session. After making my way past an Everest-sized pile of crystals in Dreamcatcher's shop entrance, I ducked under the stalactites of wind chimes hanging from every inch

of the ceiling, to make my way upstairs to the treatment room.
A middle-aged lady with coiled tangerine hair asked me to lie
down and close my eyes. I can't recall exactly what happened
next but I imagine that, while I had my eyes closed, she waved
her hands around, over and above my body, never touching me
but giving off that buzz of energy that is often experienced with
reiki. Now hold on to your hats as I tell you the part you'll either
be fascinated by or laugh your head off at. The first past life she
recalled for me was from a period in the early 1900s where I had
a twin brother who was my partner in crime as a trapeze artist.
We would swing together in synchronised beauty high above
a cheering crowd. On one occasion I lost my grip and my dear
twin's hands slipped through my fingers like a wet bar of soap
and he fell to his death. Tragic, I know, and maybe far-fetched
but I loved the process nonetheless and, even if I came away not
100 per cent wedded to the story itself, it massively piqued my
interest in past life regression. It could also be tenuously linked
to my omnipresent need to make sure everyone in my life is OK
and safe at all times, who knows?

I more recently spoke to the incredible Rhonda Byrne,
author of *The Secret*, and she talked passionately about how we
never die as our 'energy' (insert here 'spirit/soul' or whatever you
are comfortable with) can never die. You don't have to believe in
reincarnation to be on board with this one as none of us truly
know where our energy goes once the physical part of us dies.
Could it embody another physical form or just weave into our
complex universe in inexplicable ways?

Mum (gosh, this is such a Lin-heavy section, she's going to
love it) also used to open my eyes to alternative possibilities on
our evening walks. Eager to break the mundanity of suburban
routine, instead of settling for *Coronation Street* after our Linda
McCartney sausages, we would stomp around the mean blocks

of Ruislip at dusk. These chats would veer off into the deep expanses of life's unimaginable possibilities as Mum reached for the stars above the mock Tudor maze. On one occasion Mum stopped in her tracks and looked around. I mimicked her stance and looked for what had caught Mum's eye.

'Do you feel it?' she whispered. I stopped and looked into the distance with a little more focus and … I did, I did feel a shift in something. This is where things get a little weird again but, you know me, I love weird. The air seemed thicker, time seemed to have stopped. We both marvelled at this secluded moment, just me, Mum and this strange shift in energy we were both feeling and possibly even seeing. Everything looked a little more hazy than normal, a little purple even. Team cynical will of course say there must have been a nearby bonfire or a heavy mist en route but it didn't feel like that. Team cynical, I love you just as much as those who are nodding their heads right now having experienced something similar. We can of course continue to look exclusively for the scientific explanation for everything, but maybe there is a little room for intrigue, magic and the totally weird that is left unexplained too. We felt something inexplicable on our nightly walk that summer's evening. An invisible movement and an all-encompassing shift of sorts. The delicious juxtaposition of the extraordinary in the setting of the totally ordinary.

Something Bigger

My unusual experiences as a kid and teen are not limited to these two isolated moments. These often inexplicable or deeply connecting moments are woven through my life like a silver thread, reminding me of the beauty, strangeness and hugeness of life. I'm yet to make sense of all of these moments so hope to learn as much as I can during this process. Maybe you'll have had similar experiences that I'll be able to help you make sense of too, or maybe all of this is new to you, in which case, HOW BLOODY EXCITING! I'm buzzed for you and what you're about to read and hopefully experience too.

Do not fret, this book is not going to be exclusively my trippy experiences from the Pinner High Street days; spirituality of course goes way beyond a few freaky experiences and a local crystal shop. We have so much to cover and so much to learn. I'm the most eager student, notepad in hand, eyes wide, ready to go. **I feel very lucky to have gained insights and teachings from a plethora of experienced, wise and incredibly smart individuals from varying backgrounds with differing expertise, who can guide us through theories and practices to help us connect with life, ourselves and others.** They will share their knowledge and impart advice on how we can look after our energy/soul/spirit, which will subsequently help us remember that we are connected to everyone and everything. I hope this book will also act as a reminder that spirituality is for everyone no matter where you are from, what you've got going on, or what you currently believe or don't believe.

Even though I've been borderline obsessed by this stuff for most of my life, I still have so much to learn and so much to unpick. I have a kaftan full of questions and my excitement is of seismic proportions, so shall we crack on?

Are you ready to see past the human body and mind so we can have a poke around in the other bit? Are you ready to experience something bigger than us?

PART 1

LOVE

Is there anything bigger than love? It's all-encompassing and the catalyst to life itself but when we can't see it, life can feel barren, brittle and unforgiving. Love is safety, comfort, reassurance, motivation, community-building, miracle-making. It is omnipresent and everywhere, so why at times does it seem to vanish completely?

When we are lonely, depressed or full of rage, we are blind to love's power and mass. It seemingly dissipates before our very eyes at the mere whiff of negative distraction. Life's distractions can be so big that we forget it is our lifeboat whenever we need it – we just have to remember that it's not always exclusively an exterior source of love that can carry us through life, it is also always within.

We often think of love as a rather one-dimensional proposal. It's all red roses and romantic dinners backed by a sunset. We forget that love is the driving force behind each unfurling flower and pulsing through every jolt of hysterical laughter. We usually only recognise the romantic or family aspect of love but it has so many other sides.

It's so powerful that when we refuse to see it, we create a vicious friction that separates, causes suffering and sparks war. In those moments where we are blind to the love that is around us and within us, we lose our connection. Self-loathing or judgement upon others blocks us from the abundance of life.

Self-love is a term that's been thrown around a lot in the last couple of decades but have we really noted the powerful nature of simply loving oneself? I think not, as we're living in one of the most divisive eras – a time in which we use social media to compare ourselves to others and use labels to exclude and discriminate against others. We've lost sight of the love we need for ourselves and others.

My relationship with love has changed over the years. At times I merely viewed it as something to get drunk on. I would crave kisses and human touch and the thrill of feeling my heart flip upside down with lust. An intoxicating, heart-thumping love was all I desired and the only kind of love I recognised outside of the grounded, long-lasting love for my family. Self-love was not in my orbit for a long time. I assumed I would like myself more if I was loved by another, maybe even lots of others. As my TV audience increased, I expected to find more acceptance of the bits of me I didn't like. Maybe if others loved my insatiable enthusiasm that I felt out of control of, I would like it more too? Maybe if my characterful nose and bulbous eyes were applauded, I would find it easier to look in the mirror without judgement? I learned that lesson the hard way and have only really started to understand the power of self-love and acceptance recently.

How we get to that place is another story. My own rollercoaster of self-examination has been one of severe self-loathing at times and I'm so desperate to settle into a calmer plateau of self-acceptance. I assume that once I get there my relationships will be better, my love for the planet will be more respectful and my understanding of love in all its many guises will be cemented. **I believe love is where it's at when it comes to living a spiritual life of connection and meaning.** *It's often the answer to so many of our problems but so often we forget it's for us, due to feelings of unworthiness, and can't perceive it in others as we only see our differences. To help us peel back the red shiny wrapper of love so we can feel it more, see it more clearly and understand its potency I am going to explore several different subjects with some incredible people I've met over the years, to help us on our merry way. Here's to love and a deeper, more meaningful life.*

SHAMANS

Love is complicated but essential for connection to that something that is bigger than us. We often feel confused by love and so devoid of it, and maybe we can attribute some of that lacking to the modern world. We value success, an accumulation of 'stuff', and power, over the abundance of love that we have access to whenever we want. It's long been the work of shamans to help others tune in to that love globally and internally, with historic practices and treatments. I have been fascinated with the mysticism that surrounds shamans for as long as I can remember. So often we are coerced into believing there is only one option in life. We are exposed to limited choices when it comes to health, happiness and connection. The confines lie in the hands of the government, media outlets and monster brands. We are subconsciously imbibing messaging and rules without even recognising that our beliefs are changing by the minute. Looking to the esoteric theories and ideas that might not dwell in the mainstream has been essential for my wellbeing, ongoing recovery from mental illness and connection to the hugeness of life. There simply is no better place to start than with shamans and their beautiful look at love and life.

Where Did It All Begin?

Shamanism is said to have originated in Siberia yet, once commonly recognised, it became apparent that it was conducted the world over in many cultures. The practices involved have been used and cultivated for thousands of years in India, by Native Americans and in South America, with cave art depicting shamanic rituals dating back as far as 30,000 years ago, yet there is also evidence of shamanism being widely used throughout Asia, Tibet, Hungary, Sweden, Central Europe and Africa, to name but a few. The exact origins and dates are unknown but it's certainly been a spiritual path for many which at times indigenous tribes have had to fight for, as throughout history those who have not understood its power and importance have either dismissed its validity or taken from it without acknowledging its origins. Many individuals still practise shamanism today to help people connect with nature, spirits, community and themselves. But what is it? How do they carry out this ancient work and what does it look like?

Calm and Connected

The work of a shaman may differ in practice but most would align with the idea that their work is to act as a healer. Using a plethora of skills, honed over many years, the shaman employs rituals, psychic ability, acupuncture, energy work, sound bowls, herbs, tinctures and reflexology, among other esoteric practices, to heal physical, emotional and mental pain, problems and trauma. The time spent with a shaman will differ depending on their particular teachings and perhaps even where they are based geographically. Their work is in conjunction with that something 'bigger': it's tied tightly to the power of the land

and nature and has always to work in harmony with it. The shaman's work is also a direct communication with all that is usually unseen by the human eye: spirit, energy and psychic ability. It's a powerful concoction of ceremony and healing on a physical level interwoven with a deep understanding of the hugeness of life.

I've met a couple of UK-based shamans over the years and have been helped massively with examining my own resistance to accepting love. It might be helpful to meet one in this book for a deeper understanding, so keep reading to get a glimpse into the world of Wendy Mandy. I first heard of Wendy via Russell Brand's brilliant podcast, Under The Skin. I was curious and fascinated listening in on their conversation and felt a sense of peace immediately wash over me. Whenever I listen to wise people talk, I feel calm and connected as the little worries and insecurities I carry daily dissipate. They cannot stand the heat of wisdom and truth. All the rubbish and modern-day debris just falls away. Coincidently, or perhaps fatefully, shortly after hearing Russell's podcast episode a great friend of mine, breath-work coach Rebecca Dennis, suggested I have a session with her friend who was a shaman. And guess who that friend was? ... *The* Wendy Mandy.

Wendy doesn't have a website and minimal results come up when you google her, which made me even more intrigued. It's all word-of-mouth stuff, which is wonderfully old school, yet it's almost impossible to get an appointment with her as she is booked up for months in advance. In a completely jammy move, I managed to get an appointment after Rebecca and Russell put in a good word, so expectantly awaited my session with Wendy a month down the line. Wendy has spent most of her life working and living with tribes around the world – the Kogi of Colombia, the Samburu of northern Kenya and the Yawanawa of Brazil to name a few. Wendy is currently writing a book about all of the amazing people she has worked with, learned from and taught over the years, which I cannot wait to read.

Energy and Power

Wendy's practice room is rammed with beautiful books on every subject from natural medicine to astrology. There is a treatment bed next to a cabinet of well-loved rattles and sound bowls, with a painted ceiling above depicting flying creatures in red and blue. It's a hypnotic space that keeps your attention and intrigue, with eyes darting from one curiosity to the next. I lay on the bed with a towel over my bare legs, feeling slightly insecure as I always have freezing feet, which at the end of the bed actually look tinged with purple. I could have painted my toenails too but, hey, there are bigger fish to fry today.

Sat by my aforementioned violet hooves, Wendy instantly gets to work rubbing life into them – the most heavenly moment of my day so far. I LOVE having my feet rubbed. I turn into a sort of stoned, purring cat with slurred words and squinty eyes. My body relaxes entirely as Wendy asks me some questions and I rattle off my list of worries and past regrets that I carry around with me daily in a cumbersome and perhaps unnecessary backpack. Wendy is small but also huge. Her tiny frame is almost unable to carry the size of her energy and power. It spills out into the room and makes me feel safe; my own torrent of insecurities wrapped up in her knowledge and total understanding of life. Phew, what a relief. If only momentarily, I feel a weight lift.

After the most heavenly foot rub that seems endless but simultaneously way too quick for my liking, Wendy steps up to my side and places two fingers on my pulse points. I am familiar with this technique as my dear friend Gerad Kite, who also practises five element acupuncture, initiates treatment by checking the energy in the pulse points too. From my under-standing, this is where the acupuncturist feels for blocks in the body. Still woozy from the foot-caressing, I am startled when seconds later an acupuncture needle is plunged into my ribs and twisted, releasing the most powerful whoosh that feels like a firework going off internally, sparks fizzing out to all corners of my body. My eyes widen to saucers. This happens maybe five more times on differing points over my body – my shoulders, my feet (YOWTCH!) and the hollow between my shin bone and calf muscle. Discombobulated and desperately trying to catch up with the constant stimulation of needle to skin, I feel like cracking up with laughter, or maybe crying, perhaps both.

All the while Wendy is pressing me on the past troubles I've mentioned to her during the blissful foot rub. She is constantly excavating, trying to work out the root cause, the pain point, the twisted knot that needs untying.

Next, rattles. I close my eyes as Wendy shakes a large, cacophonous rattle all over my body. My ears follow the sound and at times it's overwhelming. The noise fills up my whole body, making my solar plexus tingle. I'm told to imagine myself at a specific age that relates to the start of some self-limiting beliefs, and as the rattle works over my body I'm to imagine that image dissipating entirely. There is such relief when the noise stops that I exhale deeply, yet not completely as instantly some celestial gongs reverberate in place of the crashing rattle. The sound bowl responsible for this beautiful noise is placed on my tummy so I can feel the sound vibrations in my bones. My tummy is such a delicate spot. I'm sure many of you feel that way too. It's my squishy bit, where my babies grew, that I try to cover in large pants and high-waisted jeans. I don't like being touched there at all, not even by my poor husband, but this was different. This was comfort. This was protection and a dissolving of something, possibly some of those insecurities. I open my eyes to a blurry vision of Wendy sat at my feet having just rubbed her own blend of rose oil into my not-so-purple feet. As I awaken to my surroundings my resounding thought is: 'What the fuck just happened there?'

I slowly sit up as Wendy comes into focus. My heart and head feel slightly lighter. I float out of the door and on to the busy streets of London, which feels like being plunged into ice-cold water. My eyes adjust to the light and speed of people passing. A newborn mole blinks into the madness. The cab ride home is a moment to reflect on how I rarely choose to seek this peace and connection. My inclination is to follow the modern world in its busyness and pace. My body still vibrating from the treatment, I vow to choose peace over stress and seek more moments of connection.

A Chinwag with Wendy

Location: Wendy's kitchen, surrounded by plants, photos of friends from all over the globe and little bottles of rose oil. As soon as that rose scent hits my nostrils, I relax.

Me: Wendy, what exactly is a shaman?

Wendy: A shaman is a person who walks between worlds. So, what are these worlds? These worlds are this physical world we live in now; here is a table, the sink, this water; it's the physicality. Then the other worlds are the worlds we can't see. We only use about 5 per cent of our senses, we are using a very, very small amount of who we actually are. We are only using a very small amount of our perception. So, a shaman like me, somehow through experience and all sorts of learnings, has come out of that small perception into other perceptions. So I can see and feel how plants talk to us, how animals talk to us and how elementals talk to us, which are spirits of the natural world. This world is a dot in the universe which is a dot in the universes. A child knows that: they lie on their back in the grass and look up at the expansive sky and say, 'What are those stars?', but we lose that perception because we're rushing around in this space-time reality chasing our tails. We don't spend enough time wondering and being.

Me: So that expansive thinking that you use and work with, is that available to all of us?

Wendy: Yes. Recently I treated an eleven year-old boy who was a drug dealer. When he came in, he had taken a lot of street skunk which had been grown with a lot of pesticides. That kind of skunk is not marijuana so it causes psychosis; he was in a mess. I knew he was stoned when he lay down on my treatment bed. I worked with his feet and got him relaxed and then I did the first acupuncture needle and he said, 'What the hell is that? That's better than drugs.'

And I said, 'What do you feel?'

And he said, 'I feel high.'

So I asked, 'In what way?'

He replied, 'I don't know, a relaxed high?'

So I told him, 'Five element acupuncture has connected you. Can you feel that? You're connected to something. Can you feel it?'

He said, 'Yup, usually I have to get really stoned to do that and actually it still doesn't feel like that.'

Anyway, cut to today, he's now free from drugs and he has a lot of support and I'm training him to be a boy that can get the others away from trying to get that high by smoking skunk. They know something is missing, so they're smoking to find this thing that they know is out there. They're trying to connect with their spiritual self but they're going the wrong way about it.

Me: Aren't we all doing that to some extent? Aren't we all trying to feel connected but we do it by drinking to get drunk, eating too much addictive sugary food, sex, buying shoes we don't need and so on? How have we got to this place where we have lost touch with nature and our spiritual selves?

Wendy: Totally. That's what I'm writing about in my new book. One of the key points is that disassociation from each other and nature. We have lost our right relationship to each other and nature. That has happened over the course of 12,000 years. We've lost that everyday relationship with each other. We have to change so much: our educational system, the nuclear relationships in a family; we saw this in lockdown as we lost our support systems, our tribes. That's why we saw so many lockdown problems during the pandemic, like a rise in online shopping addictions, porn addictions, and mass consumption of alcohol. We have been hypnotised. The biggest addiction is perhaps social media. We have to understand that it is an addiction which is replacing our ability to tune in to ourselves. It is very 'other'.

Me: What do you mean by 'other'?

Wendy: Social media produces a huge codependent relationship with lots of others that we don't know instead of a relationship with ourselves. We can't take social media away from people but we can ask them to spend some of their day doing things that are off screens, which requires discipline. Wake up and do something positive, without your phone. There are so many ways to do this, the big one being the rise in modern-day meditation. That's the new spirituality.

Me: Is having a good relationship with yourself imperative when it comes to living a spiritual life?

Wendy: Yes, but it's also about discipline. If you're in a habit, it takes nine days to get out of it with discipline. You have to write discipline into your relationship with yourself. That's how you'll move away from your addictions that are connected to the 'other', again, 'other' meaning anything outside of yourself. Plug away at it and keep going until you have that relationship with yourself nailed and then you will notice the sort of stuff I notice. People ask me, 'How do I become a shaman?' I say to them, **first of all connect to YOU with compassion. It's all about compassion.**

Me: Is fear the biggest thing stopping us from having a relationship with ourselves?

Wendy: Fear is the absence of love. Love is what you feel when you meditate. You feel consciousness, God, spirit, the carnival, whatever you want to call that thing; whatever you call it, you feel that!

Me: When you're treating people, what is it that you're looking to do in those sessions?

Wendy: I look to put that person in touch with their original essence that knows everything: that baby that came into the world from God/source/love, again, whatever you want to call it. Everyone has that in them and I want to put them back in touch with that. I want to move them past the addictions, past the programming, past the childhood, past the trauma, and ignite that connection.

Me: How does the physical element of your practice help with that?

Wendy: I tune in via the feet as the feet are a map. It's called reflexology; your ears, hands and feet are a map. Reflexology has been used for thousands of years. I can tell what is happening mentally, physically, spiritually and emotionally with you through your feet. Then I take your pulses which are in the wrist and those are six pulses that were conceived in Daoism 10,000-odd years ago. Your body is an electrical mechanism that is a mass of moving particles that create this field, so this is a way of tuning into that field. Where is the blockage? It's like being a good plumber. What is the original cause of the original blockage in this person? The needles are used to ease these blockages. I'm going straight for the essence of that person. It manifests in both the positive and the negative; it's quite polarised. So, Fearne, your element in five element acupuncture is 'wood'. (Peculiar, as that's my married name.) There is earth, wood, metal, fire and water and you are wood. Each person embodies one of these elements. Let's look at the positives and negatives of that element. You're very dynamic, like the season spring, like a snowdrop pushing up through the ice of winter. You're the planner, creator, OR, on the flip side, you're stuck, angry, frustrated, bitter. (Side note … I think that about sums me up!)

Me: YES, that is exactly what I feel like in life.

Wendy: What we have to do is work out where your emotional scratches are. For you, Fearne, your emotional scratches are that you feel unfairly accused.

Me: YUP!

Wendy: And misunderstood.

Me: YES! Often we don't know what we are like as individuals as we are so used to other people's versions and projections of us instead of tuning into who we really are.

Wendy: I think you might like my mate Mark (not his real name in case 'Mark' isn't comfortable with me telling this pretty hilarious story) who is coming here in a bit. He is the owner of a restaurant chain and I mentor him. He is an Enneagram 8. Do you know yours?

Me: Weirdly, three people this month have suggested I do the online test to find out what Enneagram number I am. I am yet to take the test so I have no idea.

(A side note for you all. If you haven't already looked into this yourself, an Enneagram is used to define nine interconnected personality types, numbered 1–9. But it's deeper than that. It is an ancient method that could have originated in around AD 400, though the exact origins are unknown. I'll dive into this subject later in the book, I promise (see pages 131–51).)

Wendy: I've studied it and I used to use it a lot in my work. I'm an 8 too. We want to punch our way through life asking others, 'So, where are we going?' You want an Enneagram 8 on your raft as they'll sort it all out. The downside is that 8s are so vulnerable as well as strong. So you become highly defensive. If you allow someone into your life and they give you hell, you want to literally exterminate them.

Me: Ha! I think I know a few more 8s!

Wendy: The shadow side of an 8 goes 'FUCK YOU'. Each Enneagram has positives to honour and negatives to learn from, much like the elements in five element acupuncture. Wait until you meet Mark. He's going to come in here and be so loud and funny and possibly embarrassing.

Me: Oh, I can't wait.

Wendy: What we all have to do is look for the things in life that are stopping us from connecting to that something bigger, the things that get in the way. Those things are a horrible white noise that'll stop you connecting with others, nature and yourself. It is always something that has happened in your past. If your mother was jealous, you'll have a tendency to let mother-figures in who might not have your best interests at heart. If your dad was absent, you'll have the tendency to invite men who are detached into your life. For me I have to be careful with little-brother-figures due to my own back story. My tendency is to let them off the hook so I have to watch that. These are the banana skins in life.

(Doorbell rings.)

I sit up straight, oh gosh, I think it might be Mark.

Wendy: Hello, Mark!

Mark: Do you like my trousers, Wendy? They've fallen down.

Wendy: Oh NO!

Mark: Have you got anyone else here?

Wendy: Yes.

Mark: Hahaha. As I came in the door, they just fell down.

(Mark has now waddled into the kitchen with his trousers round his ankles and his boxer shorts on full display. Mark cannot pull up said trousers as he is holding a huge box with both hands, which is precariously piled with fresh vegetables. I'm not sure whether to look away or help.)

Mark: This is not deliberate, I promise. My God this is not going well.

Me: Mark, nice to meet you. I'm Fearne. Mark, pull your trousers up.

Wendy: Pull them up, for goodness sake. Now go in the other room, Mark.

Me: So, my last question is, what is the one thing we can all go away and do to cultivate a relationship with ourselves that in turn allows us that connection in life?

Wendy: Compassion. Compassion. We are so hard on ourselves. Let's say that I've just had a row with my neighbour. They were being really noisy and I slightly lost it. The first thing is to just be kind to yourself. Think, 'OK, that wasn't great that I lost it there', and then calm down and practise self-love. **We are all so hard on ourselves. Just spend five minutes making a tea and talking to yourself like you would a best friend.**

Me: Wendy, thank you. I know I need to practise this, BIG TIME.

• • •

It seems the resounding takeaway from this chat is that for us to live a spiritual life, one that is connected to others and nature, we first HAVE to cultivate a good relationship with ourselves. I'm scared yet excited. It seems achievable but I have a horrid feeling I have a nihilistic and unkind relationship with myself at times. In the name of connection, I know I have got to lose some of the very ingrained negative stories I put upon myself daily. I've made small efforts to do this in the past yet it's never stuck. Now I really have no excuse. I also want to bring my kids up to love and accept themselves fully. How can I expect them to if I am not demonstrating this in everyday life? Change is desperately needed.

Day one of my 'self-compassion experiment'

Saturday, 6:30am

Within seconds of opening my eyes I notice that my brain has gone off on a negative rampage. I'm berating myself internally for having slept in my kids' bunk bed again, the voice acerbically whispering to self that I should be stronger and should have nailed this sleep thing with my now eight-year-old son years ago. I stop mid-sentence to examine the cause behind this self-flagellation. As guessed, I have a pretty unkind relationship with myself. Is this the block that is hindering me from connecting with the beauty and magic of life? Could it be that simple?

My shoulders slump – this is not going to be easy. In the kitchen it's still dark outside, the street lamps illuminating tiny raindrops. The kids are already fighting over what TV show they're going to watch and I can feel more self-berating coming on: a heaviness that ignores my intention of making delicious pancakes for their breakfast but instead focuses on more perceived weakness on my part, for not being stricter about when they can and can't watch TV. I try to steamroller this familiar inner monologue with kinder words that assure me it's no big deal; that I watched tons of TV as a kid and now as an adult would way rather read a book. It's a pointless worry. Bloody hell, this is already exhausting. Why can I not give myself a break?

Starting with My Hands

As I stir my way-too-strong coffee I notice the cracked skin around my thumbs, the skin that I pick and peel and bite when anxious. It's almost comforting even though I know it's a small moment of self-destruction. That will need to go too. I have vats of hand lotion upstairs that I never use. I haven't painted my nails in weeks and, as superficial as this might seem, I think my hands could do with some self-love. Maybe if I start with hands, work my way up to 'self' and then start thinking about the other bit, my soul/spirit, I'll get there incrementally.

The next nasty moment I notice self-loathing creep in will be no surprise to anyone. It'll also possibly be your biggest trigger to letting the self-love slip: social media. This one is a low-hum self-loathing. It hums so constantly that it's easy to overlook. It's a slow crumble from the inside that at first goes unnoticed. It begins with curiosity but incrementally morphs into comparison and then total despair. I close Instagram and slam my phone down a little too hard on the kitchen work-top. The berating continues as I reflect on my own lack of discipline. It's the weekend. Why am I allowing myself to squirrel down this vortex of other people's supposed lives/arguments/thoughts and projections? Must. Be. More. Strong. Willed. This is the discipline Wendy spoke of. A discipline that gets us away from our addictions which are hindering our overall connection. At this stage I'm not sure whether this inner pep talk, after said Insta-binge, is coming from a place of love. I'm not sure the discipline is coming from a place where I believe I deserve better. I think it's coming from a place where I believe I'm a weak, pathetic person. Oh boy, this is all so much harder and so much more deep-rooted than I had imagined.

Fear and Loathing in My Local Park

A wintery afternoon brings more cloud but simultaneously a desperate need to get out in some fresh air, as both kids begin to climb the walls. They've already turned the kitchen into a giant game of 'The Floor Is Lava' with every cushion from the house, even my favourite tasselled and more-decorative-than-practical ones, and have strewn them across the crumb-infested floor to use as platforms to escape the lava. WE NEED TO GET OUT OF THE HOUSE. After a twenty-minute struggle to find the exact socks that Rex 'needs' for our local park adventure we are out into the grey, damp air, feeling relieved, ejected from the mess of home on a lazy Saturday and into a world of trees, local squawking green parakeets and little streams that Rex loves to jump over.

During the global pandemic I noticed several things subtly change in my kids' behaviour: Rex's sleep almost immediately went out of the window and Honey's fear of dogs escalated to extreme terror. I imagine the general anxiety emanating from every human affected many kids in myriad ways, yet here I am again blaming myself! I'm taking responsibility for a whole pandemic and its effects on my kids as a small, unassuming Yorkshire terrier approaches us. Tail wagging, eyes bright, she wants to make new friends. Honey clambers up my body like a koala hugging a tree and screams in my ear. Poppy the dog, whose owner is desperately shouting her name, runs closer with glee, mistaking Honey's sheer panic for excitement. I'm flustered, each scream a punch to the nervous system, mainly because I'm lumping self-blame on to the drama of it all too. What could I have done wrong to create this fear in my little girl? What fear of mine is she picking up? I skip to my own fear too quickly. A little worry escalates into: 'I'm getting it all wrong'. BINGO, this is the core problem. This is the root of my self-loathing. I believe that I am the only one getting life wrong and everyone else is acing it. Phew, I'm so glad I got to the bottom of this one on day one of my exploration into self-compassion. Now I just have to work out how the hell to climb out from under it.

I flesh it out with my friend, the exceptional author and activist Sarah Wilson, who articulates the exact feeling. In her sun-drenched Australian accent she says, 'Fearne, you feel like everybody else got the guide book to life and you didn't.' THIS. IS. IT! Thank you, Sarah.

● ● ●

It's getting lighter earlier… the spring promising to break through. Maybe it'll be easier to channel self-compassion with a little blue sky overhead. On awakening it's easy for my mind to start compiling lists of all that I need to do today. I pause and wonder, 'Is that the most compassionate way I could start a new day?' I don't think so. Maybe affirmations could work and get me in a positive headspace? I've read every Louise Hay book going and I know I feel better when I train my brain like a small puppy to create new, more positive neural pathways. 'I love and embrace myself, I love and embrace myself, I love and embrace myself.' This was the affirmation that came to mind without much thought. These were the words I needed. I can't say I wholeheartedly believed them but maybe that's the point. I lay there wondering if it is possible for us to truly connect with the things and people we love in life without self-compassion? Without self-love, we would be oblivious to the fact that we are made of the same stuff that the glistening stream water is made of, the same stuff that those I love are made of. It would mean seeing myself as separate to it all. A spiritual life surely has to be based on the principle that there is no separation at all. We are love, we are beauty, we are one.

I'm starting to really recognise why I have to make this mission of self-love of paramount importance.

Celebrate Yourself

Most of this stuff seems to be just bad habits. Stuff picked up along the way in life and then used as a case against myself. I record an episode of the Happy Place podcast from home with a wonderful guest. I press pause on my usual instinct to pick apart the bits I could have done better; instead, I take two deep breaths in and out and, as I close my laptop and put away my microphone, I allow myself some positive focus – the energy of this episode was good. The guest was open, relaxed and smiling, and maybe I played a part in that. Maybe I helped to cultivate an atmosphere that was relaxed and safe so they could talk about life on a deep level. Maybe I'll allow myself to celebrate that a little.

I used to celebrate every victory yet today I rarely celebrate a thing. I remember so clearly a warm summer's day when I was twenty-three, when I celebrated myself fully at 11am with a crisp glass of champagne in an empty bar in London. I had just interviewed Princes William and Harry for the first time. I had been invited into Clarence House to conduct an interview about the tribute concert they were putting on for their late mother, Diana, Princess of Wales. It was an out-of-body experience from start to finish. Acutely aware of my missing t's and lack of experience talking to people from the upper echelons of society, I floated through the whole day. I grinned too much, stared at their faces in disbelief that I was in the same room as them, but somehow managed to stay on track with my carefully handwritten questions, which I had practised in the mirror for weeks on end. The whole interview was cheery and, looking back, probably quite sweet. I sashayed out of Clarence House, my cheeks aching from the permanent smile, and walked in my new shoes and most sensible dress, in a hue of burnt orange, down the street to the nearest bar. I swigged back the bubbles and looked up to the ceiling to thank whoever might have been 'up there' helping me out that day. I felt grateful for the opportunity and was more than happy to raise a glass and say cheers to my own moment of success.

Where has that version of me gone? I'm aware of an incremental wave of outside verbal abuse and bad mental habits on my part, which have knocked any celebration out of me. Instead, now I sit and wait for the abuse. I hand over all power to strangers to tear me apart and tell me how awful I am. I'm lucky in the fact that my audience these days seems to be fairly on board with my work, so the abuse is limited, yet I have been through phases where strangers and the press have mentally tortured me to the point where I felt I couldn't carry on with the job. That in itself would be a whole other book, as the amount of times I have been ridiculed, mocked and, I would go so far as to say, at times bullied by the press is unreal. I'm no victim and I'm aware that this is the nature of the beast; I'm also incredibly aware of how there are far worse situations in life to deal with, but I can't say it hasn't affected me and my own self-worth. I'm usually on high alert, ready to second-guess the shit that might fly my way. I've taken this to the extreme and no longer really celebrate any successes or moments where things have gone well. It feels like I might be tempting fate in doing so. **Changing this mind-set doesn't mean I'm wanting to fling myself into pure self-adoration and indulgence all the time, I just want to mark the bits of life where there has been fluidity and joy.**

After years of exterior noise and judgement, and a gradual move away from traditional broadcasting and its exposure, I'm now ready to claim back the bits of me that I had given up and handed over to others: the parts of me that might have been deemed annoying; the parts of me that were suggested as being stupid and useless; the parts of me that were mocked and ridiculed. I want them back. All of them, and I want to celebrate them. Why have I let someone else's definition of me, based on little fact, corrode my actual personality? I wonder how much you have let this happen to you too? I have a feeling that before I can claim this stuff back, I might need to feel a little bit angry first. I can feel rage in my neck just thinking about all of this. As I sit in my little office post-podcast mulling this over I can feel my neck muscles tighten into stone. Maybe I need to excavate all of this shit first so I can make space for self-love. Or maybe this anger isn't about other people and their opinions at all. Maybe it's anger towards myself for letting them do it? I'm going to have to get quiet and work out who this anger belongs to.

Loving the Younger You

I'm not great at meditating. I have a feeling this too will have to change during the writing of this book. I'm sporadic with it and use it more as an SOS rather than a daily practice. I'm not sure why I'm so reluctant. I have interviewed countless people over the years who can testify to its importance and impact. I have spoken at length with monks who have gone into four-year-long retreats, meditating for up to six hours a day. I know there is peace, epiphany and contentment to be found with meditation but I keep myself busy instead. Maybe this is a chicken-and-egg thing. Do I have to get self-compassion first to then allow myself the time to meditate each day, or do I have to start meditating to get the self-love?

There is a whole section on meditation on the way (see pages 45–71). On this occasion I make a good choice. Normally I prefer a guided meditation, something from YouTube, with a guide that has a soft voice that isn't creepy or too forced, and gentle music in the background. I can follow their words which helps to keep my untamed mind on board with the letting go bit of meditating. Today I need proper peace so I choose to brave actual silence and being fully with myself. I'm not just seeking relaxation and rest here; I'm seeking answers too. I perch on the small, round ottoman covered in cat fur (like most of my furniture) that's in the kitchen and plant my feet firmly on the ground. One big breath in and a tidal wave exhale as I instantly push away the thought that I'm being self-indulgent taking this time out when others might be sat hunched over laptops, in hospitals doing vital work, teaching children and doing other helpful stuff. I quietly ask myself a question: Who is this anger for? Who does it belong to? Then I sit with it. The thoughts come in: 'I could be dealing with the Mount Everest of laundry downstairs right now.' No, that's not a useful thought. I let it go and just focus on my feet on the floor. I need the bombardment of everyday mental chatter to subside so I can listen to my intuition. There is anger. I can feel it threatening to attack my neck again but what is it? Who is it for? The mockery and public shaming at times has made me want to punch through walls but these people are faceless. Bitter people behind keyboards letting their own tiny thoughts grow in size once typed letters appear on screen. Can I be angry with people I don't know, will never meet and who have no actual bearing on my life? I don't think so. I'm concerned I'm thinking too much. I'm cognitively trying to Mrs Hinch this moment. I'm attempting to sort through all of this rubbish to get a clean result. Maybe if I just focus on the rage without the stories, I'll be able to let go some more.

With the anger bubbling and the burn in my throat another feeling arises. Foolishness. I feel silly. I sit with all of it without resistance. I want to get curious about it, not push it away. The longer I sit with it, the more I realise that there are fewer thoughts and inconsequential daily worries. I'm just with the anger. Minutes pass but I'm not sure how many and then the clouds start to part. I can see the rage in all its glory as something separate from me entirely. It's a huge burning ball that I'm hurling at myself, more specifically at my younger self, the part of me that I believe was naive and clueless and mirrored most of the things that were written and said about me. Some of it could even be true but does that make me a bad person? I don't think so. Show me a person in their formative years who hasn't made mistakes or been naively excited about the newness of adult life. I'm not sure any of us could find one. I let my mind settle on an image of me in my early twenties. Plump under-eyes and rosy cheeks, severely layered hair, permanent grin, dancing into fire without knowing it would be hot. Without letting judgement overshadow this image, I just sit with her. God, I hate bits of her. I can see how I've tried to run away from her so desperately. I've read, studied, thought, listened and learned to try and not be her. Using books, knowledge and sensibleness as my weapons, I've tried to plaster over the naivety and foolishness that come with giddy excitement.

I stretch my arms above my head and wiggle my fingers and toes to come out of this twenty-minute meditation. I blink my eyes open with the newfound clarity that I need to start loving me in my twenties. I'm still on the run from her and her Avril Lavigne get-up, but I'm now aware of it and I know where the anger lives. In the process of sprinting away from her, I've given up the good bits she had as well as the bad. I've said goodbye to spontaneity and giddy excitement and replaced it with caution and at times cynicism. I actually feel a bit sorry for younger Fearne. Why have I abandoned her so willingly? Can I accept her without using sympathy as my means to make the peace?

Make More Mistakes

Often we feel heavy from our past. The version of us that walked the planet a decade ago still taps us on the shoulder to remind us of our mistakes. It's a hard shadow to live with. This morning I was thinking back to me in my twenties. What a very different person I was back then. I believed in a linear kind of success and placed so much of my self-worth in its hands. I was so willing to change who I was and compromise my own beliefs to feel accepted. My twenties were packed with full-throttle fun, gin, fags, usually a bruised heart and very little sleep. Never quite in one time zone due to working here in the UK and also in the States, my watch was constantly being wound forward or back. At the age of twenty-six I had ticked a huge goal off my list, hosting a primetime TV show on NBC in America. I was a cohost performing to millions of people weekly, with the confidence of someone who had yet to deal with life's big pitfalls.

Although a very sunny memory all round, this morning I was looking at this time with a fresh set of eyes. Each filming day I would sit in the make-up chair and let Wendy, the make-up lady, turn me into someone completely different. Back then, American TV was all glamour, so within an hour I would turn from Eastcote's very own, Fruit of the Loom-wearing scruff-bag into Pamela Anderson's younger, less buxom sister. Halfway through the transformation Wendy would wield her giant airbrush and spray foundation at my face like she was putting out a fire. After the massive fake eyelashes were glued to my upper lids I would be stuffed into a skimpy, strapless dress and doused in hairspray so my perfectly curled locks would stay ten centimetres away from my own scalp. I would look in the mirror and think, 'Who the fuck is that?'

I was unrecognisable to myself yet totally lacking the confidence to challenge the TV executives who insisted on this new, dialled-up version of me. Today I would be like, 'NO WAY, MATEY', while hurling a padded bra to the floor. I will not morph into what people need me to be. I can only be me, the real me: the one who was under the lacquered hair and thick foundation back in my twenties but was too scared to reveal herself. My lack of confidence led to me making several mistakes and bad choices that have followed me through life. My lack of self-worth has led to me looking outside of myself for validation, always to my detriment. I can often look back at this version of myself and talk about her cruelly and focus more on the regret and mistakes made rather than the progress and lessons gained afterwards. Having had some pretty game-changing conversations with friends over the years, I've settled on a kinder dialogue with young Fearne. I refuse to call her names and put her down any more. It's no help to anyone and really rather narrow-minded. Simply put, **I would not be the me I am today without the me I was back then. Go easy on your previous self. Thank her/him.**

Just Stop

I've hit a wall. Tiredness has taken over and is creating an inner friction that I liken to the noise of sandpaper on wood. It's putting me on edge and everything feels tricky. I'm not good at surrendering. I would rather stagger to the finish line on my knees than take a moment's rest and I think that is again due to a lack of self-compassion. The kids are at school, I've had two Zoom meetings and recorded an interview for my Radio 2 show and yet I'm reluctant to rest. I empty the dishwasher, my feet flopping about in sliders that I'm practically dragging across the floor. I know, I'm being dramatic, but you know when you've hit a wall, and are shattered, everything feels dramatic – a severe lack of self-compassion stopping me from, well, stopping.

The dishwasher is empty but I cannot be arsed to fill it again and leave a treacherously tall pile of dirty plates in the sink. Time to surrender. These last six days I have gotten a little better at self-compassion. I've placed more importance on it and can see how it makes room for joy, laughter and connection. As I stare into space in the middle of my kitchen, my intuition is scream-ing at me to GO AND REST! An act of self-kindness is needed and I'm going to rally against habit and get in the bath. As soon as my skin hits the hot water I crumple into the relaxed state my body has been craving. Why didn't I do this an hour ago? Why do I often seek stress rather than allow myself some comfort? This old belief system is still at work with the tape replaying the story that I am unworthy of comfort, but I still have time to change it. I'm too tired for any more self-analysis today so just sink into the bubbles and let my mind go with it.

Soul Connection

Jesse, my husband, and I have been obsessed with a TV show called *This Is Us* this year. It's more than a TV show. It's life depicted with every ounce of rawness. It's therapy disguised as TV. Pain spills off the screen and tears roll down my face every night. I can only handle one episode at a time due to its power and potency. If you haven't seen it, I won't spoil the plot line for you but in Season 2 there is one episode that freezes your body, it's so painful. I felt like I hadn't drawn breath in minutes but the intensity was broken by Jesse getting up and walking away. I snapped out of my fixed gaze and followed after him.

'Sorry, I just can't watch that tonight. It's too much.' His deep brown eyes were gazing down at the floor. My husband lost his mum to a drug overdose sixteen years ago. Shock and grief twisted together in a life-changing hurricane of hell. We talk about Krissy all of the time. We talk about her with the kids as if she is still here. Nanna Krissy is a part of our family and our daily lives. Jesse is open and willing to talk about her too, which might have tricked us both into believing grief was something that could fade with time. Grief might not be living alongside Jesse all day, every day, but it is there, under the surface, in his decision-making, in the music he makes. This particular episode of *This Is Us* touched on something that was lying dormant in Jesse. We cried together, we talked about it all, we sat silently and let it percolate. I felt I could 100 per cent be there for Jesse and with his pain. I could create space for this big emotion and listen to him.

A couple of weeks ago, when I myself had been triggered and subsequently sank into self-loathing, I don't think I would have done quite as good a job. Sometimes I get caught up in how well I'm supposed to be doing at work – how many people are listening to my podcast, how good the guests are on each episode, what people are feeding back to me – and I try to find meaning in it all; yet this unexpected, quiet moment with Jesse was truly meaningful. The unforeseen grief spilling into our lounge and the conversations and closeness that followed felt like actual connection. It wasn't just my mind that was able to find the right words to soothe my husband or my physical body instinctively moving to rub his back in the appropriate moments, it was a connection with something else entirely. Whether it was with our souls, our energy, maybe even Jesse's mum's energy entering the picture, it was deep, real, unrivalled connection.

MEDITATION AND YOGA

What do spirituality and wellness have in common? What do you think? Your answer will be as valid as mine of course but, for what it's worth, I think they're wholeheartedly connected. To me, they have to work in tandem and I'm not sure wellness can be fully reached without spirituality. Spirituality is not much mentioned in the conversation around wellbeing, but I can only talk personally and say that I know I could drink all the green juice in the world, do Pilates daily and cover myself in reishi mushrooms and I would still not feel 'well', unless I felt connected to that something bigger. I could be 80 per cent wheatgrass and amazing at handstands but still feel empty inside when I turned the bedside lamp off at night. Yoga and meditation seem to be the easiest way to marry the modern-day iteration of wellness with deep-rooted spiritual concepts that have been around for aeons. Having these two pillars of wellness, yoga and meditation, promoted heavily today is no bad thing as it normalises them and gives people more tools with which to cope in life, but sometimes, through the filter of the modern world, the meaning and spiritual side of both get lost.

Yoga is perhaps misinterpreted as something to get 'good' at while meditation is seen as a tool we can use to then achieve and do more with less stress. I'm pretty sure neither of those outcomes were in the original plans.

Balancing Act

I'll cut to the chase. I love yoga and practise it regularly but often skip meditation as my ego gets in the way. My ego has a habit of listing other activities that I could be doing to distract me from taking the time to stop: washing, reorganising cupboards, doing as many emails as humanly possible, sometimes just eating biscuits, anything to avoid meditating. I have a big inkling this might need to change for me to really engage with everything I've talked about in this book so far.

I was twenty-nine when I went to my first ever yoga class. My friend Amy, who also worked at BBC Radio 1 at the time, asked if I would like to join her favourite local yoga class after work one evening. I turned up late and rushed to the back of the class. I didn't own yoga leggings so instead wore running shorts and a Kurt Cobain T-shirt. In front of the mirrors stood a magnificent woman with the biggest blue eyes framed by eyelashes so long her blinks seemed to last for seconds. Her soft American accent calmed my I-hate-being-late racing heart and drew me into the delicate, profound words she was speaking. She spoke for maybe ten minutes about the intentions for the class, which sounded lovely but, to me at this point in my life, unrelated to the physical bit we were about to get into. By the age of twenty-nine I had spent a lot of time sweating in gyms I didn't want to be in – Beastie Boys blasting in headphones, wiping down sweaty machinery that someone else had just let loose on. I knew there had to be other options when it

came to moving my body. I was also bored, so bored of view-
ing my body as something that needed punishing through grit
and hard work on a running machine. Yoga, from the outside,
seemed like a gentler, kinder practice.

Every single position the mesmerising teacher Zephyr (now
a great friend) glided into looked simple but felt truly unnatural to me – a horse trying to move like a puma. It just wasn't
working. I had done a lot of ballet growing up but the discipline needed seemed to be the complete opposite to that of this
new, alien style of movement. I looked around the studio at the
women and the odd man, folded like origami, with utter lust
My frustration simmered on the surface of my skin. I don't like
being bad at things and due to the aforementioned assumption
that when it comes to yoga, there is good yoga or bad yoga, I felt
I was failing. Point missed entirely. At this juncture in life I was
aiming to be accomplished at yoga only on a very surface level,
yet to understand the deep-rooted values set thousands of years
beforehand. We see someone on Instagram, pencil still, upside
down in a handstand and think that until we can reach those
heady heights we won't be 'good' at yoga. I felt like this for years.
I would fall out of balances or simply not be able to contort my
body into the spectrum of shapes I was seeing around me.

Body Bliss

About three years ago, seven years into my practice of yoga,
something clicked. My stolen moments of movement, away
from the chaos of family life, started to feel different. Each pose
gave me the opportunity to explore my own physical capabilities and quieten my mind; each pose an opportunity to let go
a little more and enter new territory. I started to notice that in
moments where I felt out of control I could move with purpose

and lose the mental chatter. These days, I might be able to knock out a few complex poses and balances that look impressive on a digital grid but it's not about that for me any more. It's the feeling of the practice, not how impressive it looks. The results I'm aiming for steer so far from the land of six-packs and ripped triceps; I simply want to feel good. In my practice today there are moments where my body and mind feel aligned and I experience snippets of bliss. I still have a gelatinous postnatal tum and I can't do a handstand (I'm not sure I ever will at this point) and that's fine. Yoga is now a place of stillness, exploration and calm that I so desperately crave in life.

On a practical note, yoga has become much more accessible to the masses these days with free classes on YouTube or subscription apps, which means you don't need to join a pricey yoga centre or buy a pair of hamstring-hugging leggings that vac-pack your buttocks. I still mostly practise in my pj's, in my kitchen amid a sea of Lego and dried-up cornflakes ground into the floor.

Falling Off the Wagon

Yoga has become one of the most obvious visuals of wellbeing in modern society, which again is brilliant but also presents some tricky territory. When yoga is used without the deep esoteric, mystical meanings behind the movement, some communities feel uncomfortable as they see their heritage being profited from and commodified. Generations of ancient communities, notably in India, have used yoga as part of daily life for centuries, so having an understanding of the culture and heritage that come with yoga offers gratitude and respect for the practice itself. I think it's always a good idea to learn what you can when it comes to a new practice that has its roots in history and spirituality.

Having a deeper connection to its foundations will always offer you more to learn from. Alongside this, I do believe movement is for everyone, so if you just want to learn some simple poses to get you started and to help ease physical pain or stiffness, then yoga is a great discipline.

One way of understanding how yoga can help you connect more with the world around you, and connect with yourself, is to look at the meanings and intentions behind the movements. For that we need an expert and I have just the chap in a few moments' time.

First, let me explain how I have fallen off the wagon when it comes to meditation. I used to meditate all of the time as a teenager and young person in my twenties. Before mindfulness apps were even a thought and Headspace was just a space, I would sit on my bedroom floor, light a candle and tune into my own and surrounding energy. It was something I looked forward to, a space ensuring the time to pray for others in need, as well as to ask for personal guidance, a hybrid prayer/meditation mashup, if you will. My mum would often play me meditation cassette tapes ('80s kid to the core) instead of story tapes when I was young, so the notion was introduced and normalised at an early age (see page 7). I inherently know that it works for me, I'm pretty sure it works for everyone, so why are we not all doing it, all the time? Surely we would save money and time if meditation was further normalised and encouraged from a young age? Think of all the stress-related illnesses that cost the NHS a fortune today: all the arguments we get ourselves into with others as we're not reacting in a grounded way; **all the time lost worrying about things that are out of our control anyway. All of this can be lessened and channelled with meditation.** It's the Zoom call to the universe, your direct link to wisdom, answers and calm. Again, while considering the micro and macro elements of life –

that wisdom we seek, that strength we desire, that calmness we crave – it's inside all of us. Meditation is our direct line to it. That concept is obviously not promoted anywhere near enough as a lot of the world today relies on speed, absolute digital connection at all times and as much information as possible. We place academic intelligence above all else and think of wisdom as a fanciful idea that might perhaps come with age.

As I've said, I'm almost annoyed at myself that I've fallen off the wagon so catastrophically as I was so tuned in to my practice back in the day. My own excuse seems to be the arrival of kids. I whine about the lack of time to meditate to my deeply spiritual and regularly meditating brother Jamie, who consistently replies saying, 'If you say you have no time to meditate, then you need to meditate even more so.' Ahhhh, irritating but also truly spot on, Jamie Cotton. He knows his spiritual onions. **So, if I understand the benefits and know that meditating will help me deal with the chaos of life, why am I not doing it? It's my ego. My shouty little ego comes along to inform me that I'm far too busy to be wasting time like that.** I mentally run through the huge list of tasks and chores I have to do before the sun sets, which exclude me from having to meditate. Arrogant! I think back to the days when I would use meditation as a fun and regular pit stop and can easily recognise that I dealt with life differently.

There really are no more excuses.

Jambo Dragon

Let's meet Jambo Truong, who is a teacher in anatomy, bodywork, ceremony, meditation and yoga. He was born into Chinese traditions where he was introduced to meditation and chanting at a very young age. He has always felt intuitive and tuned into something bigger and now uses this in his work and everyday life. One of his earliest memories is his great grandmother's funeral, which was the first spiritual ceremony he attended. He has clear memories of seeing his great grandmother in his bedroom after her funeral, to the disbelief of his family. Because his family didn't believe in these visits from his late grandmother, Jambo recalls her spirit moving further and further away each night until she no longer appeared. A variety of similar experiences played out throughout Jambo's childhood and young adult life. He always felt conflicted as he would experience the inexplicable but his accounts retold would be rejected by his family, even though he was being brought up in a very spiritual household. At the age of fourteen, Jambo started working with ritual and ceremony of his own accord to connect with his intuition and his spiritual beliefs. He built altars in his room and would meditate for up to an hour a day with his grandfather by his side. At the age of twenty he studied reflexology, which he was not only passionate about but also proved to help him with his own physical pain. At the time he had terrible sciatica which he was medicating with painkillers provided by his then nurse boyfriend. The reflexology remedied his pain and boosted his passion for learning about natural medicine and helping those who needed it, initially in rehabilitation centres, working with addicts. He has since gone on to study many methods of healing which he now uses widely in his workshops and classes.

Me: Hello, Jambo. I'm so glad to meet you.

Jambo: Thank you, same here.

Me: Jambo, when you're working on physical healing, say with reflexology, what is it that you're trying to do?

Jambo: If you think about all the energetic systems in our body, the chakra system, the meridian system, they are an interpretation of the blueprint of human potential. So, I decide with each individual how to work with that blueprint. I can see where they are in relation to their blueprint. We are aiming for homeostasis. We are encouraging homeostasis by shaking up the jigsaw puzzle of the physical body. We all need to regularly keep doing this as we are dealing with constant external forces: the pandemic, the world of online, meeting new people. We are affected by the outside world constantly so we need to keep checking in to help us get back to balance.

My aim is to bring people more harmony in life. We are all made up of components of a physical, emotional, psychological and spiritual body. So the true meaning of health is a balance between these four natures of our being. We will all have a tendency to lean into one of those four elements more than the others. Some people will lean into the cerebral but will not care for their physical body at all. Others will watch out for themselves emotionally but ignore their spiritual life.

Me: I can see how this is true in my own life. I adore yoga but I didn't get it at first. I didn't get the spiritual side, I only strived for the physical element. I would compare myself to others and their yoga standards but I've let that go now. How can we use yoga or physical movement to cultivate our relationship with spirit and nurture our soul with physical movement?

Jambo: An example is, when we meditate, and for me that means taking my retreat each morning with 100 Malas, that's a long time sitting. My back hurts, my shoulders will ache, so to facilitate my meditation I have to do the asana part, the movement bit. That's the most obvious example. The second thing to mention is when we look at mental health we exist only in the realm of the mind: constant rumination and thought, where we lose touch with what we are actually feeling. Also, if you are exclusively working in a spiritual sense, doing rituals, and ceremony, you won't be grounded. Connecting exclusively to the spiritual world means you'll be flying all over the place, life becomes a disembodied experience. Without the physical vehicle there is no home for the spirit to live in. This 'meat vehicle' I'm living in right now is the one vehicle that my spirit said, 'Jambo, in order for you to be you, to do what you need to do, and to be brilliant at it, you need to be this shape and this size.' This is what I was given to deliver what spirit has asked me to do. If I don't honour my body, I won't be able to do any of it.

Me: Simplifying it, is incorporating yoga into our everyday a way to have acceptance and a relationship with our physical body; to understand it better?

Jambo: Yes, and to appreciate it. If you have legs, it doesn't matter what size they are, have respect for them and appreciate them.

Me: You know what, in the writing of this book and in my everyday life, I think I have overlooked how much I'm trying to dive into the spiritual with total disregard for the physical element. I almost detach from the body at times with a desire to experience the mystical, but I now understand that without my body none of it is going to happen. I need to explore that notion when I'm practising yoga. I'd love to talk to you about meditation. We've seen a rise in the normalisation of meditation in recent years, it's been talked about more, commodified in ways too, but still so few practise it daily. Can I admit something to you? (Takes deep breath) I currently only really use it as an SOS in tough times (cringe).

Jambo: WRONG! You should not use it as an SOS. Said with love from my heart, Fearne.

Me: I know. Help me, Jambo.

Jambo: I've been meditating my whole life. In my thirties I started experimenting with the more Western practices I was witnessing around me. I was placing more importance on the physical side of things. I was more interested in learning how to perfect a hand-stand than cultivating a full-bodied spiritual practice. I let my daily meditation slide and I started to see negative outcomes instantly. There are so many reasons why meditation is a good idea. In the West we think it's all about closing our eyes and trying to relax. It's so much more. It fundamentally helps us to have a relationship with our ego. Let's go back to yoga for a minute. If when we are practising yoga we focus on joy, total bliss in the moment, we welcome spirit in: we can embody spirit. If we are suffering in our yoga practice, pushing our bodies and in pain, there is no room for spirit. Spirit wants to be here when we are having a good time. Meditation is the same. It allows us to connect with this feeling on a deeper level. It enables us to detect what is standing in our way of the perfection of the present moment of life. Let me give you an example. You're on holiday with one of your best mates. There are wildflowers, vibrant colours, birds with three heads. You're in awe, thinking, 'Wow, I've never seen so much beauty in my life.' Your friend on the other hand is saying, 'When can we go to the pub? I'm bored and hate walking.'

Me: This sounds like being on holiday with kids.

Jambo: So that's what your ego is trying to do all day. You could be in a state of enjoyment with your work that day, while taking a walk, making love to your partner, and the ego jumps in and tries to ruin it all. **Meditation allows us to bring our ego in and say, 'Come here, babes, what's up?'** It's that communion with all fragments of ourselves that allows us to become more whole.

Me: Oh, I love that. I've had a slight revelation. I was still of the thinking that meditation was mainly for me to clear my mind and try to find peace, but what you're saying is that it's actually about listening to our ego and having a conversation with it. It's about having a dialogue with it and a relationship with it. Ironically, it's my ego stopping me from meditating in the first place. My ego constantly says, 'Oh no, you have so many more things you should be doing, tidying the kitchen, finishing emails, going for a walk.' I clearly need to meditate ASAP so I can listen to why my ego is telling me this.

Jambo: That's right. You cannot have a human experience without spirit. Ego can be called many different things; you could call it karma but you could also call it trauma. The ancestral trauma you're carrying, trauma from your own parents, trauma from your own previous lives, determining how you're going to live your life. All of those examples are aspects of the ego. It's the relationship of ego and spirit. It's impossible to just be with spirit. Ego is the best friend that we can have as it will keep letting us know what is in our way. Spiritual cultivation is possible only due to the ongoing relationship and dialogue with the ego, as it's telling you where the blocks are.

Me: So the ego is giving you direct information as to how you can grow and progress? I'm starting to get this. I'm not looking to lose the ego or to feel angry that I have one, it's more an appreciation of it and learning to work with it. It's impossible to clear the mind completely of thought and ego I should imagine?

Jambo: It is possible – the day you die.

Me: Ha! Right, OK.

Jambo: Also when you're asleep the ego disappears. That's why we're able to have these crazy experiences that we call dreams. We are able to have dreams because our ego has stepped out of the way. When you're meditating forget about clearing your mind, just try and be your own best mate.

Me: Is part of the process an aid in helping us to find an equal balance between ego and spirit? I can see in my own life the times when ego has taken over but also times when I've been so in spirit and flying all over the shop. Do we use meditation to find that equilibrium?

Jambo: Yes, it's called the middle way. You'll have imbalance if you go too far down any direction; the middle route is the balance. What is the middle way? It depends what's on your own personal spectrum.

Me: I guess going into anything too extremely in life creates imbalance. One of my big questions for this book is this: can we start to integrate the traditional, esoteric, spiritual learnings into the jarring modern world, with its stresses, fast pace and digital inflections? Is it even possible?

Jambo: Some of my own teachers are very orthodox and we have to be mindful when we talk about some of these traditions because they are so sacred. They have come from thousands of years of sacredness and we need to have respect for them. Many of my practices are secret and I've been sworn to secrecy with them. In China, historically many traditions were driven out, so many traditions are very secret and hidden still today because of this. I've spoken with many of my teachers and have initiated conversation around updating and moving beyond some of the older teachings because otherwise they'll get even more lost. I can't share these ancient teachings unless we change some of the rules. Some of the teachings have been lost because in the dynamic of the master and the disciple, if the master is dying, unless the master decides that the disciple should hold these teachings, they will die with the master. I don't want any more of these teachings to die. I want to share them with the masses.

Me: It's such a tough one, as I'm sure you want to continue to completely honour the teachings but also to share them to stop people from suffering, inflicting pain on others and also the planet.

Jambo: It's taken me time to convince my teachers but we have to move forwards. Even moving these sorts of teachings online is a big change. We have to get the message out there in the modern world.

Me: I want to learn from people like you, Jambo, and also learn more about all of these teachings with the utmost respect. I guess I'm trying to do that by listening and learning but sometimes I worry about sharing these ideas because I'm not sure where the boundaries are. I don't want to steal from the sacred in any way.

Jambo: This language you're using comes from modern-day discussions around cultural appropriation. I have a problem with it. I know we're discussing spirituality but when looking at all religions and methodologies, they adopt from others. All traditions merge and get adopted and have done so for thousands of years. Some traditions come from a reaction to others. Historically, religions will have adopted traditions or reacted to them in an opposing way to carve out their own method for doing things. For example, you'll see similarities in traditions within Native American life and Aboriginal communities, due to the element of people starting to travel and migrate hundreds of years ago. Cross-pollination and ideas being transferred is ubiquitous in all teachings.

Me: That has been magnified today due to the internet I guess. There is cross-pollination everywhere, culturally and spiritually.

Jambo: It's a combination of understanding and learning about differing cultures and practices but also sharing the message so that globally we can find more peace.

Me: Well, I've adored listening to you talk today and have really got an understanding of meditation now. I know I can't put meditation off any longer. Thank you so much, Jambo.

Meditating Challenge

I set myself a challenge (yet simultaneously worry the framework of a challenge is missing the point altogether), a challenge to meditate every day for a month. I'm of course hoping to carry this on forever but let's learn to walk before we can run, eh? I'm not sure if this is cheating but, being a huge fan of Deepak Chopra and his books, talks and teachings, I opt for an online podcast he has with daily fifteen-minute meditations. His voice is like a warm bath. Within minutes of hearing his soft vowels, my neck muscles start to loosen up. I feel excited, buoyant even, that I'm already a changed woman. I am a daily meditator (even though I've not even started). Along with excitement there is a twang of nervousness as I don't want to listen to my ego. At the best of times it's self-obsessed, lives in the victim and loathes rather than accepts. I'm not sure how I'm supposed to converse with it or even make peace with it. Jambo's words, 'Come here, babes, what's up?', ring in my ears. I need to comfort this tortured ego like I would a lost friend. I need to meet with it and let the spirit meet the whingeing. I really have nothing to lose.

Day one of meditating goes a little like this:

Spiritual self: Oh, Deepak's voice is already bliss.

Ego: I fancy a hot chocolate.

Spiritual self: Sshhhhhh!

Ego: I'll look forward to one straight after.

Spiritual self: Just focus on Deepak's voice.

Ego: I forgot to post about this week's Happy Place podcast on Instagram, I'll do that after.

Spiritual self: Ego, why do you feel the need to keep looking for things to do?

Ego: I don't know, I just like it.

Spiritual self: The point of this is to not 'do'. Just listen.

Ego: Maybe I could do a ritual for my upcoming fortieth birthday. All my mates could do it with me.

Spiritual self: I know you're looking for a loophole here, trying to keep it 'spiritual', but can you just pause for a minute.

Ego: It's a good idea though, isn't it?

Spiritual self: Deepak has just revealed today's mantra. It's SO HUM.

Ego: Oh, I like it. SO HUM.

Spiritual self: SO HUM. SO HUM.

Ego: This meditation is quite long. How long are we doing this for?

Spiritual self: SO HUM.

Ego: I'm not sure I can do this every day.

Spiritual self: SO HUM.

Ego: Definitely treating myself to a hot chocolate afterwards.

Spiritual self: SO HUM. SO HUM.

Ego: SO HUM. SO HUM. SO HUM.

. . .

I got there in the end. The first ten minutes were like taming a tyrannical toddler.

Day two. SHIT I FORGOT!

Day three. Work was so busy. Husband away. SHIT I FORGOT!

I know that I have to think of meditation like brushing my teeth. I want to get to the place where it is impossible to forget as it's just a given. The safest bet seems to be to do it after the kids have gone to bed. There is little excuse at this time of the day and I'm hoping that it'll ease me in the direction of bed too. Today I worked a pretty long day with back-to-back meetings bookended by school runs and feeding the kids. Come 8pm, when the house is silent for the first time since 6:30am, the temptation to put the TV on and zone out is overwhelming, yet I know I have twenty-one days to implement this new positive habit so I'd better start somewhere. I sit down and ready myself to meet with my ego. Deepak once again offers up a mantra, which is a wonderful tool to bring your mind back to a simple line of thought.

My ego is noisy today and self-love is low on the agenda. A lot of rabbiting on in the pockets of silence. Whenever Deepak leaves a sliver for solitude my ego jumps in to fill it. Now I'm observing my own thought patterns it's almost comical to watch these ego-led thoughts jump to the forefront. The thoughts come thick and fast and oscillate between worrying about what I have to line up for the next day and the utterly irrelevant that is lurking in the crevices of my mind. I pull my attention back to the mantra and smile at this ridiculous game of mental sheep-herding. In this moment I realise how much I need to do this. My mind often goes about its business completely ungoverned. I rarely try to quieten the ego because I'm so often led to think that all its thoughts are based on fact and truth. I'm enjoying questioning all of it now.

There is a little more ease to this fifteen minutes of mind-wrangling as **I keep in mind Jambo's instruction that this isn't about losing all ego-based thoughts; it's about observing them and listening to them to see what is really beneath.** I have a strong inkling that what lies beneath is a want for control.

When life is busy, which seems to be all of the time at the moment, I crave control. I want to feel like I can manage and cope, so the omnipresent lists and solving of logistical problems become my comfort blanket. In that moment of realisation I feel like this could be the spirit meeting the ego. It's listening to its chitter-chatter and acknowledging its cry for safety. Can a heap of lists save me? Can constant rumination fend off the uncertain future? I doubt it. My spirit knows otherwise and during this meditation gently whispers to my ego that I have to lean in more to hope and less into lists.

But What About Now?

My dive into meditation continues in fits and starts of practising and forgetting. I have a way to go until this feels like just brushing my teeth in the morning. On the days that I do, I notice a fair amount of ego-wrangling beforehand that is becoming tiresome. My ego really doesn't want me to do it. Sometimes my life feels like a spinning top moving without pause. My ego willing it on to keep whirling, backed by a fear of what stopping might mean. Once I've pushed through the inner argument of the ego and the spirit and am sat on the floor ready to surrender, I experience five minutes of discomfort. Five minutes of wanting to jump up and keep 'doing'. 'Being' feels unnatural and nerve-racking as my ego lists things I could and should be doing instead to keep up with the pace of life.

Why is sitting in the moment so tricky? For many of us the ways in which we work will have exacerbated how little we live in the NOW. The digital world usually either pulls us back into the past or propels us into the future. We are rarely encouraged in our online worlds to sit, steadily, in the present. Eckhart Tolle has outsmarted his ego by living his whole life committed fully to living in the moment. He has allowed allocated time for future planning – trips, meeting up with friends, holidays, etc. – but for the most part he is sat, happily, and contentedly, in the now. You might ask, what is the point? Isn't it fun to look ahead and feel excited about something? It can, of course, be but it can also lead to disappointment if things don't unfurl as imagined. Eckhart's thinking is that we should instead just enjoy the moment fully when it arrives. Living in a mindset that is always focused on the past or the future invites anxiety, anger, dissatisfaction and fear into the equation. Eckhart talks passionately about negating those emotions by sitting in this very moment. Maybe try it now. If you sit and think about what is happening NOW and now only, are you scared without looking forward or back? Are you angry without looking forward or back? Is it possible? One certainty is that meditation brings you squarely into the NOW. If you keep directing your thoughts back to your breath or a simple mantra or just the state of listening that Jambo talked of, then we can train our minds like a muscle to sit in the moment rather than racing to the past or future.

The Brain Game

As the days rumble by, my ego gets softer. It isn't so desperate to shout and moan and I don't feel like jumping out of my skin each time I sit to surrender to meditation and some time out.

This is perhaps a small and insignificant example but on one particular morning, some ten days into my more committed daily practice, I notice that before a scheduled Instagram live, I feel wonderfully calm. Normally I'm slightly on edge, hoping the live session is warmly received and that I am not judged or ridiculed. My insecurities normally rise to the surface and teeter on the edge, hoping to push me into despair, yet today I feel totally normal. My head isn't racing to find problems of future worries that are yet to come to fruition. I feel so noticeably different that I start to worry that perhaps I should indeed feel more, well, worried. Isn't that how so many of us live these days? In a state of raw panic, where edginess and an omnipresent sensation of stress are never far away, even if we have nothing to really apply it to. In moments of calm we often question if it's OK to lean into the serenity. Today I do, knowing that it's not just the 'magic' of meditation that has brought me here; it's the willingness to listen to my ego and look beneath its shouts, rather than being completely controlled by its impulses.

Often when we feel out of control it's because we are being steered by our ego entirely. We have lost sight of the bigger picture and all spiritual connection. I'd previously overlooked how this meeting of my spiritual self and ego in meditation could help me cultivate more hope and faith in life. In those moments where I'm wrestling with my own ego-led desires or worries, I'm now able to see, with more clarity, that it's not ME that's impatient, restless and scared, it's a cluster of old thoughts and habits that keep me wedded to the pace and stress of the modern world. I am not my ego; it's a part of me that I cannot deny or ignore but it's not fully who I am. **My thoughts are not who I am. They again are manifested by my life experience but not the entirety of me.** When I'm meditating, I can now make that separation and watch and listen to these thoughts and worries rather than have them pull out emotions and reactions that aren't always helpful. If my ego is bellowing that I continue working without a break and push through a giant headache so I can keep on top of things, I can now see the years of moments in my life where I have felt lesser than or overlooked, and know that it's these old thoughts that are speaking. If my ego is overly defensive and plotting an imaginary text message to someone that I'll never send, I can see, when in meditation, that I'm hurting and looking for a vent to release some of this tension.

Senior monk Gelong Thubten teaches meditation the world over and is committed to giving people the power and knowledge that we can all choose happiness in certain situations. He says in his book, *A Monk's Guide to Happiness*, that 'meditation helps us to access what feels like a deep well within, filled with nourishing water that we can drink whenever we want'. How beautiful is that? Even if it doesn't feel like it, we all have love and comfort bubbling within us for the taking, in all its nature and abundant glory. We have mostly been tricked by modern-day advertising that we have to buy this sort of feeling with a shiny car or latest on-trend jacket. We all know that we might feel happiness for a fleeting moment while donning the aforementioned trendy jacket but that happiness is ephemeral. The happiness Thubten talks of is omnipotent and omnipresent and, most importantly, free. Social media has perhaps put even more focus on accolade, with status and busyness taking centre stage on the grid. We make mental connections and assumptions that lead us to believe that we might find eternal happiness if we are the big boss, the CEO, the shiny celebrity or busiest business owner. Is that a guarantee, though? Again, probably not. I know loads of 'important' people who are bloody miserable. Thubten continues: 'Instead of feeling like our lives are spinning out of control, with stress, loneliness and dissatisfaction dominating our minds, we can become more connected within, more centred, even in busy situations.'

Thubten's words prod me with a much-needed reminder that my mind isn't in control of me, I'm in control of it, and with a little meditation brought into the equation I have a chance to understand my mind as well as the tools to train it.

Soothing Sound

Meditation is never just one thing. We often feel put off as we believe we have to settle on one idea of what meditation is and looks like. Having the concentration span of a month-old sausage dog has meant that I've really needed to try out many methods to keep me going back to it. Sound meditation has been a source of real comfort and joy for me. Being a music lover, I instantly feel every cell in my body relax if I hear the right notes in sequence. My thoughts are quieter and less urgent as my mind drifts into pure bliss when I pick up on nice sounds.

But what is sound meditation? I dug a little deeper into this subject, to see how we can bring it into our everyday, and spoke with Jasmin Harsono, an intuitive wellbeing guide, sound artist, author, speaker and founder of conscious lifestyle brand Emerald and Tiger and community platform Breathe Love.

I hosted a sound bath (another name for sound meditation) on my Instagram page recently and zoned out so much that I forgot I had to sit up at the end and talk to the lovely lot who were watching live. It's pure sensory bliss.

Me: Jasmin, what is sound healing/meditation?

Jasmin: Sound healing has been around since the beginning of time. It has been used in ancient cultures, such as the Egyptian, Tibetan, Mongolian and Mayan, and practised by shamans and medicine people worldwide throughout the centuries.

We use sound to heal in various ways – celebration, ceremony, expression – and to communicate.

We are all made up of energy and vibration; sound is innately part of us. It connects us to our emotions, feelings, memories, thoughts, and even deeper at a soul level, and it expands way beyond what we sense, hear or feel.

During a sound meditation, the practitioner uses the power of intention combined with the resonance, meaning and healing vibrations of usually live sounds to help the participant, or participants, receive what they need at that time; for example, deep relaxation or rest. The participant is taken on a sound healing journey where healing sound vibrations and frequencies are shared via sound instruments and tools. The sound tools are crystal bowls, a gong, drum, the voice, tuning forks, chimes and more, which help people centre into their bodies and shift their energy and vibration back to a balanced state.

Our orchestral bodies

Every instrument played in an orchestra has its own sound and vibration. When played in tune with all the other instruments, the whole orchestra feels at one. However, if one or more instrument is playing out of tune, the orchestra as a whole sounds off – they are not playing in harmony with one another. Once the instruments are all back in tune, there is harmony again, a perfect symphony.

The same applies to our body and how sound helps to get us back into balance. Our bodies are made up of our skin, cells, tissues, muscles and organs: they all have their own vibration and, when in harmony with everything else in the body, there is balance, ease and flow within. If something in the body is out of balance disease may show up. Our bodies are comprised of four layers: the emotional, physical, mental and spiritual body. Sound meditation helps to realign and bring our body back into a state of wholeness so that all parts of the body are working in harmony together, just like a fully tuned orchestra.

Sound meditation is often referred to as a 'sound bath' because, when sound is shared, we are bathing our bodies in it as we would bathe in bathwater. Our bodies are made up of around 60 per cent water; the sound vibrations flow through the water within our body.

Sound meditation has grown in popularity in recent years as we seek ways to de-stress and tap into a holistic way of living. Those who are new to meditation and are curious about it often find sound meditations easier to experience because there is less instruction and doing. They can relax into their surrounding space and body, and surrender to the sounds playing. The sounds help lessen the distractions of racing thoughts and other things that make it hard to settle into meditation.

Sound healing is scientifically proven to shift our energy and bring harmony to our body, but not every experience will be blissful. Our bodies are likely to be holding stress and tension from past life experiences. Sound meditations may bring awareness to that tension, we may find that the experience is overwhelming or emotional. At some point in the coming days, weeks and months, sound healing will support us back to our true state of being as we let go of what no longer serves us and remember our power, wisdom and potential.

Most people find sound meditation relaxing; there are lots of benefits, including:

- Aids the body's natural ability to heal.
- Regulates breathing, brainwaves and heart rate.
- Produces a sense of calm and wellbeing.
- Reduces tension, calming the nervous system.
- Promotes deep relaxation and healing sleep.
- Aids a meditative state.
- Deepens mental clarity.
- Promotes a sense of connectedness and higher power.
- Deepens spiritual connection and practice.
- Reduces stress and anxiety (lowers cortisol levels).
- Increases creativity, focus and clarity.
- Decreases tension and fatigue.

- Boosts mood (stimulates the release of serotonin, dopamine, oxytocin and endorphins).
- Improves sleep, increases melatonin levels.

Important note: Those who are sound sensitive should attend a sound meditation with caution. Those with metal implants or pacemakers, and pregnant women in their first trimester, should seek medical advice if they are new to the practice.

Me: How does sound help us to relax or reach a meditative state?

Jasmin: During a sound meditation, participants often report feeling safe because sound is so familiar to them, giving space to let go and relax.

The sound vibrations go deeper, penetrating the body, helping to reduce tension, anxiety and stress, promoting a deep sense of calm and connection and bringing people into deeper states of rest. Some sound frequencies can shift a participant from beta (active) to alpha (calm), theta (meditation), delta (sleep) states. The theta state frequency is 3.5 to 7.5 Hz, so if a sound therapist plays at that frequency, they will encourage the participant into a meditative state.

Me: How can we incorporate this into our everyday life?

Jasmin: There are simple yet profound ways of incorporating sound into everyday life:

Sound meditation classes and one-to-one sessions: Seek out sound meditation classes or a private session that may be offered in person or virtually.

Download a meditation: Download, stream and listen to various sound meditations online, experiment and see what you like. You will find a variety of sound meditations shared via YouTube, Instagram and more. Start small – try a fifteen-minute sound meditation before bed to help ease you into a deep, restful sleep.

Nature sounds: Healing sounds are all around us. I recommend getting out into nature as often as possible and consciously listening and connecting to the sounds of nature around you, such as birds singing, rain falling, the wind moving through the trees, and the flowing ocean waves.

Our voice: Our voice is an instrument that I consider to be the most essential sound tool; through our voice we can create a sound meditation of its own. We are sound. It is not about sounding perfect but vocalising sounds that encapsulate how we feel in the moment, healing tension, anger, worry, and bringing us into higher vibrational states such as joy and peace.

Start by simply humming a couple of times a day; feel the vibration. Do this in the shower or when walking the kids to school or cooking dinner. Experiment by changing the tone and pitch of your voice, hum softly and then hard. See what resonates. Breathe through the experience.

Soon you may discover that sounding through your voice becomes an integral part of your everyday life and helps shift your energy flow. You may even start to experiment by trying other vocal healing techniques, such as chanting and singing sacred mantras and songs, toning, intuitive voice and more.

Finally, if you are interested in playing sound meditations at home, do your research to purchase sound healing instruments from reputable and ethical manufacturers. Slowly build your sound kit, become familiar with your instruments and create a deep connection to your sound tools. Get your family and friends involved and start creating sound together. It is honestly part of our heritage to come together and connect through sound.

Simply Listening

These last few weeks of giving myself that time at the start or end of the day has calmed a part of me that felt wildly out of control. Before chatting to Jambo, I was still working on the assumption that I had to rid myself of all ego and negative thought when in meditation. This led to me feeling like I'd failed before I'd even started. Now, in these brief moments of stillness, I simply listen. I listen to my inner moaning and groaning and ask my ego what is up. It's allowing me the freedom and room to forgive myself more deeply for past mistakes and a willingness to have more self-compassion and compassion for others, knowing that we're all in the same boat. We are all part spirit and part ego, bumbling along on this complex planet, trying our best, making mistakes and looking for love. My ego is probably always only looking for love, it just goes about it in a strange way. It shouts for it, craves it and sometimes wants to attain it through power or control. The part of me that is pure spirit IS love so can always offer up the right words, level of comfort and clarity when my ego enters the room. No one of us is more spiritual than the next person, some of us just have a louder ego.

THE LAW OF ATTRACTION

When we are talking about that something that is bigger than us, we might naturally assume it lies in the mystic or in the unknown. This might make spirituality seem more appealing to you as it alludes to magic and a greater power, but for some it might also be daunting if you find it hard to believe that anything other than the human experience exists at all. This is where the law of attraction comes in. It might at times seem like pure sorcery as you witness new outcomes and sizcable life changes but its roots are in the practical. It's all about thought. When we look at love and those times where it feels absent, it's usually purely down to our thoughts.

I learned so much about this subject when the wondrous Rhonda Byrne came on the Happy Place podcast as a guest. As a big fan of the book *The Secret* I was buzzing at the opportunity to chat to her one-on-one. Speaking to Rhonda is like talking to a celestial angel. Her energy is so light and beams out of her smile, and her passionate cadence is infectious to the core.

Dreaming Big and The Lord of the Flies

As a teenager I naturally understood the law of attraction without even knowing what it was. As an individual I'm not special,
I'm not the most talented, I'm not even the most determined, but
I am a big dreamer. Sat in English lit classes in Year 10 of senior
school, I did little else. I have such vivid memories of staring
out at the gloomy steel sky that canopied over the concrete car
park below; a cacophony of grey. There had to be more colour
out there. I knew that there was and I spent 90 per cent of those
lessons imagining it in HD.

My dreams weren't based on arrogance or believing I
had something special to get me there, I just daydreamed so
hard that my mental fantasies felt real. Instead of listening to
my long-suffering teacher, Mr Conn Iggulden (who is now a
best-selling author and probably completely in shock that I now
spend most of my time writing too), passionately waxing lyrical
about *The Lord of the Flies*, I would transport myself to a world
away from Eastcote. Instead of itchy tights and a stiff white shirt
with a collar that felt like it was made out of cardboard, I was
wrapped in a silk gown, walking red carpets, with camera bulbs
lighting up like firecrackers ahead. As you've probably guessed
from reading this book and possibly my others, I'm not so interested in that part of the job any more but, back then, as a brace-
wearing, mascara junkie fourteen-year-old, it seemed like a much
better option than Piggy and his asthma inhaler. I dreamed
myself into the job. I believed it so much that the lines between
my reality and the ongoing fantasy in my head were meshed like
a tangled fishing net. I saw no other option so that's what the
universe offered up. It didn't, of course, hand me a silk gown and
Leonardo DiCaprio as escort but did present opportunities for
me to work my way into my heady fantasies. Auditions started

to show up on my radar which were the perfect chance to see if I could really fill showbiz shoes. That's the point at which hard work and a willingness to learn had to be applied, but I think I was only open to those audition opportunities because I had an inner belief that being in the industry was an option for me in the first place.

Me and my thoughts conjured up all manner of weird and wonderful events for the next fifteen years. My head was constantly full of bountiful dreams so vivid that I had almost lived them before they happened. I interviewed on the red carpet at the Oscars for two years running, worked on TV shows in the UK and America simultaneously and had the world's best musicians play huge hits a mere metre away from me in the Radio 1 Live Lounge. All of this was dreamed up and explored mentally before it unfurled in reality. I was practising the law of attraction before I even knew what it meant.

Beaten by Life

In my early thirties I sank into a depression. It was quick. Shock, trauma and a complex head-fuck of circumstance and confusion wrecking-balled into my life. The manifesting stopped in a heartbeat. One minute it was there for the taking, the next I couldn't even remember how to do it. I think I subconsciously assumed my luck had run out. At this point I mentally departed from my own story and saw life as something that was there to test and attack me. I simultaneously felt wildly out of control and assumed that the unknown quality of the future would always result in something awful. Manifesting took one lonely seat at the back for a very long time.

That was ten years ago and only now, due to the writing of this book and the extent of investigation and exploration that

I've been on, do I feel it's possible to engage with manifesting again. FUN!! I had forgotten how much fun it is.

Because I'm focusing on love in this section, I'm acutely aware that to be back in the mental space where I can manifest, I need to believe I deserve to have my positive thoughts come to fruition first. There is little point in me having dreams and desires only to then extinguish them with a torrent of self-loathing. As we've already learned, **lifting one's self-limiting beliefs and allowing some self-love to surface equals opportunity.** As my self-worth slowly surfaces, people just keep showing up in my life at the right time, to guide me and teach me, so I can write the best book possible. Of course, there is effort involved and a lot of hours at my laptop to get the job done, but it's all fun and I'm not having to email hundreds of people begging them to be a part of this book. I've fallen back into a more positive habit of believing anything is possible and that life doesn't have to be one long struggle.

Bigger Than Us felt like it had already been written and was just sitting inside of me waiting to be released on to the screen of my laptop. I could picture it sat there on a bookshelf, full of stories and hope, before I even stumbled upon the title. I felt the presence of many great contributors before a single connection was made. My mojo is resurfacing and, my God, I'm relieved. The pivotal point has been letting go of a lot of negative beliefs I had grown used to.

For the last ten years I had become way too comfortable believing that I don't deserve help. It's been my number one nemesis and, because I was certain that I don't deserve help, I didn't receive any or if it did show up I would push it away. Being an all-or-nothing person, I've taken this to the extreme. Not only have I shunned help but I've attempted to help others even when I have little to give. I would hand over possessions, thoughts and delicate pieces of myself for the consumption of others, feeling I wasn't worthy of holding on to them myself. It goes without saying, I love giving, but during my thirties it was sometimes not coming from the right place. I handed over my power again and again, because I thought so little of myself. Ten years lacking self-love means that I can look back and spot numerous patterns that I know no longer serve me. Relationships and one-on-one dynamics would often result in resentment due to my lack of ability to set healthy boundaries. The relationship I had with myself was often fraught due to my willingness to let every single outside opinion in. I had no clue that there was another option – to exercise autonomy when it came to what I took on board. My lack of self-worth led to the assumption that I had to imbibe and believe every outside opinion.

My moods were often irregular due to my shaky foundations and lack of self-belief. I left jobs because of it, turned down work, tried too hard in friendships, stopped socialising at points. Ten years of feeling like my heart was beating outside of my ribcage due to nothing more than a thought. ONE thought: that I didn't deserve any better.

We usually make things more complicated by blaming circumstance or other people for our suffering but often it's one or two root beliefs. Mine has been easy to trace as it's been so prevalent and loud. Yours might be hidden or masquerading as something else. Your negative root thought might be self-loathing masquerading as bolshy confidence. Your negative root thought might be that you're unlovable yet it masquerades as shyness. **Only you'll know what is lying beneath the stories we tell ourselves.** There is usually just one little belief controlling it all.

Writing this book has helped me look closer at what is fact and what is fiction in my life. My self-loathing is all fiction and, guess what, so is yours. I know, I'm making it sound too easy, but all those things you hate about yourself are total lies. They're nothing more than learned stories and habit. I don't want to make it sound too simple as I know only too well that these thoughts might have been with us for decades. Discipline and hard work have to be in the mix to ensure we drop these stories and choose the truth over the fiction part, but it is 100 per cent possible. The foundation of self-love or acceptance is distinguishing fact from fiction. Are you a horrible person? I doubt it. Are you too loud or did someone just say that to you once? Are you useless? Of course not, everyone can find their purpose. What is true and what is a bloody big lie?

The Big Secret

So, is it really that simple? That our thoughts are determining so much outcome in our lives? And how does this help us cultivate a more connected and spiritual life experience? I know just the lady to ask. I know you've been waiting for her since I mentioned her name at the start of this section.

Rhonda is one of the aforementioned individuals who came into my life at the right time. Twice in fact. The first was in my twenties when *The Secret* caught my eye in a local bookshop. Like millions of people the world over, *The Secret* became my manifesto for life and helped cement my early manifesting capabilities. More recently, due to the release of Rhonda's latest book, *The Greatest Secret*, I was given the opportunity to interview her for the Happy Place podcast – the universe seemingly giving me a little nudge to get back to attracting the good stuff in. After the recoding of this episode, I was flying. Hearing these powerful messages spoken aloud by an individual who has lived and breathed this stuff is intoxicating. My husband looked at me with quizzical eyes as I blurted out every bit of information I could recall that Rhonda had spoken that evening. I clung tight to every morsel of hope that I could go back to thinking in a positive way. As toe-curling as it can be to listen back to oneself bursting with excitement and enthusiasm, this is still one of my favourite podcast episodes to replay.

Sticking to the good old-fashioned 'don't ask, don't get' mantra, I decided to chance my luck and ask Rhonda if she would be up for another round of quizzing, this time for this very book. Luckily, I didn't have to recoil with embarrassment for pushing my luck too far, as she accepted the invitation, giving me another chance to tap into her incredible wisdom. I've only interviewed Rhonda twice but I already feel like she is perhaps my spiritual aunty. I'm not sure how she would feel about this but I'm going with it. I feel comforted by her presence and could talk to her for hours. I'm not sure if Rhonda has the time or indeed inclination for hours of chat, so I'll try not to overstay my welcome.

After Rhonda had stumbled across the notion that thought was the most powerful conductor in our lives, she set about making the seminal 2006 film *The Secret*, which included interviews with philosophers, writers and thought leaders who discussed, dissected and encouraged the law of attraction. This led to the best-selling book of the same name, which has sold over 30 million copies worldwide and still continues to change lives daily. So, let's learn more about how we can turn our lives upside down, in the best possible way.

Me: Oh Rhonda, I'm so grateful that I'm getting to chat to you again today.

Rhonda: It's so lovely to see you again. I'm so glad you're writing this book. It was always going to happen. I remember when I was writing *The Secret*, I just couldn't stop it coming through. It had always been in me. I needed to write the truth and share what I had discovered.

Me: I'm so glad you wrote it – it changed my life and that of so many others the across the globe.

Rhonda: Thank you. And I love the title of your book by the way.

Me (air punch): Thanks, Rhonda. Right, let's start with the basics – how does the law of attraction work?

Rhonda: The law of attraction operates on one thing, and one thing only, and that is thought. Whatever we THINK is what we create in our life. More accurately, it's whatever we think and then BELIEVE, but most people believe all of their thoughts without questioning them. We are creating in every single moment, every event and circumstance, we are constantly creating. If we don't understand the power of our thoughts, we will miscreate and create things we don't want. We don't do it deliberately but we have to understand the power of our thoughts otherwise we'll talk about things we don't want, and while we are talking about them, we are creating them. The law of attraction is completely based on thought. Whatever thoughts you focus on and energise are what you'll create.

Me: So much of this is down to self-limiting beliefs, right?

Rhonda: We are the cause and the outside world is the effect. So it matters a great deal what we have inside of us. We cannot experience anything in our lives that lives outside of our beliefs. Our beliefs build a wall around our lives. Limited thinking like

'I don't deserve better' or 'I will never find love', these thoughts are barriers and become true when we believe them. We need to realise these thoughts are not who we are. They're coming from a flimsy old belief and we can let it go. Any positive thoughts about yourself are true and any thoughts that are contrary to those positive thoughts are lies. Let them go.

Me: So many of us are trapped by limiting thoughts but perhaps we don't understand their potency. We forget our own power.

Rhonda: If you have a positive thought and you don't contradict it with another thought, then you will manifest the positive thought. It's powerful stuff.

Me: So many people feel like life or the universe is against them. I have felt like this at times. I guess you need one big perspective shift to believe that the universe and life are for you and with you.

Rhonda: If you believe the world is against you, then that will be your life. We are free to create our lives in any way we want. We are free to create a life of suffering or a life of joy. We have to stop creating the life that we don't want to live. It just takes one positive thought to change your life.

Me: It sounds so simple but sometimes feels so tricky. What I guess I need to understand is that this sort of thinking doesn't mitigate tough times, does it? You can't negate loss, global issues or pain, so is part of the thought process acceptance? An acceptance of the parts of life we can't change?

Rhonda: There are two parts to this. The first is that if you are really joyful and thinking positively then anything going on in the outside world won't affect you in the same way it'll affect other people. I speak from experience. When I was working on *The Secret* I was so positive. I became so diligent to my every negative thought and would just say, 'Cancel, cancel' and put a positive thought in its place. You can turn everything around with thought. The second thing to remember is that we are all creating our own lives. So, I'm creating my life but I'm not creating yours. So what happens to another person is under their creation. You cannot create in someone else's life. You wouldn't want someone else creating in your life. Here is an example. You think you've found your soulmate. You're totally in love but he leaves you and then you want to use the secret to win him back. Yet imagine if someone out there was madly in love with you and wanted to use the secret to get with you, but you didn't like them. It would be awful. It just doesn't work like that. Each of us creates our own life through the law of attraction.

Then, on a mass conscious level, we are also creating the events in the world. Some of the things that we see as a negative event are actually a blessing. For instance, what we've all just been through with the pandemic has been so difficult for so many people and there is a lot of fear, but it's also a big wake-up call for us as a human race. We have been given an opportunity to live without fear. This is a global wake-up call that we need to live in a place of joy and revel in the miracle of life and this world.

My mind is racing at this point. Hearing Rhonda say these powerful words might be hard for some of you to read; at points I found it hard to hear. Do we create everything in our lives? Surely there is bad luck too but listening to Rhonda's last point on how we frame tough times I think I'm starting to get it. We might feel sad or angry that certain things have happened to us but were they the lessons we had to learn? Have we had the gift of growth from them? I recall some situations in my life that have caused great pain and suffering and, although I certainly didn't actively want them to come into my life and I can't with clarity see the moment I manifested them into reality, I can see the gifts and learnings from the darkness and trauma. Like me you might want to re-read this section or maybe come back to it at another time when you've had a chance to think about the lessons you might have learned from the tough parts of life.

Me: We've placed so little emphasis on joy lately. Fear has been so emphasised this last year.

Rhonda: Joy creates. If you are in joy, it creates more joy. Most people think, 'I'll be happy when I meet the perfect partner, get the best job, live somewhere else', but you have to be in joy and feel happy first to get all of that stuff.

Me: What if someone out there thinks they have been trying to manifest good outcomes but it hasn't been happening – what is going on there?

Rhonda: They're not believing they have it already. They're noticing that they DON'T have it and are in lacking. If you believe you have your desire already, then it'll manifest so quickly, but if you're constantly noticing that you haven't got it, you will continue to manifest the absence of it.

There appears to be an idea of time but time is just a concept. There is no time. Look at gravity, it's not working in the past or the future, it's operating in the moment. There is no time for the law of attraction: there is only this moment now. Therefore, we have to imagine we already have our desire now. It is good to use your senses as well when you're imagining, so you can really feel like you have it. Touch, smell, sight, sounds. Imagine it all. Imagination is simply thought in picture. Many spiritual teachers say visualise and then let it go. The letting go represents forgetting about it, which means you won't obsess about that thought and allow any space for contradicting thoughts. We are always creating a situation where we either 'have it' or 'don't have it'.

Me: How did having the revelation about the law of attraction change your relationship with life?

Rhonda: My life did a complete three-sixty. I wasn't spiritual before *The Secret*. I thought bad things could happen at any moment out of the blue, but when I understood the law of attraction I realised how powerful we all are and also that we never die. The body might die but we do not. The body is not who we are. My entire life changed at this point. I was previously in so much debt, my health was in a really bad way, but when I discovered *The Secret* and the law of attraction everything negative just left. My relationships changed, my health, my finances, my relationship with life itself. I even regenerated my eyesight. I understood that I had been told that with age my eyes would deteriorate; I believed it and of course they did. So I visualised that I could see perfectly and after two nights of doing so I put the glasses down and have never picked them up again.

Me: What the hell!

Rhonda: I had such a belief that I would do it, so it happened. I visualised reading in the dark and very small writing and didn't contradict that thought.

Me: It's mind-blowing yet weirdly simple. For people reading this who feel that this is not attainable for them, people who are stuck in negative loops, are there tips on how to get started with the law of attraction?

Rhonda: We all have negative thoughts, they don't matter a bit. It's only when we start believing them that they become a problem. Let's look at how we deal with emotions. Emotions are constantly arising in the universe but they're all very impersonal; we just take them so personally. It's just energy passing by. Say, for example, guilt is passing by, it's just energy and it's passing. It'll come in and out of the body. But usually instead we make the impersonal guilt very personal and we say, 'I am guilty.' Instead, just let it come and then go.

One other thing that helps to shift us all very quickly is gratitude. It'll shift your frequency and get you off a negative frequency where all the negative thoughts live. Those negative thoughts – guilt and blame, etc. – are on a low frequency. So get yourself off that low frequency and on to a higher frequency by using gratitude. **Lie in bed in the morning and either run through a list in your head or write down the things you're grateful for.** For example: 'I'm so grateful for my mum, she's always been there for me.' Or: 'I'm so grateful for my work colleagues because they're so understanding and supportive.' As you go through your list you'll instantly feel a softening effect all over the body but especially in the heart. This means you have disempowered the negative mind, you're off that negative frequency. I used to do this each morning when I was working on *The Secret*. I would lie in bed listing simple things I was grateful for until I had tears in my eyes and then I would get up and, with each step and foot that touched the ground, I would say out loud, 'Thank you, thank you, thank you.' It switches things up.

Me: So that helps us to acknowledge abundance to help create more of it in life. Is it cognitively rewiring in a way?

Rhonda: It is rewiring; it is reprogramming your mind. The only task our mind has is to create the life we want. But we've overcomplicated how we use it and we've empowered negative thoughts and made emotions very personal. Just remember, any thoughts that don't say, 'You're beautiful, intelligent, gorgeous, unlimited, eternal, wonderful, full of joy', simply say to those thoughts, 'Oh, wrong person, move on.'

Me: If it feels overwhelming to switch to this thinking forever, it could be a great experiment even just for a few days.

Rhonda: You'll see a difference in only twenty-four hours. It's so fast. If you start using gratitude daily, you'll see it works so quickly in shifting your mindset and the outcomes in your life. As well as gratitude we can focus on love. When we look out at the world, it might not seem like it, but it's all just love. So, in a similar way to how we use gratitude, we make a list of everything we love. **You can do a love rampage. You can say, 'I love it when we have a blue sky. I love it when the traffic runs smoothly like this. I love this music I'm listening to. I love this podcast. I love the birds flying overhead.'**
You'll fly to the highest frequency by doing this as love is our true nature. Love is inside us always but our mind and negative thoughts cover it up. You just have to be aware of your thoughts and know the negative ones are not the truth. Don't identify with them. Do a love rampage and you'll get off that negative frequency.

Me: A love rampage, I adore this! I feel so lucky to have talked to you today, Rhonda. What a gift!

• • •

After our chat I have so much more clarity on how the law of attraction helps us to live life with a spiritual outlook. It cultivates hope. It's the match to the kindle that lights the fire of possibility. By training our minds to focus on the positives we instantly create hope. Often we lose connection to that something bigger by no more than our self-limiting beliefs and our self-limiting beliefs can only enter the room when love is absent. **The law of attraction brings us back to a place where anything is possible because we believe we are connected to something other than our own minds.** Again, it's so wonderfully simple but we all know how impetuous our minds are.

Within moments of this conversation finishing, it is quite apparent that I am going to have to completely retrain my brain from its current operating system. Two minutes after our conversation I find my mind dishing out thoughts of a negative nature: 'What if Rhonda thinks I'm an idiot?' And, 'Did Rhonda think that was a total waste of time?' I know negative thoughts are human nature but my propensity to believe them is rampant to say the least. I'm going to have to monitor my thoughts like a pet owner might keep a constant eye on a new puppy, so it doesn't chew the sofa and shit everywhere. My brain is the most out-of-control puppy. We've all got a little head start on this one due to Wendy's wisdom earlier on, but to progress we now have to interrupt any negative thoughts and question their validity too.

The Easier Option

I instantly text four friends who I know are having a rough time for varying reasons and relay every glorious word I can remember that flowed from Rhonda's mouth. I speedily punch the touchscreen, unable to get the profound to them quickly enough. Two of my friends have lightbulb moments about their own life on hearing Rhonda's answers, and the other two can't believe how simple it is but still feel they're unable to achieve this constant positive state. It does, on paper, all look so easy, so why are we mostly awful at this? On reflection I think we've just gotten used to believing the negative. It's simply an easier option. It takes much more effort to constantly look for the gifts in lessons and the silver linings. We also live in a world where negativity is completely the norm. Newspapers are full of nega- tivity. So rarely is there a heart-warming story, miraculous event or tale of altruism reported in the papers. Hence why I mostly avoid them. We've warped the word 'news' to have exclusively negative connotations. How weird. Negativity is so regular that we don't even notice it as negative. Positive stories or outcomes seem elusive and buried under sensationalised reports and fear- mongering. We might even assume positive outcomes are only for lucky people, but surely we have much more say over the amount of this ungoverned negativity we let into our lives? Understanding how powerful these negative thoughts are is key, so we can then step back and look at them under a magnifying glass to ask, 'Is this really true?'

Changing the Story

Sometimes we build whole frameworks around one simple negative thought. Our life's decisions are made from that one thought and how we move through the world steered by it too. **These negative beliefs feel comfortable and give us the excuse or reason to act in a habitual way.** With that one big negative thought removed, we might even feel a little lost.

For instance, for a long time I didn't believe I was good enough to be asked to do a primetime TV show. I felt 'too odd' and 'too quirky' and 'not attractive or girlie enough' so placed myself as an outsider who was always going to fail from the start. Luckily with age I have stopped believing this negative thought. At first, I felt like I had jumped out of a plane without a parachute. What was my story now that I didn't believe this notion? Why was I not getting any TV jobs? My self-perpetuated belief system and framework dissolved within minutes and I was left with a lurking feeling that perhaps I had simply changed as a person. Perhaps I didn't want to do big TV shows any more. My ego, with its need to compare and look for lacking, had cemented this thought into fact to keep me feeling like I wasn't good enough, yet that wasn't the truth. I can now see how so many other negative thoughts I've believed have stopped me in my tracks and kept me vibrating at a very low level.

If we are operating from this place of feeling lesser than, it of course hinders us from connecting with that something bigger. We might not feel there is much more to life than the human experience, or that a spiritual connection is undeserved and only there for those in need. Last night I spoke to a friend on WhatsApp about her current lack of confidence. Now, may I point out that this friend is major. She is not only gorgeous, utterly unique in her expression and talent but also a wonderfully caring person. She couldn't see any of this as she was so trapped in her negative thoughts and wedded to totally believing them. After speaking to Rhonda I felt like one of her missionaries. I pep-talked my mate through her whirlwind of negativity and gave her another perspective. Maybe her own beliefs that she is unlovable and 'gross', as she at one point declared, were a total lie. Now I KNOW these beliefs are a total lie but because she has believed them for so long it is of course initially hard for her to switch this up. I called upon Rhonda's beliefs and asked my mate to tell the universe that she is ready for self-love and acceptance. To focus on those thoughts without any other thoughts contradicting them. I know that I was saying this for me as much as I was for her. My mate's response was quick and definite. She didn't feel it was OK to ask for help or for guidance when so many others have much bigger problems. This is where things get seriously interesting, as I have also felt guilty and unworthy of asking for spiritual guidance when in trouble, as I have felt those sorts of wishes should be reserved for those who truly need it.

Having spoken to Rhonda on two occasions now I have perhaps a little more insight into why this sort of thinking is potentially very damaging to us and those around us. As soon as we slip into denying ourselves guidance we are not noticing the true abundance of life. Love isn't limited, it cannot run out. Knowledge and wisdom again cannot run out. There is enough for everyone. Also, we have to unpick our own lack of self-worth to see that choosing to stay in suffering in our own lives will not help others who are having a tough time.

In fact, if we are thriving then we will have a larger capacity to help others. So, to ask for guidance or for change and to focus on such goals only leads us to a place where we can be more of service to others and offer a guiding light of our own. Choosing to live out our own dreams does not take the power away from others to do so too. If anything, it'll encourage and inspire others to do the same. In my own life, I have been so massively inspired by others who have followed their dreams and broken down their own self-limiting beliefs. We all deserve to live out our dreams.

Mental Walls

Today something triggered me on Instagram. My habitual tendencies to feel like I'm being treated unfairly flared up like a recurring puss-filled boil. The post in question went against everything I believe about life and freedom and was presented in a way that alluded to anyone of an opposing viewpoint as being wrong. It's not just the fact that I, like most, hate being wrong; it's also tied into one of my lifelong-held beliefs: that I AM wrong. It's been one of the negative thoughts that I've harboured, which has held me back so much. I've manipulated that negative thought into solid fact. Over the years 'I got it wrong' has morphed into 'I am wrong'. I've embodied the notion entirely. At times I have been petrified that I'll be called out or publicly shamed (at times I have been, as the UK press went through a phase of really going for me in a very personal and vicious way) because I am in some way wrong.

It's a deep-rooted fear that is hard to articulate as I'm not sure where its origins lie. It's been a lurking feeling that lies completely dormant but is triggered easily when others confidently state that their way is the right way. I'm all for freedom of choice and everybody doing what is right for them but that strangely doesn't stop me from being my own worst enemy. It's driven me to aim for perfection at times and at other times to feel debilitated as I have been so terrified to put a foot wrong. In a way it's been a subconscious attempt to dehumanise myself. All humans are fallible and will make mistakes and, as we all know, we then have the option to either grow from that mistake or keep making it over and over again until, BOOM, we get the hint. Yet, even though I know this on an intellectual level I've had the tendency to override that knowledge and instead have berated myself or felt like an idiot because of the belief that 'I get life wrong'.

In John C. Parkin's brilliant book *F**k It Therapy*, he calls this type of thinking 'prison'. In some ways we'll all find ourselves in a type of confinement due to our own thoughts, but sometimes we have no idea the cell even exists. We trundle on through life and then at some point we'll come up against a big hurdle where we realise that we are the ones imprisoning ourselves in the first place. Of course, the realisation might not be instant and we'll probably go through phases of blame, shame and guilt, but hopefully with some self-inventory we'll stumble upon the fact that we have created walls for ourselves and that we have the agency to knock them down. That's what 'F**K It Therapy' is. It's saying a giant 'FUCK IT' and doing what, deep down, we really want. Saying what we really want to, creating what we really want to, enjoying what we really want to, saying no to what we do not want and essentially knocking down those prison walls. That to me seems to be the starting point for the law of attraction. First, we've gotta knock those walls down.

No Idea

The next step is to know what you truly want out of life, but what if you have no clue? What if you have forgotten what you like and what you feel will bring you joy? I have definitely been there. It is perhaps somewhat of a cliché but after I had kids I found myself all-consumed by my new role and the responsibility of it. Although at times I still felt deeply connected to that 'something bigger' and could feel the rumble of my soul swelling each time I held my babies, I also lost a sense of who I was.

When both Honey and Rex were at preschool for large portions of the day and I found myself with the odd day off work, I literally had no clue what to do. Luckily, I adore my job, which makes me a very fortunate person, so usually my tendency is to fill my day with as much work as possible, but on those rare days where I was on top of things and had a few hours to spare, I felt a bit lost. If you'd asked me in one of those barren moments what I wanted to manifest with the law of attraction, I wouldn't have had a clue.

We can perhaps lessen this pressure by working towards a goal of knowing what feeling we want rather than a specific outcome. I usually settle on peace as my desired goal. Gone are the days where I wanted high drama and a rollercoaster of adrenalin, emotions and the limelight. I just fancy a little sliver of peace. It is perhaps easier to apply Rhonda's advice when we settle on a desired emotion. I can think back to other times I have felt really peaceful and can remember how my body felt, how my skin tingled, the smell of seaside air, the sound of shingle moving beneath the surface of blue. I can get myself there and enjoy focusing on that so as not to let any contradictory thoughts swamp the good stuff.

Perhaps we can also apply Meik Wiking's research on nostalgia to help us on our way. Meik is the CEO of the Happiness Research Institute in Copenhagen and has written several beautiful books, including *The Little Book of Hygge*, *The Little Book of Lykke* and *The Art of Making Memories*. In *The Art of Making Memories* he talks about the power of nostalgia and how it can free us from the limitations of the present moment. This might somewhat contradict the widely celebrated theories on the power of being in the 'NOW' Eckhart Tolle professes will help with eliminating stress and anxiety, but Meik has the research to prove that we can boost our happiness with nostalgia. Maybe combining the two ideas is the balance. We can let ourselves conjure up happiness and connection with nostalgia, with a little mindfulness so as not to get stuck in the past or believe happiness lives only there. Using nostalgia to remember the full-bodied experience of a desired emotion could be a very powerful way for us to implement the law of attraction. As Rhonda stated in our conversation, 'You have to believe you already have what it is you want.' I suppose you could do this by using your imagination, which might be a little out of practice as we tend to use it a lot less in adult life; or perhaps call on feelings and stored memories in the senses, to focus on the desired feeling.

The Norm

I attempt to use the law of attraction to lessen the shame and worry I feel after being triggered by the aforementioned Instagram post. Isn't it weird how one photo on a tiny grid on a phone, which I could choose not to look at, can ruin a whole day? I curse myself for scrolling in a trance-like state in the first place, then I press delete on that negative thought. I remember that if I focus only on the shame and terror I feel of potentially being wrong or getting life wrong, then that is what I will experience. It's frustratingly easy yet requires mental strength to rewrite new stories but I'm up for it. Without ruminating too much I just delete the thought and cover it over, like I'm repainting a wall with a better, more positive colour. I replace 'I am getting life wrong and I feel scared' with 'I am permitted my own beliefs about life and am free to explore life however I please, in a way that'll help me to grow and enjoy this one precious experience on Earth'.

Let's head back to some good old-fashioned Danish wisdom with my friend Meik Wiking. When Meik came on my Happy

Place podcast we discussed the notion of what is seen as 'normal', as the assumptions of what is the norm in differing societies can inflict a lot of pain on those who don't feel they fit into that box. Of course, the 'norm' doesn't exist. There may be averages that can be worked out through stats research and data but that still doesn't make something normal. I believe normal is what feels right for the individual so that we can feel unburdened by comparison and continue freely in our exploration of life. If I allow my brain to wander down this new path of thought, I feel so much less stressed. My body softens and indeed, as Rhonda has pointed out earlier, my heart feels softer, towards myself and the person who triggered this surge of rumination in the first place. This might be the pivotal moment needed, so that I don't charge through the next six hours in a rage driven by my own fears of being wrong. That gear shift and frequency upgrade seem to bring about a certain contentment and clarity. I make the decision to not look on social media for the rest of the day and even manage to squeeze in a quick walk before picking the kids up from school.

Like Attracts Like

I'm put through another little test to see if I can continue to train my puppy dog mind in an attempt to get to 10pm (granny bedtime) without believing too much of its loquacious hype. Before picking the kids up I venture into the loft to find a fan. This expedition was not vital but, in an effort to tick more things off my never-ending list of hell, I rush up there anyway. On the way down, with not only the fan I had hoped to find but also a newly rediscovered old painting and a folder that could come in handy, I lose my footing halfway down the ladder, crumple like a bag of potatoes and concertina against the wall. My back slams against the skirting board but it's my big toe that gets the brunt of it. Is it broken? No, I can move it but my God it hurts. Tiny daggers stabbing at the underside of my bulging sausage toe.

Normally I would spiral quickly into a mental dialogue about how everything is going wrong and I have too much to do and no time to do it all. A sense of unabating overwhelm. Anticipating this draining line of thought, I instead laugh. I laugh at my own impatient need to get eight things done at once and view myself as this tiny ant racing around on planet Earth, rushing like time is running out but really going nowhere. It seems quite hilarious when I take that perspective. I hobble to my wardrobe and find flip-flops as shoes are too painful and laugh all the way to the kids' school. **Not only am I empowered by the new sense of agency I have over some parts of life but I'm also seeing how like attracts like, with the kids' moods following my own jovial ascent.** I'm also moving at a much slower pace once home, as my purple toe says, 'Halt!' The universe might have been sending me a gentle hint to slow the hell down, so I smile knowing that I'm being looked after by that something bigger too.

What Have I Missed?

Over the course of writing this book I have been prompted to really look at my self-limiting beliefs and how much power I'm giving them. Questioning these old beliefs has been one of the biggest life-altering changes to come from writing this book. I have slowly deleted the comments from others etched into my mind that had, up until now, sat comfortably in my brain contributing to the self-flagellation and negativity I found it so easy to slip into. I wonder how many beautiful moments of connection I've lost due to my devotion to these negative beliefs. I consider how many bright blue skies have passed me by because I was too busy lost in a head full of negative thoughts; how many smiles from strangers went unnoticed because I have been so fogged in guilt or shame; how many signs I've not spotted because I've been looking at the floor. I can also see the times that I've stayed in a loop of negativity and undesirable outcomes because I've believed every hideous thought that's entered my head. I've let fragments of negative stories extinguish love in its entirety. I don't want to waste any more time or miss any more moments of connection. My finger is hovering over the delete button awaiting any negative thoughts, like a ninja ready to annihilate any mental lies. We must all remember Rhonda's advice: that any cognitive chatter that does not align with the fact that we are all beautiful, benevolent, perfect, wise, helpful, capable humans can sod right off.

Love's Lessons

- Look at what is fact and what is fiction. What stories are you telling yourself that no longer serve you?

- Remember you are pure love and light; any other thought is a lie. Rhonda says so!

- Meet with your ego. Listen to what it is saying. What does it need?

- Have compassion for yourself. Be kinder, gentler to yourself. Talk to yourself like you would your best mate.

PART 2

AWARENESS

How often do we walk throughout our days with our heads in our phones, minds in the future and bodies detached from the elements around us? I would say most days pan out in a muffled rush where our skin is covered by element-numbing clothes and our minds are drawn to the addiction of constant distraction. Awareness takes a huge back seat and is getting more and more lost in the constant noise of the modern world.

How many times have you seen a pedestrian walk at pace from a pavement and over a road without even looking because their head is craned down in an attempt to keep glued to a screen? We are stumbling through so many situations in life with this mindset. Never-ending box sets allow us to focus on other people's dramas and not look closely at our own; clothes and comfort take precedence over feeling the brisk air on our skin, and noise from every direction stops us from listening to our own inner voice. We live in a busy, noisy, fast-paced blur which makes it so easy to skim the surface of life and its magic. We are choosing to and often paying to numb ourselves from life.

In this padded cell we've created for ourselves it's a challenge to commit to awareness in everyday life. The temptation for comfort and distraction is huge. We don't want to sit with our pain and find the connection in it and we are reluctant to look at our own lives closely because watching five episodes of Schitt's Creek is so much more fun. Awareness is not just noticing what is going on around us but also a recognition of what is behind our emotions and what is driving us to act out. I'm talking about a full HD, three-sixty awareness that enables us to have a level of introspection that helps us to connect and find meaning in life. Most of us usually have a head full of questions about why we've ended up where we are in life, or perhaps why the same flavour of trouble keeps arriving when we least expect. These questions can be answered if we have awareness.

I think most of us are trying to actively avoid awareness. It seems too much like hard work to notice our own cycles and patterns and much easier to just blame something or someone for our misfortunes instead. It also requires more effort to experience life with all of its hugeness without attempting to numb it with TV, food, shopping, gossiping, social media, etc. For example, it is much harder to sit and look at why we might feel inferior to others and what deep-rooted pain and experience has led us to that place, rather than to gossip about others in a hope we'll feel better about ourselves.

Awareness can be humbling and also lead to great change in life so we usually take the opposite option and stay numb and static. We want to avoid pain in all circumstances and that is of course totally understandable but I know from experience, and I'm sure you do too, that pain is often where we feel the most connection. We often assume that pain will alienate and ostracise us but it's the place where we find meaningful support and conversation too. I've bonded with so many people over my own experiences of depression and panic attacks, much more so than I have discussing the happier parts of life. I've forged friendships and working relationships that feel deep-rooted and honest. These transactions would not have been possible if I had not initially been in a place of pain but most importantly been willing to delve into it in a big way.

Leading a spiritual life doesn't mean that you're going to be dancing around barefoot with peonies in your hair the whole time. To me it equates to a life where all emotions and experiences are valued equally and are there to learn from. It's not about ignoring the darker side of life in favour of staring up at the stars in awe; it's about knowing when it's time to look within to poke around in our pain and when to look up with gratitude for all of it.

Awareness comes in many shapes and sizes and can be cultivated through many esoteric, beautiful and simple ways, which we'll explore together in this part of the book.

Let's get clear, get receptive and get ready to see life in all its hugeness.

ENERGY

In the Western world we are a species who need to see to believe. We want proof, stats and often a certain amount of collated data so we can call it science. If we can't see energy, how do we know it exists? I guess one easy way to recognise its power and whereabouts is when looking at the moon. That big old moon in our night skies either waxes or wanes, pulling the oceans closer to shore and back out again. That gravitation and electromagnetic pull is completely invisible to the eye but its power moves our seas. We would have to be pretty short-sighted to believe that it's only the moon that yields powerful energy and ignore our own. Energy, also known as chi, qi, or prana, when looking at all global modalities is everywhere and everything.

Have you ever walked into a room and got the creeps or walked past someone in the street and sensed their negative vibe? Have you ever been in the presence of someone who makes you go weak at the knees or been in a crowd that felt electric? That's all down to our individual and collective energy.

Examining energy gives us more perspective too. It takes us out of the minutiae of everyday life and allows us to expand our thinking beyond the walls of our homes, across seas to other countries, to our dear moon and other planets, to further than we can even comprehend. Energy is everywhere and can't be confined. It connects the dots of life, moves mountains and allows us to think big.

The Never-ending Cycle of Energy

Now, I know I've already mentioned Rhonda Byrne several times in this book but it's worth including her thoughts on energy here too. Her book *The Greatest Secret* explains that our energy never dies. Energy cannot die, energy just IS. Rhonda talks about energy not dying in the context of human death. When the physical body ceases to live our energy continues. Her own particular preferred methodology aligns with the thinking of reincarnation and energy taking form in another living being in a continuous circle of life. You may not be on board with that take on death but maybe you can consider a life cycle where our energy still exists after our human body dies. A constant flow of energy that is available to us all. Energy that connects all living beings, creatures and nature.

How is your energy today? If you sit very still, can you feel the energy in your body? Does it feel dull and bruised by the relentlessness of modern life? Does it feel tingly and buzzed up by what is going on around you? Does it feel contained in your body or can you feel it permeating from you and around you? How much control do you believe you have over your own energy or the energy that you are using? Do you think it is tied up in circumstance or just your own personal nature which is supposedly fixed? This is something I'm fascinated by and so curious about.

The Invisible Layer

I am unbelievably sensitive to energy. I feel like I have a few missing layers of skin on my body. I'm deeply affected when problems in society flare up, I can almost sense the shift in energy. When big news stories are circulating about horrendous situations playing out in another country or injustice snarling in the face of innocent people, I feel it. I lose sleep, feel edgy, can't think straight. I also feel utterly overwhelmed in big crowds. I spent years drinking my way through music festivals as the sheer volume of people and their energy felt like a bombardment I had no control over. I'm like a sponge soaking up whatever is nearby. My barriers are down and I'm too willing to take it all on. It's often why I'm so happy in my own company. I feel I can take a break from the relentless soaking up of energy around me.

At times I've been able to use this trait to help me in my work. If I'm interviewing someone, I can pretty much tell immediately how their energy sits that day. My inner radar picks up if there are nerves afoot or any discomfort. I can then find tactful ways to calm that person and ease them into a friendly conversation. Equally I can tell if someone is trying to drain me of my own energy source. I can literally feel them hoovering up my supply for their own needs. Have you ever met or spoken to someone who leaves you feeling drained? I know when this is happening and allow myself time out to chill afterwards so that I can recalibrate my own energy levels. Yet I've also met those who leave me boosted. Beautiful folk who, without having to say a word, create an even playing field for an energetic back and forth. **Energy is beneath words and actions. It's the invisible layer we can easily ignore if we choose phones over faces and distraction over engagement.** It's the subterranean pull that leads us to the right people and wards us off others. It's also the bit that can lead us to intuition and even psychic tendencies if we are open-minded enough. More on that later!

Let's Get Weird

Shall we get weird again? I love weird. Age nineteen I lived in a tiny flat that I adored. I had painted every wall myself and put cheap throws over old tatty sofas. I am good on my own. I rarely get bored and enjoy my own company, sometimes a little too much. This year of flat-dwelling in Northwood, five minutes from my parents' house, gave me enough time and space to turn inwards for the first time in my adult life. As a kid I had had a fascination with spirituality but now, as a fully-fledged adult in my own space, I could experiment with what that might look like and how I might use it to grow and expand. This was the period of my life in which I meditated the most. Without the distraction of social media (it was yet to exist … ah, the good old days), children to care for, and even before I had my now incredibly old cats, I could cultivate a routine that eliminated any fears and gave way for some magical moments.

On one such occasion I found myself sat cross-legged on the moss-green carpet in my hallway. There was a sliver of a window at the end of the hallway that looked out on to some fir trees and, on this night, a pretty juicy moon in the sky. I had finished filming for the day and didn't bother cooking much when I lived alone so, after a bowl of cereal, sat down with the intention of sending some good energy to those who needed it. My aunty Karen had been on my mind. Throughout my whole childhood Karen had been living in a very small terrace house on an incredibly busy main road. For a big chunk of that time, she was a solo parent to my cousin Biba, who is a few years younger than me. Later down the line Karen met her now husband Mick and that led to a brand-new cousin, Shannon. Their house was way too small for the four of them so Shannon was having to share a room with my aunty Karen and Mick. She was desperate to sell the house and find a new one with an extra bedroom but it just wasn't happening.

So here I am, nineteen years old, desperately wanting to help her in a situation I had little control over. I set about creating an energy ball. I had read about this somewhere in one of the many spiritual books I was obsessed with at the time. Hands a few inches apart I set about focusing on the energy between my palms. After a few minutes I could feel a light buzzing, an undeniable pressure pulsing against my skin – the invisible energy that was building in the space between. I pulled my hands away from each other, gradually allowing more energy into the space, only pulling them apart further when I could feel the energy filling the space. Over the course of twenty or so minutes I felt I had a beach-ball-sized energy ball, bountifully placed in my hands. I then set about filling the energy ball with the wish that my aunty could find the right house allowing her a swift, problem-free move. Once the ball was full of this intention, I physically pushed the ball towards the moonlit window like I was passing it during a netball game. A vigorous push to send that energy and intention outwards. It felt wonderful. Calming, energising, vitalising. I went to bed that night with the calm buzz of the experience still in my palms.

The next evening my aunty called round. This was the early 2000s so no one thought to call or text beforehand. A random arrival of family members or friends was the absolute norm. Her long blonde hair flowing behind her, and her tasselled poncho catching in the wind. My aunty is known for her style. She jangles with bangles and wears reams of velvet and pinched waistcoats in a nod to her '70s rock music collection. Smile from ear to ear, her nose ring glinting in my tangerine-lit doorway, she looked pretty stress-free. Aunty Karen had pitched up to tell me that she was moving. The sale of her house had gone through and the new house was ready and waiting for her. I'm not saying my energy ball had the beef and vigour to kick estate agents up the bum and get things moving entirely on its own but maybe, just maybe, my intention and focus helped align with Aunty Karen's.

I've been making energy balls ever since. Often I don't even tell the beneficiary about it. I just send it off, headed their way. It always feels nice and hopefully helps in some small way. I'm completely untrained in energy work but feel we all have the right and space to experiment and get curious about how it can help us and others in our daily lives.

Warm Hands

I've had reiki, cranial sacral treatments and energy healing many times over the course of my adult life and love when I can feel subtle shifts in the right direction or at times just pure relaxation. My mum completed her Reiki 1 many years ago so will often offer up her bejewelled hands for some soothing relief from menstrual pains or backache. She's placed her warm hands over my children to help calm them when they've been nervous and has helped friends with aches and pains too. Although not recognised by the medical world, many hospitals now offer reiki in between treatments for serious health conditions and many patients have had amazing results or have professed it helped with general relaxation. Let's trot off again in the direction of learning and meet Giselle La Pompe-Moore. Firstly, Giselle has the coolest name I think I've ever come across and, secondly, she's bloody wonderful, I can't wait for you to meet her. I was tipped off about Giselle by one of my Happy Place team members and swiftly emailed to introduce myself. Twenty-four hours later we were on a Zoom on a grey Friday talking all things energy.

Giselle is a spiritual guide, writer, meditation teacher and reiki master. She says that getting to this place was more of a 'remembering' rather than something new in her life. Since the age of six she has had premonitions. At her Catholic school she felt worried that she would be in some way punished for this innate skill, yet it continued through her childhood and teen years where she started to notice how she could freely manifest situations and outcomes in life. It felt like a secret part of her life so she buried it deeper in her adult years while working for a magazine as a beauty coordinator. Stress took over and she realised how much she was waiting for outside influences to make her feel happy. The constant searching led her back to her childhood tendencies and knowledge to then train for her Reiki 1 and onwards. She realised this was her calling and has created an incredible career and path for herself treating people who range from eighteen months to eighty-five years old. Giselle doesn't believe that reiki is the only way we can use energy to heal and teach. She says that, whether she is reading tarot, using crystals or any other practices, she is connecting to the other person's energy and channelling through spirit to receive the energy and answers. During the global pandemic she has been working with people online and healing remotely, which is fascinating and something I want to know more about.

Zoom clicks to life. I take twenty seconds working out how to unmute myself. When will I get used to this new way of life? God, I should have put some under-eye concealer on. Giselle looks radiant and I have not bothered to put my ring light on so the old eye bags are taking centre stage. I will now use all of my might to NOT look at myself and just concentrate on Giselle and her wisdom.

Me: Giselle, I'm so happy to meet you. Thank you for chatting today. I'm buzzed to talk to you.

Giselle: Hey, how are you?

Me: I'm good, excited to be writing this new book and get all of your knowledge on paper. So, first up, I want to talk about a form of energy healing I've heard of before and that's reiki – what exactly is it?

Giselle: Reiki is a holistic form of energy healing and it was founded by Mikao Usui in Japan in the early twentieth century. It is a practice to help kickstart your body's own innate healing ability. That healing is happening on a physical, mental, emotional and spiritual level and I think that's why energy healing is so fascinating. We have such a Western view of healing being purely physical. If I have a headache I get treated for the physical symptoms of the headache and then I'm healed. With reiki, because we are working on all four of those levels, we are open to how that healing will work for you. As a practitioner I'm channelling the energy. It's not for me to determine where that healing goes. If you are presenting with a headache, I'm just placing my hands and the energy will flow to where it needs to go. It could be emotional grief that's not been expressed, it could be wanting to connect to your intuition more. Reiki is about focusing on the connection to spirit and consciousness and how we can bring that into our lives. In a world that seems so divisive, one where we speak endlessly about our identities and our differences, whether it's background, politics, race, etc., with reiki you just realise we are all energy. It's the ultimate leveller. There is no difference.

Me: When you're channelling, you're not channelling *your* energy into that person, are you? Are you instead channelling the bigger energy that is universal and beyond us as individuals?

Giselle: Yes, it has nothing to do with me. It's not my energy. I'm not giving them energy and I'm not receiving any energy from my clients. I am sharing energy. It's so interesting that we can share energy remotely. People might think this is just a handy 'pandemic special' but it really isn't. We've had the ability since reiki began. I have clients all over the world – New York, Canada, South Africa. It's incredible because it just proves that we are all so connected. It helps the client in so many ways and it's like that old saying: where your attention goes, your energy flows.

Me: YES! I'm obsessed with that thought. If you set your intention or energy somewhere, that's what you're manifesting into reality. We forget this so often. We believe most things as bad luck whereas some of the time it's due to intentions.

Giselle: Intention is so vital when it comes to reiki. When I'm doing a session, my intention is to connect to reiki. It's not the tools you're using that create the magic, you ARE the magic. You're infusing your magic in the chosen practice. When we understand that we are energy, you are energy, I am energy, your pet is energy, the plant in your house is energy, we can see that we are all sharing this sense of oneness.

Me: If people reading this have not heard of reiki or energy healing, how can they incorporate this thinking into their everyday lives?

Giselle: On the outside we have our aura. The physical energy field around us. We cannot see it but we can feel it. There are seven layers to our aura and the size will differ from person to person. The energy fields closer to our bodies are heavy and dense and they get lighter and finer as they expand outwards. A great way to sense them is to go to a busy place like a big shopping mall and you just feel hit by the amount of people. You're not touching them but you feel it. You're literally bumping into people's auras. Your aura will depend on your emotions that day, what has been going on for you, if your chakras are aligned. Some of us will be more sensitive to this than others but everyone can feel it. I'm someone who has previously had a very real, physical anxiety, and I can tell the difference between that physical feeling and the overwhelm one might feel when thinking about energy fields and how they affect me. So that is our outside energy system. Then we have our inside energy system, which are the chakras, which is Sanskrit for wheel. The chakra system originated 3,500 years ago in India. We have these seven major energy centres, from the base of our spines to the crown of our heads. In reiki we are looking for an open flow between all of the chakras. If we have blockages in that flow, we will see physical symptoms or just feel very heavy in life.

Me: Yes, often we feel stuck in life but we think it's only down to circumstance, we don't consider that we might be emotionally and spiritually stuck.

Giselle: This is because usually we only think of ourselves as physical beings. This goes back to the four levels I've been talking about. The mental, physical, emotional and spiritual. They're all on the same level. Physical doesn't override the others. When we ignore the subtleties of the other levels, we are not connecting to them at all. One client came to me recently and just wanted to feel relaxed from the session as she had been feeling stressed. When my hands were moving around her body, I got to her throat and noticed my hands getting hotter. She started coughing and couldn't stop for ten minutes. The cough turned into a big cry and she had a huge release. At the end of the session, she told me she is a poet and a performer and she hadn't been allowing herself to do it recently as she felt so much fear about it. Her throat chakra was screaming out for her to communicate and express herself but she wasn't picking up on it. She had so much stress and anxiety in her life but hadn't connected the two.

Me: I had such a similar situation as I had a huge cyst on my vocal cords which led me to realise that I wasn't speaking honestly to people in my life. I wrote a whole book on it (*Speak Your Truth*, available in all good bookshops) because I was so fascinated with how this all works. Often we just ignore the energy and its flow because we can't see it.

Giselle: I think it's so prized in society that we need to have science and research back everything up but I think it's also really important to have anecdotal evidence to back things up. Why do we have this reluctance to believe things we can't see? The connection to spirit is where you'll get the trust and faith to believe in the things you cannot see. I have innate trust because I have so much evidence from this work.

Without the foundation of a spiritual life and the trust that comes with it, I can't exist. I need to have the faith and trust so that when the world is in flux or even when I'm in flux, I can come back to my spiritual practices and stay hopeful and open-minded.

Me: What do you think people should do if they think they have an energy block?

Giselle: We need to have a level of self-enquiry. Self-enquiry requires space. So often we wonder why we can't feel things or connect to what's going on and that is because there is no space – spirit needs space. You'll find it hard to connect to your intuition if you're always busy. Intuition isn't going to knock on your door and be like, 'Heyyyyy, I've got a little treat for you.' When we take a step back and create space, then we can find answers. We have to come home to ourselves and give ourselves space. The biggest question we can ask ourselves is: what is here for me that I need to see? You're almost doing a full-body scan while doing this. You might notice you're tense in your shoulders. You might at first think this is because you are just physically sore in that area, but if we probe deeper we might think, 'OK, what am I carrying here? Emotionally and mentally, am I carrying something? Why am I not surrendering to something bigger than me who can carry this for me?'

Me: Is there bad energy and good energy?

Giselle: I don't believe that there is. I think it goes back to what we were talking about earlier. **Where our attention goes, energy flows.** I have never experienced bad energy. I set an intention daily to receive what is in my highest and greatest good. That's the only intention I have in life so I get met with it. I haven't encountered negative or toxic energy because I'm not setting that intention for myself.

Me: WOW, WHAT?!

Giselle: I just don't buy into there being bad energy. If we remember we are all light, we are all love, there is just no space for it. People do crazy shit and cause harm to others and themselves, but if we strip back to who we think we are in comparison to who we really are then there is no space for bad energy there. People who move through the world causing pain usually don't realise that the pain is coming from their human selves, the physical, they are just trying to survive out there. Underneath all of that is 'the spiritual', which is being ignored. If we get back to thinking that we are one, that we are a whole integrated being, then there is space for you to think, 'I don't love this part of me but that's OK.' None of us have to be 'higher vibes only', it's actually very dangerous to think like that. We are human. We need to have the ability to be angry, to be hard, to be soft and to be kind. That's what an integrated person is. **We don't have to love all parts of us but we do have to have acceptance.**

Me: If I were to wake up tomorrow and I did a quick body scan and I could feel a blockage or something that is uncomfortable, then what? Am I to put my attention on that bit of me or is that creating a negative connection because I'm noticing the pain?

Giselle: Start with the intention. What is your intention for exploring it? It could be that your intention is to get some answers as to why it's there. It could be to gain willingness and openness to heal that part of your physical self. Healing might not manifest in the way that you want but it will manifest in a way that you probably most need. You might think the healing is for the shoulder to stop hurting but the healing might be that you need to find acceptance with the physical pain or honour that a lack of productivity isn't a bad thing. You might just need to surrender to rest.

Me: Ah, my worst nightmare.

Giselle: You might not get the answers in that moment but you might later on realise what you need to do. The attention you put on the intention is to give space to what needs to come through for you.

Me: In a global situation like the pandemic, energetically it's been heavy. What's the best way to work with that?

Giselle: Go to those four levels again. Physically, what can I do to help myself? What does my body want? Breathwork? A reiki session? Dancing? Or rest? Mentally, what do I need? What can I learn? What is my story about this moment? Emotionally, how am I? Am I missing people, stopping myself from feeling certain emotions? Can I see beyond this moment and understand that we all came here to grow and growth is sometimes created from moments of discomfort? Accept the moment and know it's OK for it to be hard. Our mind and body might tell us we can't get through this moment but our souls, who have a bird's-eye view of our past lives, present life and future lives, say, 'Of course you can.' I recently got diagnosed with a health condition and the reflection for me is that I can choose to believe that this will be awful and traumatic, but that is too heavy for me to carry. I just don't know the true outcome so I'm not going to put all of my intentions on the future as I don't know what will happen. I said to myself, 'It's going to be lighter to believe that I can heal this chronic condition', and if I keep aiming towards that, that's what I'm going to receive.

Me: Are there things like you just mentioned that we can do physically to help move on blocked energy? Shaking, dancing, etc.?

Giselle: Yes, shaking does help. Dance and shake your body to move things on. Set the intention to release anything that is not serving you. Then shake it out. Breathwork is also key as breath is energy in its purest form. Our breath is a reminder of our soul and spirit. We believe in our breath without being able to see it. Any practice you choose – whether it's smoke cleansing by burning sustainable and non-appropriated herbs or banging a drum and making sound – any of these things work if there is intention behind them, to move on your energy or the energy in a space.

Me: Of course, because space holds energy not just us. You feel that when walking into a sacred space, you feel the energy and peace there. Or if you walk into a space where awful things have happened, like, say, the Tower of London, and you get creeped out a bit. It's not exclusively a cognitive experience, it's very visceral. It's because of the energy in that space.

Giselle: I see spaces in our homes, or spaces in general, as witnesses to experiences. Your space soaks it in. These spaces hold people's energy as they're witnessing the energy. We can change that, though. With intention and people experiencing different outcomes in that space you can move the old energy on. I do a lot of work in people's new homes, to move on the energy of the previous house owners using rituals backed up by intention. Even clapping can help. Break up the energy around you by making noise. You mustn't let superstition get in the way. It doesn't have to be a certain number of claps, or a certain sound bowl; set the intention behind it and move the energy on.

Me: I have been known to grab a drum and bash it about my kids' room if they've had a bad night's sleep the night before.

I wanna move that energy on! Bloody hell, I loved this chat.
Thank you so much, Giselle.

. . .

Approximately three minutes after this conversation, and a slight
panic that I hadn't saved down the discussion for me to later
transcribe, I'm lying on the floor of my tiny office. Instantly a
lower vertebra pops in relief that it is finally straight as nature
intended rather than hunched over a laptop. The rug is itchy so
I try to bypass that small irritation and focus on my own body.
A full-body scan is needed. My mind is an X-ray machine skimming over the entirety of my horizontal body. The first thing I
notice is my neck. The back of my neck feels as stiff as a steel rod.
Without moving it at all to test the flexibility available, I just sit
with it and set my intention. I am curious as to why my neck is
refusing to be a dynamic and agile body part. I'm interested to
know why this energy block is present. Quite quickly the answer
comes. It is a feeling of holding on for dear life. My neck muscles
contract with the hope that I can keep life neat and in place without too much chaos. The world around me shows signs of pain
and a lot of noise so my internal response is to try to keep my
shit together. My neck has literally clenched itself tightly to keep
my head from spinning off my body. The muscles have wrapped
themselves around my windpipe and bones to keep me looking
only in one direction: forwards. To look the other way might just
be too painful and lead to overwhelm with all I have going on.
I breathe energy into that spot. I imagine each breath sending
blue light to the tension. I'm not lumping expectation on to the
situation. I'm not expecting instant relief but my intention has
been set. I now know there is also an element of change required.

    If I think about the four levels that Giselle spoke of, I have
to look at what is going on for me emotionally and spiritually,

as well as mentally and physically. Emotionally I know I'm a bit scared. I'm frightened that so many are suffering in the world for varying reasons. I am scared that the chaos I see around me will threaten my own levels of peace. Chaos is my nemesis. My Virgo brain needs straight lines that point to progress. All of this back-pedalling, shouty noise and chaos makes my head spin. Emotionally, like many, I feel bruised. I don't shy away from global pain and often don't put much censorship in place for myself. I let it all flood in. The initial response being panic about the pain rather than landing on acceptance or rallying for positive change. Spiritually, I have lost hope. I have let the negative stories playing out on the ... Sorry, slight interlude. Something just caught my eye. I'm sat at a floor-length window and a white moving object just distracted me. A single white feather. For me, this is a sign of hope. This feather now lying directly to my right on the grass outside is backing up what I need to do. What I need to do for my spirit and in turn my shoulder. I need to have hope.

I will dissect feathers and other signs later in the book as I'm obsessed with them, but for now I will take absolute comfort, and also a pinch of excitement, that I can safely rely on hope and something bigger than me. What am I expecting? That I can solve all the global problems single-handedly? That I can shoulder them all and process each one individually with vigour and energy? It would be impossible (and the notion is kind of narcissistic). Most global leaders prove this daily. I need to find an equilibrium in hearing about the global goings-on and then have hope that I can be a positive force for change but without being burdened by the entirety of the pain involved. Does that make sense? It does to me. This short exercise of lying on the floor and looking at my stiff old neck has led to something so much bigger.

The Shrinking Energy Field

I'm a huge, nerdy Dr Joe Dispenza fan as he is someone who has managed to bridge the spiritual world and science. In his books he leaps from mysticism to hard-fact science in the same breath and has gained a huge following of people interested in changing their own biochemistry and neurology. He talks about energy a lot and the field of energy that surrounds the human body. In his book *Becoming Supernatural* he talks about how we can change our own light field around our bodies. The energy field around our body emits light and information and he has seen in his own studies that when we are in survival mode or highly stressed we draw from that invisible energy field and it shrinks. He has also witnessed in studies that a gathering of 550–1,500 people all meditating en masse can cause the energy in the room to shift. I love this direct link between our brains and the energy around us. Isn't it liberating to know we can change it?

His studies show that learning to change your own brain-waves, using meditation, can manipulate the energy field around your body and also the energy centres within your body. This can create healing internally and a larger exterior energy field. We might not be able to see this energy field, or aura as Giselle called it earlier, but we can sense how that feels when we are around others.

The Power of Now

I was once lucky enough to watch the great thinker and author Eckhart Tolle live at the Royal Albert Hall in London. My brother Jamie, who is the direct opposite of me in every way – quiet, controlled, considered, academic – is a huge Eckhart fan

so we excitedly met on the front steps of the venue in eager antic-
ipation. I often call Jamie my very own Eckhart because if I'm
struggling with something I can text or call him and he'll give
me a short yet profound perspective to work with. We somehow
ended up with seats really near the front and coincidentally my
good friend Craig David was sat directly in front of us. Eckhart
walked out on stage to rapturous applause and huge expectation,
as most Eckhart mega-fans were intrigued to witness the great
Mr Tolle improvising without any plan at all for the next two
hours. Sticking to his ethos of living in the now, his talks require
no planning at all, he simply goes with the flow and sees where it
takes him. Now THAT requires a faith in something bigger than
us! It was magical from start to finish, with impactful moments,
naturally, scattered throughout. At one point, when he was riff-
ing around listening for answers, there was a huge mid-summer
thunderclap overhead that reverberated across the Albert Hall's
spherical roof. Goose bumps.

Near to the end of his two-hour talk his partner Kim Eng
entered the stage to host a group meditation. Now, I've been in
group meditations before at my local yoga centre, with twenty
or thirty people gathered for sound-bath meditations or post-
yoga meditations, but this was 5,000-plus people all squashed
into one space. Being very sensitive to other people's energy, I
closed my eyes and just tried to concentrate on my own breath
and Kim Eng's words to help slow my nervous system and get
me into a meditative state. Twenty minutes flew by in a heartbeat and, as Kim Eng actioned us to open our eyes, my skin
felt tingly and the air around me infused with electricity. My
brother confessed he fell asleep halfway through, which is no
bad thing and probably means he was willing to let all of that
good energy in, to totally relax him. It felt exciting yet calming and a real privilege to have taken part in such a beautiful

collective experience. Who knows where the energy of 5,000 ended up that evening? Did it spill out on to the streets of London giving passers-by a little boost? Did each one of us travel home that bit lighter and more connected? Did we pass that energy on to others in the small transactions of daily life? Maybe a bit of all of the above. All I know is that it felt powerful and important and, more than anything, meaningful.

Chaos on the School Run

It's not often that we get the chance to collectively change the energy in one space that's inhabited by lots of people. Usually if you visit a busy space, it's certain that you're walking into a blender of feelings, emotions and energies that will differ from your own. The school run is the perfect example of this. It's a chaotic mix of kids and shattered parents, dogs on leads and school bags dragging on the ground. My kids' school is very near to a playground, so more often than not a bunch of us will take the kids over for a play straight after school. The kids' collective energy feels like freedom. They've had to contain so many impulses throughout the day at school knowing that their teacher will not suffer the same attitude and rebellion as tired parents at home. The playground equals liberation. Screams and yelps and letting loose. Parents' energy in this situation tends to be a little different to that of their kids. We are happy they're enjoying themselves, alert as we transition from a day of peace back into total chaos (or a day of work that transitions into total chaos) and slightly nervous that one of them will fall off the climbing frame in the exact moment you turned away to chat to a mate. It's a cacophony of varied energy.

This week, due to the writing of this book, I've been hyper-aware of all of this. Yesterday I woke up feeling awkward. Do you ever get this? A strange feeling of being overly aware of how your limbs move and what your face is doing. A panic that you're grimacing instead of smiling and a lack of ease when talking to other people. Well, that's what I was dealing with. After I'd dropped the kids to school I had several Zoom meetings and recorded my radio show. I just about got through all of that unscathed but really felt like I had used up all of my personality units in those transactions.

The weather was fair so we ended up bundling into the playground with forty or so other families. I felt like I was getting gently electrocuted on arrival. An instant assault of energy. Both kids hurling their school bags at me, elated energy thrown my way too, teamed with the energy fields of many other parents trying to find their own comfort in such a scene. I got chatting to a mum I've known for around four years, which gave me the time to tune out of the collective energy of the playground in full pandemonium and just connect with one other. Then another mum I'm friends with came over, which meant I snapped back into the reality of the madness around me. As the other mum approached, I attempted to introduce the two of them, which went badly. The overwhelm of the gear change from working on my own at home all day to then a bombardment of collective energy made my head spin and forget the name of one of the mums. I felt light-headed, like I might faint, then just super-embarrassed.

Usually, I just walk into the playground and immediately put on a suit of armour to deal with so much energy. I click into 'mum-on-the-school-run mode' and slip into the required patter. Due to my curiosity into all things energy during the writing of this book, I didn't do that on this particular day and became hyperaware of everyone else's energy fields. Maybe if someone had said on a loudhailer, 'Hey, parents, all take one deep collective inhale and exhale', maybe our energies would have aligned, calmed instantly and felt lighter? It just shows that without communication and a collective want to change the energy, it's just a game of aura bumper cars at the fair.

Clapping and Connection

If you've ever been to see a talk, or have taken part in a spiritual group activity, the host or group leader will often start the session or day with a collective inhale and exhale, or perhaps will encourage you to say hello and introduce yourself to your neighbour to create bubbles of nervous laughter and an en masse ice-break. Any small collective moment can help our energies align and connect. I'm learning that it's not just about raising or lightening the energy so it feels better, it's about connection; the invisible glue that holds us together. I really felt this during the pandemic. In times of utter pain there usually come moments of beauty and benevolence, one a reaction to the other. Each Thursday at 8pm our whole street would line up on doorsteps ready to clap for the NHS. Every Thursday I cried. I didn't have a specific reason to cry but the tears welled up and fell. They weren't tears of sadness or even tears of joy; they felt like tears of connection. A connection to my neighbours, most of whom I didn't know before the pandemic. A connection to the street we all call home. A connection to something much bigger that we were all creating together. The clatter of palms rippling for miles was quite literally breaking up the heavy energy we had all felt during the day. We were changing our own energy fields in that moment by focusing our minds on gratitude and not the omnipresent fear. We were changing the energy in our surroundings by physically breaking it up with our hands which created noise, which of course is energy too. We were aligning with each other as we all had the same intention for those few minutes. I wish we could find ways to keep aligning with each other, without needing a reason other than wanting to collectively change energy and to increase our connection to each other and the planet.

Limitless Energy

Another book I imbibed with urgency is *The Divine Matrix* by Gregg Braden. He describes the divine matrix as the 'container and bridge' between the world within us and the world outside of us. This book is mind-blowing and requires small breaks to process the hugeness of the topic, alongside rereading sentences to really chew over their power. Gregg's description of the divine matrix is akin to a mirror, with every bit of energy reflecting what we've created back at us. I find this notion empowering as it articulates that we have much more agency over outcomes than we are led to believe. We live in a toxic sandwich of fearmongering from world leaders/the media and a constant warning of personal lack from advertisers – no wonder mental health is on a speedy decline. We aren't actively informed that we can put our focus where we choose to conjure up outcomes that differ from what we are told. It's not promoted that we could collectively aim to stop climate change with our energy and intention to make impactful differences. Instead, we are bombarded with horrific stats and few options to help make change. The horror story statistics are needed to give us a kick up the bum but with positive intention behind it as well. Fear alone cannot create change. We need the positive, powerful part of the equation too. Fear usually just paralyses us. We are stood frozen to the spot, heavy with guilt and shame. Using our collective energies positively would move fear to one side and make way for progress.

Equally, we are not told that if we lay intention in certain areas we can break the mould, do the extraordinary and challenge supposed limits. A menu of fear and lack is dished up daily via the news, print media, social media and so on, so we hold our energy in tight, hoping no one else steals it. We forget its limit-lessness and omnipotence.

Changing My Day-to-Day

Bringing things down to the microscopic I can see in my own life how this plays out. **My individual energy might not move mountains or send planets spinning off their orbit but it certainly changes how my days play out.** Today my energy has felt light. I woke up in my kids' bunk bed but quickly made the decision to sniff their crumpled cheeks and warm scalps and breathe in pure gratitude rather than feel the pain in my lower back that could turn to self-loathing that my kids are still waking in the night after all these years. I made the decision to put my intention on the positives and to keep my energy light. I have a long day ahead so need to use my energy wisely, knowing I need stamina to stay focused as there is a podcast to record tonight, at a much later time than I'd prefer. The school run was easier than normal. I remembered the bags and homework which I some-times forget, the kids were happy and Rex slightly less rebellious than normal. I knew a run would give me headspace and get my lungs pumping so I choose to put on my trainers rather than have a bath which I was equally tempted by. I'm very behind on replying to emails but rather than play over my usual fear-based mental tapes about how unprofessional I'm being, or how upset the other person is, I instead just feel glad of the peacefulness in my kitchen. I'm placing my intention in the places where I want my energy to flow.

We all know the other side of the coin to this one. How many days have we all woken in a grump, had someone beep their horn loudly at us on the school run/journey to work, with a fist shaking in our direction? Ten minutes into the journey you realise you haven't packed the kids a snack or water bottle which subsequently plays into the self-loathing that was piqued after the road rage incident. Your attention then stays in the negative, draining the energy around you. You then walk into the school/place of work with your head down hoping you don't have to talk to anyone, you get back to the car and there is a parking ticket, and so on ... On these days you can literally feel the light around you shrinking. Our attention is on the negative so our energy is used up trying to battle against life.

This is the reflection that Gregg Braden is talking about in *The Divine Matrix*. His examples are much more sophisticated than my own and go off into the incredible realm of quantum physics, which I won't even pretend I understand, but you get the gist. Energy is everywhere and everything, it can be manipulated in any which way we desire and it is limitless and cannot die. When you think of it like that, it's really quite freeing. Having a better understanding of my own energy, others' and the planetary energies at play, I have more clarity around how I can connect to that something bigger, by simply remembering I am made of the exact same stuff.

An energy exercise
by Giselle La-Pompe Moore

Find a comfortable space to lie or sit down in, close
your eyes and take a few deep breaths to ground and
centre yourself. Set an intention to connect to your
energy field and start to rub your hands together very
quickly. Feel the heat that your hands are generating
and bring all of your attention to your hands.

Do this until you feel the energy in your hands, then
bring your palms in front of one another, feeling the
energy in the space between them. Notice what you
can feel. Place your hands over your heart and imagine
a white healing light moving down into the crown of
your head and all the way through your body - allow
this energy to move through you and focus on what
you can feel as it does. Keep doing this until you
visualise the light reaching the soles of your feet. Take a
few more breaths, then open your eyes.

ENNEAGRAMS

During the writing of this book there have been several coincidences, or shall we call them signs. I've been led with ease to wise people. They've just sort of popped up from nowhere, genies from the lamp, offering help. I've been gifted books on relevant subjects at the right time and have been pointed in the same direction by several people. The more excited I get about writing this book, the more new opportunities appear. As I said at the start, writing this book has changed my life in so many ways. Hearing the word 'Enneagram' repeatedly during this writing process, from different, unrelated people in my life, seemed to be another sign I couldn't ignore.

I managed to get through thirty-nine years of life without even hearing the word 'Enneagram' spoken aloud and then, within the space of three months, four separate individuals mentioned it to me. First up was the wise Wendy Mandy from Part 1 of the book. You may remember she asked me if I knew my Enneagram number and I had no idea what she was talking about. Days later I heard the author Jedidiah Jenkins mention his Enneagram number on a podcast I was listening to. Then my friend Donna Lancaster brought up her number in conversation.

A month or so later, while having a catch-up on the phone with Gabby Bernstein she told me her number and how it resonated. If that isn't a sign for me to investigate further and learn more, I don't know what is.

What's in a Number?

So, first up, what on earth is the Enneagram? Out of sheer curiosity I've gone off down a rabbit hole of trying to figure this out myself, but as illustrated in the previous chapters, you can rest assured that an expert is also on hand in this section. The Enneagram is a system of personality typing that describes patterns in people and how they react to the world around them. An online questionnaire is your portal to your assigned number and archetype. The numbers 1–9 relate to a personality type and a detailed description of how that person might move through the world. This is the list of numbers and their titles:

1. The Reformer
2. The Helper
3. The Achiever
4. The Individualist
5. The Investigator
6. The Loyalist
7. The Enthusiast
8. The Challenger
9. The Peacemaker

You may instantly connect with one of those titles and think you can predict where you might sit in this tally of nine but, wait, this is so much more than you think.

How is a personality test helping us lead a spiritual life, I hear you cry? I know, we could all easily go and buy a teen magazine and do one of those multiple-choice quizzes to find out our personality type and save ourselves the hassle of having to delve into Enneagrams, but that would be too easy and would be massively missing the point. My understanding, so far, is that once we have our assigned number with its list of traits, we can see what is blocking us in life; what fears are blindsiding us; what barriers we might have in place due to how we perceive the world. Understanding our own limitations gives us the option to make changes as to how we view the world. **Our perception of the world around us dictates so many of our life outcomes.** It will act as a driving force behind how we connect with others, ourselves and the planet. If leading a spiritual life has many of its roots embedded in connection, it's probably a good idea to know what limitations we have in place.

People Pleasers

It's also not just some kooky test that a scientist or modern-day expert has whipped up to gain a following. This has been going for thousands of years, with the origins dating so far back that its conception isn't entirely known or understood. Some assume ancient roots in Babylon some 4,500 years ago, yet others place its roots in ancient Greece around 2,500 years ago. It's even thought that Italian writer Dante had a vast understanding of the Enneagram as so many of his characters embodied the qualities directly linked to the nine personality types. In the modern world the spiritual teacher George Ivanovich introduced it as a spiritual symbol in the 1930s and it reached the United States in the 1960s. Its background is eclectic and has been honoured by people the world over from many differing cultures throughout time, but how can it help us today, in this complex modern world where most of us have no clue who we are? We are perhaps more confused in this era than ever before. There is much more pressure on us to show the world who we are yet in turn we get lost in the circus around us. We are too eager to people-please and fit in, so give over parts of ourselves to ensure we aren't left behind. We look up to those who appear 'perfect' on social media and try to emulate their projection by changing ourselves. Do you know who you are? Sometimes I think I have a jolly good idea of who I am and at other times I feel I'm sinking into the silt of life without a clue.

Nature or Nurture and Messy Hair

When I observe my own kids, with their unique personalities and outlooks on life, I wonder how much of it is learned from me and my husband, and perhaps our circle of loved ones, and how much of it was already there. Rex and Honey couldn't be any more polar opposites if they tried. Rex is urgent, chaotic, a creative cannon ball of energy and fun. He never stops, constantly on the lookout for the next opportunity to be inspired and stimulated. He hates rules, actively loves to smash through them and then watch the unfurling repercussions … oh, and he never brushes his hair. His hair is a visual nod to what is going on inside. Beautiful, untamed, frenetic, charismatic chaos.

Honey is considered, organised, thorough, deep-thinking and respectful. If she sees a line, she won't dare cross it as she desperately wants to make sense of life and its unwritten rule book. Hair, flame-red and curly yet always somehow smoothed down and in place, in a necessary attempt to contain the mess of life. She quietly sings throughout the day, making even the most mundane into a melody.

They're my chalk and cheese, butting heads most days as they stubbornly hold on to their view of the world around them and their own big personalities. It's easier to observe and dissect my children's personalities than my own as I have the luxury of distance. I can sit back, secretly side-eyeing them, like a stealth wildlife documentary maker. When it comes to my own personality, it's much easier to feel confused. Who the hell am I? In Russell Brand's audiobook *Revelation*, he dissects his own outward projection and feels equally as flummoxed. He talks of moving seamlessly from the Cuban-heel-wearing, huge-haired prankster to slipper-wearing, kaftan loving, countryside dweller. He fully embraced and embodied both lives and truths yet can see the pivot of change where he shed one skin and grew another. I can see my own phases with crystal-clear lucidity. Loud, desperate for approval, pink streaks in hair, ripped tights, and multiple tattoos, all made up a large part of who I used to be. Now comfortably in a new chapter, I'm mostly make up free, desperate for tranquillity and more interested in other people's stories rather than my own. So how can I work out who I am if I am forever replacing the ephemeral cloak of personality?

Life's Big Mirror

Most spiritual work encourages us to look at ourselves in the mirror. The Enneagram seems to be a shortcut to really taking a look at ourselves with absolute clarity. Although I've always had a deep interest in spirituality, over the last ten or so years I've been much more committed to the idea of it being a part of my everyday life. Doing a lot of therapy has meant I've had little choice but to look in the mirror. To peel back the layers and dig deep beneath trauma, confusion and mistakes made means you have to have a jolly good look at who you are. Sounds so simple, right? Wrong! It's bloody hard. First you have to peel back about twenty-odd layers of life's wallpaper to get to the real story.

So much of who we think we are is actually based on a reflection the world chucks back at us. We might define ourselves as bossy because someone once told us we were. We might proudly announce we are good at organising as the whole family often leans on us to make shit happen. We might make decisions based on the idea that we are shy, as others seem to be louder and more outgoing around us. How much of this is based on the truth? I imagine very little.

Retrospectively I can see periods of my life where I actively tried to change my personality, in an attempt to rewrite it altogether. I've had such a large mirror placed before me due to the nature of my job. Since the age of fifteen, when I started out in this weird world of broadcasting, my understanding of myself has been warped into circus-mirror distortion. My personality became a movable part of me that was made up of tiny fragments of outside opinion conflated with my own true sense of self. Other people's view of me became almost more important than who I felt I actually was. I would dye my hair a new colour and rinse off the old, boring version of me in the shower at the same time. I would tattoo my body to write something more interesting into my story. Yet it's been a full-circle process and, as I turn to face the next decade of my life, my forties, I can see how I'm returning back to an old version of myself, the one before I was submerged into the public eye, yet hopefully with a little more wisdom. If there has ever been a time to know myself, it's now.

So, Who Am I?

This year has been transformative for me in so many ways. Writing this book has propelled me closer to the mirror to really look at who I am and what I'm doing with this precious life. I'm now so close to the glass that the crow's feet and forehead lines are in high definition, and I'm cool with that. I am still walking, with curiosity, down the path to meet the real me: the version of me that has shed all old stories and expectations; the real me who isn't defined by outside influence or societal norms and has made peace with the messy bits of myself while acknowledging the good bits with less cringe factor. God, getting older is great!

I am realising that, most of the time, when we feel a discord in life it's because the personality we have created gets in the way of who we really are. I need to get out of my own way! You need to get out of your own way!

The Questionnaire

Before I speak to our Enneagram expert, Robert Holden, I'd better do the online Enneagram test that will assign my number and list of traits associated. Twelve dollars later and I'm standing at the foot of 105 multiple-choice questions. Having done badly at school I panic that somehow I might fail, even though these are questions about me. I'm instructed not to give too much thought to any of the questions, to work intuitively. I race through the questions fervently, eagerly wanting the results. Before I know it, thirty minutes have passed and I'm now awaiting the important number outcome. Two of my friends have said they think I'm a number 8, the Challenger. Wow, that sounds powerful and a bit exciting, yet I'm not sure I feel quite as strong as they perceive me to be.

An email pings into my inbox and I open the file attached with the results. I feel as if I'm about to find out whether I've gotten into university or not. No mention of university but the Enneagram has spoken and I'm a 2, the Helper.

The Helper

I don't know any 2s, so quickly read up on what this all means. It states all of my best and worst traits. I'm caring, empathetic, warm, thoughtful, generous and tactile yet also seductive, people-pleasing, worried, possessive and insecure. I literally couldn't have said it any better myself. Each one of those labels hits my heart and head with total accuracy. There is a detailed description to accompany the breakdown of traits which is entirely spot on throughout, as if I have been closely monitored and cognitively dissected without knowing so. A small section mentioning a 2's hidden side is so nuanced yet totally accurate that my jaw drops slightly. So hidden in fact that I feel I'm learning something new about myself which is also, weirdly, completely familiar. It talks about my apparent ease with others yet a hidden feeling of insecurity, assuming others might not want me around. I haven't been able to articulate this social discomfort before. I haven't even known what the feeling is. Every time I've been to a friend's house, and it could be a really good friend I've known for years, I leave worrying that they don't like me or are thinking I'm too boring to be around. I'll recount my every word spoken and worry that they would have preferred the company of another instead. It's like I'm already envisioning their rejection, so meet it face to face before it comes to light. There are more detailed breakdowns on how I expect others to mind-read what I'm thinking, which has been the cause of much stress in dynamics over the years. On countless occasions I have felt pure rage that someone hasn't mind-read me and done what I was expecting. This misplaced anger is actually probably directed at myself for having not opened my mouth when I needed to. I've even actively asked someone if they wanted a lift somewhere while simultaneously sending psychic messages that I haven't got time to and can't be bothered, yet when they've said they would in fact love a lift, I've felt total rage at the cheek of it. It's actually quite hilarious.

There are big reveals too: a 2 only believes they will be loved if they are completely available to attend to the needs of others. This one punches me in the gut. I have known this in my soul forever but haven't felt able to change it. I have thrown everything at people I love, or even like, so they hopefully reciprocate the feelings I have for them. I haven't felt 'enough' just turning up to a new relationship empty-handed. I have handed over the keys to my heart, car and soul so many times. I feel a little sick in my tummy about it. It's, at times, led me down the path of resentment and completely ruined some relationships too.

Wow, this Enneagram situation is riveting and revealing and a little spooky. I feel like I've been sliced open, investigated and understood to my core. This test has revealed parts of me, which were hidden in habit and moments of socially conforming, that I didn't even know were there.

This intricate analysis of my number and who I am already feels helpful but I want to get to the bottom of how this can really help me lead a spiritual life, so I'm going to meet with Enneagram expert Robert Holden to pick his brains.

Me: Hey, Robert.

Robert: Nice to meet you, Fearne.

Me: So I've done the test and I'm a 2.

Robert: How did that read for you?

Me: Terrifyingly accurate, Robert!

Robert: It's all to do with how you feel on the inside. Only you will know if the outcome resonates.

Me: It's already helping me to understand so much more about myself. There were some reveals which have helped me cultivate a better relationship with myself.

Robert: Most of us have a self-image, which classically we call the 'ego' or 'persona' or 'mask', because however much we try to inflate our self-image, it's really only an idea and it's something to grow out of. If we are interested in growth, we will always willingly outgrow the sense of who we are and what we are capable of. The growth is exciting when we think of that which is 'bigger than us'. When we say something 'bigger' it isn't separate from us. I think it's actually our true identity. I was trained in psychology. Soul wasn't a word used. I would study Freud, neurosis, psychosis, misery, depression.

Me: Fun.

Robert: All misery. Then I created something called The Happiness Project on the National Health Service. It was an eight-week happiness programme and within this work I started to explore the notion of outgrowing who we think we are. That's why we have to find the tools that work to help us.

Me: The Enneagram is doing just that. It's helping us understand our own limitations which derive from ego.

Robert: Exactly. Our ego is the sense of a separate self. That's what the literal meaning of an ego is. The sense of separation is what Einstein called the 'optical illusion' because none of us are separate. The great heartache for the Enneagram number 2 is that YOU know we are all connected. You think, 'Why is it that so many are acting like we are not connected?'

Me: You're right – this pains me so often on a very subconscious level.

Robert: That's one of your gifts that the Enneagram is showing you. You're the last type to forget we are all connected. It's your soul gift. Each number on the Enneagram has a soul gift.

Me: Ego seems to be one of the barriers that we use to block our connection to spirit, universe or that something bigger. Is ego the culprit?

Robert: The ego tries to do life by itself. It often suffers from what I call 'dysfunctional independence'. For example, the Enneagram type 2, the Helper, likes to help but not to receive help. You say, 'I'm OK thanks, I don't need any help, I can do it all by myself.'

Me: Yup, that's me!

Robert: Helping is your joy but if you are working from ego trying to do it all yourself, you wear yourself out. In my work I was trained to diagnose and then 'fix' people. Essentially my model was a self-improvement model. Eventually I realised that no amount of self-improvement can make up for any lack of self-acceptance. If you're on a self-improvement path you will feel like there's always something left to improve. I felt it in my own life, too. The gap didn't narrow and I wondered why, as I kept trying so hard. Then I realised that I was stuck in a paradigm and that I was trying to improve upon a person that I hadn't even got to know yet. The Enneagram, which is the oldest self-awareness tool on the planet, isn't trying to improve you, it's trying to help you see you.

Me: Now, that is super-cool. So, wait, to have self-acceptance, you have to have self-awareness? I know that might sound obvious to say but I'm not sure I've understood entirely until now.

Robert: The Enneagram helps with this. It's a strange paradox but the more you judge yourself, the less you know yourself. If, for example, I only judge you, I can't *see* you. I can only see my judgements about you. Then I can pat myself on the back and think, 'I'm so right about her.' Similarly if I look in the mirror with my judgements about myself I may think I'm seeing myself but I'm just seeing my judgements. We have to go down a path of enquiry and instead of trying to improve ourselves we look to find ourselves interesting. What would it be like to find yourself interesting?

Me: Do you have to have an element of self-awareness to even do the online Enneagram test? What if someone in denial about a part of themselves, or even worse someone totally deluded, does the test? Surely the outcome won't be a true reflection of who they are?

Robert: This is a great question. If you come at the Enneagram with wanting to fit into a certain image that you're selling to the world, you'll guess the answers rather than answer authentically. The great thing is, it looks like a personality test but it's so much better than that. It's also not typing you as you cannot type the soul. It's typing the ego operating system. Your operating system kicks in with a 2, the Helper. It's not you, it's the operating system you work with.

Me: I get it now. I constantly wonder if the aim in life is to work out who we are, or is the liberation in knowing we cannot?

Robert: There are certain enneatypes that really want to know who they are. For example, type 5, the Investigator, is desperate to know, but each number comes at wanting to understand who they are in a different way. All of the numbers have a driving system in them. The Enneagram helps you to operate that system. Usually, people work out how through heartache and mistakes made.

Me: Yes, so many times I have let my desire to help others wear me down and then I feel resentment. I have let ego drive the number 2 in me, rather than feeling in control of it. How will ancient people have used this?

Robert: The desert fathers and desert mothers around about the third century were trying to work out how to bring divine consciousness down to Earth using the Enneagram. They understood there was an access to universal inspiration, what Louise Hay called her 'inner ding'; the infinite intelligence. The desert fathers were saying, 'OK, we have this universal inspiration on our side but why do we still feel so lost, and unloved?' They questioned that if heaven is on Earth why did it feel like hell? They wondered how to create a spirituality that helped realise heaven on Earth.

It is designed to help three main blocks in each person. The first is the basic fear that we carry in our nervous system. It's not logical, we all carry this in our bodies and we carry it due to the concept of separation. The second block is a passion, a source of suffering over the heart. The third is a fixation, a mental glitch or habit in our thinking that gets us into trouble. The Enneagram helps us meet our basic fear, see the passion over the heart, and it straightens out our thinking so we can tap into the gift we have to give.

Me: My initial reaction on hearing about the Enneagram was that this would help me understand who I am, defined by a number and certain traits that I needed an understanding of, but what I'm hearing now is that it's actually a tool to help us recognise the blocks and fears that are stopping us from true connection – is that right?

Robert: The Enneagram offers us the most insightful lens on our inner blocks. Success, happiness, peace of mind, it will reveal how you're blocking all of these things in life. It doesn't just stop there, though. It also highlights what your gifts are. Your gifts are weirdly the things that you're blocking.

The ego is afraid, full stop. That's where it operates from. When we are working from ego we will block our gifts we have to offer, but when we work from love we remember our connection and soul gifts. We make a decision – we can either function or grow. We can function in life yet still go home feeling empty. Or we can say, 'Right, now that I'm functioning, what if I start thinking about growth?' This is where the Enneagram comes into play. Every type has a virtue. The virtue is the part that heals us. So each number will have a way to transform the ego, and the idea that we are separate from life, into an illusion. If we know there are nine operating systems within the Enneagram, we can actually step back and think, 'In some ways, none of this belongs to me. It's mine to work with but this is exciting because

I can wake up from this.' It gives you self-awareness, it helps you to make better choices and, ultimately, it's a path of growth. It's helping you to grow by recognising your inner blocks but it's also helping you to recognise your big gifts and own them.

Me: This has helped me really understand that connection just equals oneness, which is the same thing as love, and the rest equals separateness and fear, which is essentially the ego. Boom. I love this!

Robert: Yup there are fear decisions and there are love decisions. The Enneagram enlarges your way of seeing the world and the decisions you're making and where the decision is coming from, a place of love or fear. Love is oneness. If we look at the Enneagram diagram, it looks like a circle with the numbers 1–9 around it – the nine different ways humans will operate.

The Enneagram

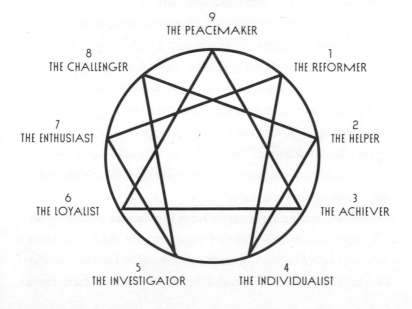

9
THE PEACEMAKER

8
THE CHALLENGER

1
THE REFORMER

7
THE ENTHUSIAST

2
THE HELPER

6
THE LOYALIST

3
THE ACHIEVER

5
THE INVESTIGATOR

4
THE INDIVIDUALIST

The Enneagram is telling us to stop playing small by just aligning to one type and instead be the whole circle. The circle represents oneness and wholeness and infinite potential.

Me: Be the circle! My new catchphrase in life! Robert, thank you so much.

• • •

My head is exploding. My temples are actually throbbing as I try to process the hugeness of the Enneagram. I feel optimistic and liberated that I can now see what is blocking me in my pursuit of true connection. How ironic, but simultaneously wonderful, that our blocks are also our gifts. My gift is to help people, but my block to truly connecting is also my drive to help others and not accept help myself. I feel simplified in the best possible way. I've been X-rayed and the results are in – my block and gift are the same thing: helping others. Gosh, I'm so much simpler than I thought. If I unwrap some of the pickles I've gotten myself into over the years – the broken relationships, the misunderstandings at work, my confidence thinning out into nothingness – it's all down to this very block: I cannot accept help.

This realisation stings a bit. This story is so obviously threaded throughout my whole life yet I've not seen it clearly. I've made each mishap so much more complicated than it needed to be. I've dissected whole chunks of my life, personality and others when I could have saved hours of rumination by understanding that it all boiled down to one thing – my block, not accepting help. This block could sound worthy or even heroic at times but I know this feeling intimately and it's so much uglier than that. The unwillingness to accept help has at times led me to be very judgemental of others and also left me astonished when asked for help when I'm not expecting it. I love to help but sometimes it's on my terms only. My block has stopped me from connecting with people on so many levels and has made me shut up shop when things get too tough. Rather than unfurling a quivering hand, a gesture suggesting I need help, I've instead clamped up like a Venus flytrap.

I've also tried too hard in an attempt to prove to others that I don't need help. I've boasted, unwittingly, about how capable I am. This has proved little but most definitely demonstrated to others that I am so capable they can lean on me heavily. It's come to be expected that I am a capable person who will get shit done, without your help, thank you very much. EXHAUSTING. Why do I do it to myself? I've gotten into such a bad habit with this that I've now taken it to all new levels of believing I don't deserve help. I am a person undeserving of any help at all. What is this blocking me from? It'll be the same thing, whatever your block is – true, beautiful connection. Your block might be different to mine, you might even be able to see it without doing the Enneagram test, but had you considered whether it's also your soul gift? Until now, I most definitely hadn't.

I Have a Gift

Now that I understand my block entirely, I can also be very un-British and exclaim that I have a gift! My gift is to help. The very thing that is blocking me from connection is the thing, when used properly, that connects me to everything. I know I love to help but, as I've mentioned previously, without any boundaries or limits. It's exciting to think that if I truly get this ego operating system working smoothly I'll be able to use my passion for helping others to give me a much more meaningful and connected life. Yes purlease. When I'm not using my gift of wanting to help properly I sometimes feel incredulous when people don't thank me for doing something for them (even when I've instigated the help). I have to work out what the sweet spot is. Is it the bit where someone thanks me? Nope. Is it the bit where I feel like I'm using my time productively? Maybe, but I have an inkling it runs deeper than that. Is it a true leveller, where I subconsciously understand that we are all connected, with interwoven lives, thoughts and outcomes? I think so. I long for that feeling of connection with others at its deepest level. I don't just want to help others to feel boosted; I genuinely want to see those around me thriving. I want to thrive alongside others. One big thrive-off – getting high on our own connection and progress.

I've perhaps unknowingly started to use my gift over the last five years. Starting my brand Happy Place has given me the perfect arena to practise helping people every day with the conversations and storytelling I hope to showcase on the varying platforms I use. I've found a new purpose in the work that I do and I regularly feel pumped knowing that a podcast I've recorded or piece I've written has made someone smile that day. Yet now I have this new information, that helping is indeed part of my life's mission, I want to up my game and wildly experiment with how I use this gift. Anyone else still cringing when I use the word 'gift'? My toes are still slightly curled up in my shoes, so let's try to shake off the Britishness and just accept **we ALL have gifts.** What is yours? Do you already know? It's probably something you do without thought. Yet if we put thought and intention behind these actions, think of the positive change we can make to our lives and to others. That's exciting.

Getting Help

Our gifts may vary in theme but the outcome is always the same: connection. It's our one-way ticket to feeling connection with the people, planet and universe around us. When did you last feel truly connected? Submerging my pasty, vitamin D-deficient body into the freezing spring sea last month was an episode of true oneness. I felt like I was the ocean. I let its chill flood my body and my brain shut off from the human reaction to scream the cove into silence. I staggered out feeling reborn and somehow welcomed by the irregularity of the dancing waves behind me. I have also felt true connection in the tiny moments of union when I've had the opportunity to help someone else or been helped by another. As previously mentioned (maybe too many times) I'm useless at accepting help but sometimes you have no choice. Sometimes, a true mate who can see through your bullshit is willing to put themselves on the line to ensure you get help. For example, the time a friend booked me a doctor's appointment when my ongoing low mood was clearly morphing into full-blown depression. She could have continued listening to me repeating myself on the phone about how I couldn't cope but she didn't. She picked up the phone and booked me an appointment and drove me in the pissing rain to make sure I got actual help. I'm not sure I've ever felt more connected after a large spell of total helplessness.

There was so much meaning in that quiet moment of friendship. There was no huge gift in a box with a ribbon, or Instagrammable moment. It was a secret phone call to a doctor, and a silent car journey with a heavy cloud of grey overhead. It was quiet but so jammed with meaning. Connection has to be in tandem with meaning. Without the meaning it's all just a pantomime. You could experience more meaning in smiling at your elderly neighbour over the fence than you might being cheered at by thousands of people. It's not about numbers, size or visibility – it's about meaning and seeing the hugeness of the tiny moments in life.

Oneness in a Divided World

This need for oneness seems disturbingly relevant today as we live in such a divisive time. Or perhaps there have always been blatantly opposing ideas, rubbing up against one another, but we're now in a time where social media, the TV and our phones magnify the huge canyon between opinions while inflating acerbic sentences and hateful actions. If you are to believe what you read in the papers and see on the news, oneness seems like a far-fetched, foolish ideal that we will not, in our lifetime, experience. And perhaps it is a huge ask or desire that we see union on a global scale, but what about in our own lives? In our own tiny ecosystems, which start in the home but spill out into our social and working lives, can we create more oneness and harmony there?

Ironically, I think the way we can start cultivating this is by letting the idea of who we are slip away entirely. **When we are vehemently tied to a specific idea of who we are and what we stand for, we can easily jump to judgement of others.** This is what Robert was explaining during our chat. If you only look at someone through the lens of judgement, then you are not seeing them at all. Can we get out of our own way to truly see others? It might be tough to stare those in the eye who think, act and move through life in a polarising way to you, but if we try to lose judgement it might be possible to see the pain beneath the anger, the insecurity beneath the shouts, the fear beneath the snarl. Can we use what we've learned from Robert and view

others with their gifts and blocks? Can you look at the friend
you fell out with and see their gifts and blocks? Can you look
at your neighbour who aligns with a differing political party
to you and see their gifts and blocks? Can you find oneness in
a world where everyone moves in a different way? Can you do
perhaps the hardest job of all and look in the mirror and see
your very own gifts and blocks?

ASTROLOGY AND PLANETARY MOVEMENT

This book's purpose is to get us all looking at the concepts that are bigger than our own individual thoughts, and it really doesn't get any huger than those glorious planets and moons orbiting around the solar system. We are so used to the tiny things and thoughts in life. Guzzling down titbits of info from tiny screens, worrying about the minutiae of everyday life, fretting about a chipped tooth, one too many biscuits eaten, a flat tyre ... and we totally forget about the HUGENESS of the universe around us. We almost ignore its relevance and possibly its existence. I'm guessing that for us all to live a spiritual life we need to start thinking big. We need to expand our minds and open our eyes and hearts to the gargantuan space and energy around us, which spans from our tiny human bodies all the way out to the furthest reaches of the solar system, and beyond.

I've long been fascinated with astrology yet know so little. It gives us the best and biggest opportunity to have awareness that goes way outside the lines of our own small lives. When we look up with wonder, it's so much harder to get bogged down with the smaller stuff we are so focused on. When imagining Saturn with its glorious hoops right above our heads, it's so much harder to get stressed about your kid not eating vegetables. First, let's cover the obvious bits: star signs.

I'm a Virgo. A supercharged Virgo. Under the description of Virgo in any horoscope, they might as well just have a photo of me. Most would summarise a Virgo as practical, sensible, loyal, meticulous, neat and tidy, organised, and single-minded when it comes to the pursuit of improvement. I tick every box going. Tick, tick, tick. My husband often says I should have a bottle of surface spray surgically attached to my right arm as I'm perpetually determined to get a glossy kitchen worktop. My step-kids roll their eyes as I clean around their plates while they're still eating. When I walk into a room in our house, I do a subconscious scan and within seconds I can spot if something has been moved or hasn't been put away. I am Casa Wood's very own Sherlock Holmes, piecing together clues as to items' whereabouts and how they might have got there. Everything in our house, and in my life, has a home and if it's out of place I crumble. It feels very inbuilt. I cannot settle and feel calm unless my surroundings are in order. Outer chaos, inner chaos and all that jazz. My mate Giles, also a Virgo, is exactly the same. He once bought me bamboo kitchen cloths as a gift. I've never felt more seen!

What's in Store

Looking at family members and friends in my life they seem to fit quite neatly into their horoscope boxes too. My husband is a Scorpio and the list of traits commonly associated with this sign again ring true – honest, brave, jealous, secretive, intuitive and adaptable. I would say Jesse embodies all of those in ways.

My mate who is a Leo loves the limelight, my mum who is a Gemini illustrates extremes in opposing ways. There has to be something in it, right?

Whether you class yourself as a spiritual person or not, you'll have an understanding of your zodiac sign and will perhaps at some point have felt curious about what is on the horizon for you. I always find horoscopes in red-top newspapers slightly jarring. Something so historic, mathematical, esoteric and spiritual squashed between pages of scantily clad models and sports reports. It's like seeing a monk at Disney Land. Yet isn't that also quite brilliant? Something that's been around for thousands of years has found its way into everyday life so wonderfully and has become the norm. Whether you believe in horoscopes or not, they'll sure get you thinking.

I used to LOVE nothing more than poring over *Sugar* magazine as a teenager, lapping up every word of my monthly horoscope. With a mouth full of braces, hair tied back in a velvet scrunchy, I clung on to every word. If my horoscope that month said love was on the horizon, I was a sniffer dog, on the lookout for a new match. If I was directed to take more chances, I would say yes to everything, quite literally using *Sugar* magazine as my personal lighthouse to guide me in life. I remember specifically reading (now, this is before the internet, guys, so I couldn't just google this stuff) that Virgos were well suited to Pisces; in fact, that they might well be soulmate material and, guess what, Taylor Hanson (from the band Hanson, 'MMMBop', etc.), my teenage heart-throb, was a Pisces. I was elated and immediately started to plan how our wedding would play out.

Even now, I'm partial to flicking to the back of a mag to see what's in store for me. This month, mine reads that I'm to pause the pursuit of demanding people's attention. I need to sit back and let them come to me. As much as I can see the relevance of this reading in my life at the moment, I wonder how much of it is true? How much of it is helpful? And how does it help us lead a more spiritual life?

Where Did It All Begin?

Astrology has been used for thousands of years to guide and give comfort to differing cultures the world over. The people of ancient Mesopotamia, geographically known now to be modern-day Iraq, believed in the premise of astrology with records dating as far back as 1500 BC. Their basic belief was based on the idea that if there was a 'bad sign' in the sky, there had to be a reflection of that on Earth, and vice versa. In around 550 BC, after the Persian Empire had invaded Mesopotamia, we can see the first birth charts documented on tablets of stone. This is the earliest recorded sign of a civilisation believing that the arrangement of planets in the sky would dictate something about that individual's personality during their life. Around the same time, the Egyptians had created their own version of astrology, using rising stars as a way to tell the time and which also led to certain rituals. A little later down the line, in around 323 BC, we can see clear records of the twelve zodiac signs and associations, which merged with earlier ideas created by the Mesopotamian people and the Egyptians. The theories developed over the years, with great focus on which planets ruled over certain signs and how the solar hemisphere of the chart related to the soul, mind and spirit, whereas the lunar hemisphere related more to prosperity, the body and matter.

What we now commonly call our star sign is related to where the sun sat in the sky on the day we were born. We've seemingly run with the star sign above all other aspects of the chart, such as the moon's position and other planetary coordinates, but why?

The most obvious reason is that it's the easiest and most accessible part of the birth chart to read. With thirty-odd days to play with, anyone can work out what star sign they are from their birthdate alone, so at some point in the modern world a monthly prediction was written up in magazines and suchlike for all to imbibe.

Over time we have seemingly devalued what we can learn from the movement of the planets and sun and prefer to look at phone screens and laptops. This kind of depresses me. As little as I know about astrology and the movement of the planets, I do know that I want to spend a lot more time looking up rather than down. I would way prefer to be guided by the celestial movement above than by Instagram or Facebook. I would way rather be guided by something as historic and esoteric as astrology and planetary movement than by newspapers and websites.

Get to Know You

As yet I'm not sure how astrology is going to assist me on my spiritual quest but my guess is that it's going to help me get to know myself much better and I think that so far I've realised that that is a fundamental when it comes to committing to an everyday spiritual life. The more willing we are to really look at ourselves, look beneath the pile of stories and beliefs we have in place about ourselves, the more deeply we can live. Decision-making becomes easier because we know who we are; saying no isn't a problem because our own boundaries are in place; dreams and desires have total clarity as we understand our limitlessness; and, in that place of knowing, we might just find acceptance – true acceptance of ourselves, our true nature and all that comes with that... the mistakes made, the slip-ups, trip-ups, clumsily spoken words and negative thoughts. Perhaps learning about what was going on in the sky when we were born, and how energetically that has affected our true nature and how we react to the world, might just help us get to know who we are that bit better.

Introducing Paula Shaw, another wonderful person I was tipped off about through my friend Rebecca Dennis. Paula is a spiritual teacher and guide who uses birth charts and tarot to help guide people and give them a deeper connection to life. I've had a few personal sessions with Paula over Zoom, as she resides in Australia, and they've been so helpful and encouraging as her readings have given me confidence in decision-making and direction in life.

At 8am UK time my screen pings to life to show Paula at the other end of the day, on a warm Australian evening.

Me: Hey, Paula. It looks lovely and hot in Australia this evening.

Paula: Hey, Fearne. Good morning to you.

Me: I'm excited to talk to you today. I've seen horoscopes mainly as a bit of fun over the years but obviously there is a lot more to it.

Paula: When it comes to star signs and the zodiac chart, we have to remember that star signs are exclusively looking at the position of the sun in the sky, relative to when you were born. It's not very personal as it covers a whole month of dates due to the slow movement of the sun. It's kind of missing the point as star signs don't take into consideration where the moon and other planets were on that day, or how full the moon was on that date. Using exclusively the star sign, we don't get to see people's personal cycles; there's so much more in a complete birth chart. If you know the exact time you were born you can get a much more direct reading. Astrology predates modern religion. It's been going for millennia, so there's so much history and knowledge, and the fact that it continues to intrigue us suggests to me that there is something to astrology that humans continue to be fascinated by and gain benefit from.

Me: How do you work out your whole birth chart without spending loads of money getting someone with the skill set to do it?

Paula: There are now apps you can use to work it out if you have the exact time of birth, as if the time is even a few minutes out it will mean your chart will read completely differently.

Me: As impersonal and lacking in detail as star signs might be, I am very much a textbook Virgo, so what's going on there?

Paula: Astrology is the correlation of celestial events. The sun, when looking at astronomy, is of course the centre of the solar system. It literally lights up the whole of the solar system. When you bring that notion into looking at your star sign – your sun sign – Virgo, we can say your whole psyche and personality are influenced by the essence of Virgo. So most people relate to it. It's the flavour of you. Do you mind if we do your chart now? What date were you born and at what time?

(I furrow my brow and seriously wonder if I have ever even bothered to ask this question of my folks.)

Me: Third of September 1981 and the time ... I literally have no clue (I say with a tinge of embarrassment). Let me text my mum now.

(A speedy text is pinged off to Mumma Cotton.)

Paula: I see astrology as a map. Your personal birth chart is a photograph, a snapshot, of what was going on in the sky when you were born. What we do is look at the relationship between all of those planets, the sun and the moon, to get a sense of what could be shaping your personality and the events of your life. We piece it all together, taking into account all of the bigger cycles, like where the moon was in its lunar cycle.

One example you may have heard of is the 'Saturn return', which happens to everyone around the age of twenty-nine, thirty. It's a big turning point for everybody. It's where we move into another life cycle. Most people will have a story about this time in their life. A big change, marriage, kids, a depression, job change, etc.

Me: THIS IS ME! At twenty-nine I had all the best stuff and all the worst stuff happen to me. At twenty-nine I had one engagement end, then I met my husband which was wonderful, but that also was the start, a year or so later, of a big, bad depression that lasted some time. Looking back, that period of depression was essential and transformative in so many ways and has totally shaped who I am today. So this isn't about reaching a human age, this is relating to one complete cycle of Saturn around the Earth starting from the date you were born?

Paula: It takes twenty-eight to twenty-nine years for Saturn to do one complete cycle back to where it was on the day you were born. I can imagine that our ancient ancestors would have naturally observed this movement from the sky as Saturn is one of the five planets visible to the naked eye. **Science has somewhat overtaken our desire to look up at how the planets are**

moving. Science is brilliant, of course, but we have lost a lot of meaning and history along the way.

Me: I know, I never give poor old Saturn a thought. I'm too busy worrying that I'm late for the school run, or that I've pissed someone off. I forget to look up. How can we start to honour the bigger picture in our everyday life? How can we honour the natural cycles of the Earth, nature and the solar system in our lives?

Paula: The best way to immediately start observing cycles is to follow the phases of the moon. It's easy. It's there in the sky to see. The moon moves the tides and we are made up of approximately 60 per cent water, so to think it doesn't have any impact on us humans on Earth seems strange to me. If you ask nurses what happens on a full moon, most will tell you they notice changes in patterns of behaviour at these times. I've met many non-believers in astrology who share that they have noticed strange sleeping patterns, heightened emotions and increased dream states during the full moon. This might all be anecdotal but I've honestly noticed everything seems amplified at the full moon and at the dark moon, which is the new moon. Everything is dark during a new moon and the world feels more quiet and still.

Me: Yes, not to exclude the male readers of this section but, for women, we of course have our own monthly cycle too.

Paula: Yes, there is research that suggests there really is a connection to our hormones that are activated by the lunar cycles. Yet, it is more pertinent to look at the 'relationship' between our cycles and the cosmos. It's not a case of 'the planets are doing this to me'. We can't blame nature or these natural cycles, we have to honour and observe the relationship we have with all of it. The laws of nature can teach us so much. Look at the example of how a caterpillar changes into a butterfly. I learned recently that a caterpillar in chrysalis form doesn't just evolve and grow inside the cocoon, it turns completely to mush and then reforms. Ask yourself now, how many times have you hit rock bottom, not knowing who you are any more, yourself turned to mush, then to reform and grow into something new and greater?

Me: I have been such a pile of mush at times and, yes, I can see my own transformation mirrored in that natural cycle. This conversation has taken a turn I wasn't expecting. I was planning to ask you about how the planets affect us, but I already understand from talking to you that that is the wrong angle to take. This is about us honouring our relationship with nature and those cycles that are so much bigger than us. Learning from them and seeing how they might be mirrored in our own lives. Science and the human ego seem to have overridden the natural cycles. We want to be in control and think we can look away from it and do as we please. It's a huge, ugly shame.

Last week I was chatting to a mate about the magnolia tree in the garden. It bloomed recently and made me so happy, but one week later all the gorgeous pink petals had dropped to the floor. I was gutted to not have that view out of my window and was telling my mate Henry about it on text. He told me that it was a reminder to enjoy the moment, not hold too tightly on to things and to let the flow of nature in and out of my life, learning to honour the transient nature of everything.

Paula: Exactly. Astrology is a chance to look at the connection we have to the whole universe. We are not separate from it. Astrology has helped me to trust in the cycles. You know the saying, 'This too shall pass.' There are times when I'm going up and times I'm going down, times of regression and times of having to rebirth. It's helped me to understand that we are all different too. Our charts are different, so we are all different, and this helps me practise patience and compassion. I can see this most immediately in my own children. It's also taught me to surrender. We have to surrender to the laws of nature and its cycles.

There is a connection to the celestial bodies and meaning behind it all. **I would much rather live in a world where Venus is a goddess and everything has meaning than just believe we are all simply matter, hurtling along through space.** No, no, I can't look at life like that. Our ancient ancestors would have used the planets we can see with our eyes, so Jupiter, Saturn, Mercury, Mars, Venus and the moon. Ancient astrologers would observe their movement in correlation to events on Earth. So, take for example Venus, she isn't visible all year; she goes from the evening star to the morning star, and the ancient people believed in a certain meaning behind Venus. Love, relationships and connection were all intertwined with her story and movement. They noticed that when she wasn't visible in the sky something would change and shift in the collective. I myself observe these cycles. Right now, Venus isn't visible and I'm seeing a lot of people feeling like there isn't much magic about in life. The ancients would do this constantly.

Look at all the stone circles, like Stonehenge in your home country. They're designed to connect us to the equinox and solstices, which are connected to the seasons. Communities would come together and celebrate the seasonal shifts with ritual and ceremony. They would share food and knowledge and stories to connect with each other and nature. The rhythms of natural cycles were honoured and we just don't do that any more. We aren't wondering what happens when Venus isn't visible.

Me: God, it's so depressing, isn't it? We are ignoring so much magic.

Paula: If you are distracted constantly in the modern world, highly charged and anxious, start looking at natural cycles and the planets – there's something so beautiful and calming in/about them.

Me: We don't even honour the basic nature of how our planet works any more. We don't even have to eat seasonally as we can order strawberries in the winter from another country, boxed in plastic and delivered to our door. It's a huge discord we've created for ease. Or, if I wanted to ditch winter in November, I could fly over to you in Australia and have back-to-back summers by hopping on a plane. We are actually rallying against the natural cycles most of the time.

Paula: By doing that, what are we seeing? More people having lifestyle health issues. Physical and mental issues have all risen hugely and are mostly related to lifestyle. We are not in rhythm with what is natural. Our rhythm is now consume, consume, produce, produce. I'm so passionate about ritual (more on this coming up in the book on pages 225–47). In the UK at the turn of the Industrial Revolution you guys had over thirty bank holidays, 'holy days', a year, a number of which were aligned with equinoxes and solstices. Once the factories started up, and possibly due to the war, these all began to be whittled away, in an effort to keep people working.

Me: What the fuck?

Paula: They wanted people to keep working in the factories. A new kind of greed for more and more emerged. And, look where we have ended up. In a perpetual cycle of produce, consume. Where can astrology be useful right now? It can help us to connect to the world we actually live in. What can that lead to? We might start to listen to our intuition. To ourselves. We might wonder, 'What is in me? What wants to come forth?' Astrology is a way for us to listen and hear the answers. If you're in the metaphorical factory all day, you will not be listening.

Mo: The 'factory' is now the phone, isn't it? Our phones, our laptops, are that constant distraction. We think that is where the answers might be. We've disassociated and devalued the natural because we've placed so much importance on money, titles, accolade, status and hierarchy.

Paula: This is why we have to start looking around us. As I mentioned, we can do this with the moon or some visible planets in the sky. Plug into it.

The moon has a twenty-nine-odd-day cycle. When the moon is a bright circle in the sky, we call it a full moon and that's when it is directly opposite the sun so it's fully illuminated. When it's a new moon, you cannot see it because it's right next to the sun so it's not getting the light. In between, the moon will wax from a new moon which means it's getting bigger and then after it has reached a full moon it starts to wane again, which means it's getting smaller through the gibbous and crescent phases. **So, when the moon is new, it's when you set intentions. You seed ideas and questions and start observing. It's a quiet time of contemplation. The nights are darker and quieter. When the moon is full it's like a spotlight shining up all the bits of your life you're hiding from. It's a time to let go of all the**

crap you can see in your life that you don't need. The moon is there, in the sky, giving you permission to do so. It's an act of power and you can work with it through the moon's cycles. Your whole life can become one big ritual.

Me: Oh, my mum just texted me. Hold tight. OK, Mumma Cotton says that I was born at 5:25pm. I had no clue!

Paula: OK, let me work that out.

Me: Another thing I wanted to ask you is, whenever I dip into looking at spirituality, I start to wonder how much of our life is mapped out by destiny versus the autonomy we have over making decisions and the butterfly effect of life. Is there even an answer to that?

Paula: My honest feeling is that no one can completely answer that question. It's the great mystery and I don't want to live in a world where that mystery is absent. I think there is an aspect of our lives mapped out by rhythms and cycles that have been in motion forever – most would call this karma. Yet I believe we have free will as to how we respond to events in life. If we don't contemplate concepts like astrology, then we can feel quite lost, powerless and stuck in situations. You'll have the experience without the meaning behind it. You create free will by understanding you have the freedom to react to situations in life with wisdom and kindness rather than reacting from a place of trauma. Astrology gives us the insight and perspective to look at our reactions and not be trapped or defined by them.

Mystery is such an important thing to honour, too. Art, music, poetry, they all help us to feel the connection but we will never truly understand the full story behind the mystery of it all.

Engaging with the mystery and mythology through things like astrology, ritual and self-healing actually inspires us to create reality and not just wander along aimlessly in a meaningless world of materialism.

Me: Our brains literally can't cope with the hugeness of life. My brain hurts even attempting to think about it.

Paula: So, let's get the rest of your chart sorted. You were born at the first quarter moon, so as the moon was starting to wax (get bigger). So the moon was moving from a new moon and progressing to a crescent, so you're curious and someone who wants to go out into the world and learn and progress. Your moon is in Scorpio. As we know, your sun (star sign) is in Virgo. This adds to even more precision in life.

Me: Help! This explains a lot.

Paula: Scorpio is deep. The moon is your eternal experience of life. It's the most intimate heavenly body connected to planet Earth, it moves the water. It's emotion and feeling, it's internal and feminine. With a Scorpio moon you feel everything deeply.

Me: YUP!!! That's me. I'm like a watermelon with no shell. I feel every pinch, pull and punch.

Paula: You have really strong Libra here too in your tenth house, which rules your public persona, so you're able to interact well with people, like the hostess. You carry yourself with grace and have a way with the public where they can easily relate to and connect with you. But the Scorpio moon helps you see bullshit.

Me: YES! BS detector constantly on.

Paula: Libra in your chart allows you to see other people's weakness or strength, you could take them out but you choose not to. This often creates some struggle for you too, as the Libra in your chart stops you from creating strong boundaries with others. Your north node, which is a very karmic point of the chart, is in the ninth house in Leo. You have a strong desire to take people to a place where they can talk about and understand subjects that are taboo. It was always going to fire up in your life at some point.

Me: Yes, that's really unfurled in my work in the last few years. Boundaries are indeed my weakness too. I'm awful at them. I'm really trying to get better with this. It's all so fascinating. Thank you so much for all your wisdom and thought today. I loved chatting to you, Paula.

● ● ●

Approximately four seconds after my conversation with Paula I downloaded a lunar cycle app. Why have I not done this before? Why have I got an app that shows what the weather will be like so I can work out what I can DO during my week but not a lunar app that predicts how I might FEEL during my week? Why have I got apps that track packages I've ordered but not one to track the phases of the moon? I'm so out of whack with the natural rhythms of our universe. I think most of us are. We're one big heaving mass of consumerism as most messaging we receive daily keeps us in a loop of destructive distraction from the truth. The truth that lies in the natural cycles of the universe.

Down by the Seas

This conversation also coincided with a trip to the British seaside and my favourite coastline in the world. Dorset is home to the Jurassic Coast and some of the most sensational scenery going. Dare I say it's my spiritual home. I feel comfortable, clear and calm held in the curvature of Lulworth Cove. I feel inspired and connected beneath the handsome arch of Durdle Door. Day one of the trip and we handily find ourselves under the quiet sky of a new moon. I slept like shit the night before we left on our family trip as I've been a bit of an anxious traveller since the kids were born, but as soon as I set foot on the beach on the first day of our holiday, I feel grounded.

My friend Ella and I decide to swim in the sea. It's April, the sun is pulsating in a duck-egg blue sky but the early spring wind shimmies around our bare shoulders as we tiptoe to the pebbled edge. It is colder than I could ever have imagined. We inch into the glossy water and it feels as though millions of tiny daggers are at our skin. We are breathless, panting, and by now bobbing like two hyperactive townies in need of a reset. My legs and arms flap about as I try to focus on the shoreline. No words come out; they're all stuck behind huge pants of life-saving air. I ungracefully flop out of the sea and run my numb feet along the smooth pebbles to my towel. I yelp with glee. I'm alive. In that moment I feel fully awake and in tune with what is going on around me. My eyesight sharper, hearing crystal clear, lungs free from London smog, body light and tingly from the adrenalin and blood rush. I stand on the beach, towel gripped by two ice-block hands, looking at the sea.

The tide is in as it's morning time. It's covering life and beauty below. The natural cycle of the tides pulled by the moon, which I would never normally bother to give a thought about, are now indicating that this could be a good moment of reflection. A sliver of time to think about the beauty and mystery that could be lurking beneath my tired everyday thoughts. Work had been very busy in the run-up to the trip and often in these moments I get lost in a vortex of stress and worry and forget about the hidden gems of life. Sea, I will listen to you, I promise. I vow to race into its cold grasp every day this week.

Newness Under Every Rock

That afternoon the tide has drawn back, revealing a city of rock pools and slimy, glistening seaweed. Rex is in his element. My Pisces boy is obsessed with the water and all its inhabitants. We race across rocks, our feet darting from rock to rock like a giant game of hopscotch. Our eyes alert, looking for movement below. We crouch down at tiny pools of life; each rock pool, its own little world, full of colour and movement. We lift up slabs and find tiny crabs with grey shells and extra-large pincers. We watch sea anemones with their scarlet dancing tentacles, swaying in the water's movement. We discover magic and newness under every rock. I decide in that moment to watch the tides this week and promise to keep turning over rocks in the sea and in my own life. Which metaphorical rocks in my mind have I left unturned? Which rocks have I ignored altogether? Where could there be more magic and more beauty undiscovered? At one point Rex finds a huge crab with a rusty, sturdy body. We sit in awe of this new friend and talk about what species of crab he might be and what he might like to eat. It's a magical moment in my favourite bay I will never forget.

Our discoveries that day, and the beauty we saw, were only available because we chose to crouch down and look. We sat and waited and honoured the nature around us with curiosity, and then the beauty revealed itself. The reveal was only possible because of the moon's pull dragging back the sea to unveil the multicoloured life beneath. I am already learning so much from slowing down and looking around me.

Happy Faces

That evening, with wind-kissed cheeks and salty lips, I sat and looked out of the window at the bay nearby. The tide had now been guided back into shore to protect the life beneath its surface. The adrenalin of travelling that morning had subsided and I found the blanket of darkness above me comforting. The new moon was a time for quiet introspection. No TV or screen to distract me, just stillness and the moonless sky. I asked some questions quietly: why do I keep myself so busy at home? What am I actively trying to disconnect from? How much longer can I really go on like this? I'm sure we can all relate to that line of questioning. We celebrate busyness in the Western, modern world. We congratulate those who never take a day off to stop and look around themselves. But why? Why are we congratulating those who are the most distracted and disconnected?

The next morning I walk down to the beach with gusto, knowing I've made a sacred commitment to the sea. My swimming costume is already on underneath my tracksuit so there really is no going back. I watch some locals in their seventies sat on the wall near the steps down to the beach. Happy faces, smiles broad, looking out at the most familiar of views that brings so much joy. No race, no rush, no push or shove, just happiness in the observation of the mighty sea. Why are we not openly celebrating these souls? Those who choose to sit and take it all in. Those who learn by observing rather than striving. I'm already feeling much clearer about all of this.

Whisper to the Sea

Today I walk into the water with purpose. I don't pant in panic or throw my arms about like a distressed squid. I let my body fall naturally into the arms of the sea and take commanding breaths of air into my lungs. I swim gently, my goose-bumped body moving gracefully through the water, with ripples trailing off behind. I feel calm, I might even look like a local who does this every day.

By day three I manage a six-minute swim timed by my step-daughter Lola and her best mate Skye, egging me on to stay in the tit-curlingly cold waters for as long as I could. After three minutes I feel completely fine. I somehow make it to six minutes and feel tranquil to my core. I trust that the sea will hold me; I trust that I will learn more from these six minutes than the sixteen minutes I spent on Instagram that morning; I trust that I am not separate from the water or the moon that pulls it.

Towards the end of the trip the moon is waxing in the sky. On an evening walk I can see its little sliver of crescent shaped light in the onyx sky, hovering above the mighty cliff face that stares out to sea. With its new light come more curiosity and answers. I whisper out to the endless sea, 'What am I distracting myself from?' After all, any time we are not following the natural cycles of the Earth, planets or moon, we are merely distracting ourselves from universal truth and our own truth. The answers came slowly and were actioned by small glimmers of magic. A streak of pearlescent moonlight on the sea below, a flock of birds in formation above, the sound of the waves crashing against the rocks below. Ego. Ego is blocking me from so much in life. The need to keep up with the speed, to be seen as someone who is on top of everything, to achieve and keep pushing and suppos-edly to feel like I am a person who is going somewhere. Ego blocks most of us from connecting to what is going on around us and hides the secrets of our truth. Sometimes ego is conflated with the concept of arrogance, but ego is simply the times when we get in the way of ourselves, when our own ideas and story of who we think we are overshadow the truth. I know in this moment that I need to let go of a lot of stories and work with my intuition and the truth of who I am.

No Baggage

Back from the trip, with a nose splattered in freckles, I'm clinging on to the sound of the waves and the feeling of the icy water licking at my toes. I'm checking my moon app daily to help me include ritual into my week. Today the moon is nearly a half crescent. I'm halfway between the stillness of the new moon and its introspection and the spotlight that will show up my unanswered questions for me as the moon reaches full.

I follow an author and meditation teacher online called Kirsty Gallagher who uses the moon for guidance in her practice and teaching. Today her post on Instagram states that the Aries new moon energy is strong and that should help us to turn the page towards a new chapter. Being a romantic and fantasist at heart, this excites me greatly. I have always loved the idea that newness is on the horizon. A brand-new me, with new ideas, no baggage and endless possibilities. I think it's why, when I was a kid, I used to love going abroad so much. I would almost create a whole new identity for myself for a week of camping in the south of France. I would turn into the sort of person who would wear an anklet and eat brioche for breakfast. I think I still do this now to some extent. My week in Dorset proved to be a time of renewal in many ways. I stripped myself of London's velocity, make-up and also my bra for the week and sank into a slower and simpler pace. I became the sort of person who wears the same jumper every day and swims in the icy sea without a single yelp. So who is this new me? What is this new chapter? Kirsty asked this question on her Instagram page just yesterday, encouraging her followers to dig deep and think about what this new energy could do.

I feel I am shedding some old skin. This tight, often uncomfortable jacket I have worn for years, the one that keeps me tied to the narrative that I have to always put myself out there and strive and push myself, is slowly slipping off my shoulders. Sometimes when I'm asked to go on to TV shows or take part in big televised events, I feel the urge to say yes out of fear. It's not a 'yes' backed up by passion and desire, it's one that reeks of fear that if I say no, I will disappear. More recently I haven't minded saying no at all. I think this might be my new chapter. The moon is shouting at me to stop saying yes out of fear and to listen to my gut and go with the natural cycles of life. My own life cycle is in motion constantly and I've very much passed through the stage where I feel I have to be seen to be doing certain things to be validated by others. I'm now moving naturally into a new quieter, slower phase where the pauses in between work or excitement are much more nourishing than the activities themselves. Thank you, moon, for prompting me to look at this page turn and how I might steer my own life in this direction with even more confidence.

To Be of Service

Kirsty also mentions this week that the moon is in a sextile aspect to Venus and Uranus. I have no idea what this means but Kirsty goes on to explain that Venus wants us to put ourselves first and Uranus wants us to push boundaries and shake ourselves back to life so we can live authentically. Most Brits reading this will at first shudder at the thought of putting themselves first. Many of us will have been brought up by parents or carers and grand-parents who lived through wars, or were brought up by those who were, so it's all about the other in the dynamic. Perhaps parents who were the first generation to emigrate and settle in the UK, far from home and feeling unsettled. Through little choice the generations before us had to be stoic and put others first to get through the horrors they witnessed or the fear of starting all over again. We are perhaps carrying a diluted version of this thinking but it's there all the same and at times can stop us from doing what is right for ourselves to grow and expand and also simply rest. Remember what Wendy Mandy said in the section on shamans (see pages 17–43)? Self-compassion is where it's at. Unless we put ourselves and our needs first, we are of no proper use to anyone or anything else. First, we must honour and love ourselves. Again, as Brits, our toes curl at the thought but we have to try as we collectively know the other way isn't working. This isn't about being selfish or self-centred; the main goal is to be part of a collective mindset and cause, so once we've strengthened our own reserves we have the capacity to help others and be of service.

Authentic Self

Uranus has got me thinking (is a sentence I never thought I would write). I really am heading towards a much more authen-tic version of myself. In my twenties I often felt so out of place in the world of TV that I thought I had to present myself and look a certain way to be accepted into an environment that felt at times totally alien. I pushed most spiritual beliefs to one side for portions of this chapter of my life and became somewhat tunnel-visioned. To be honest, the world of TV still feels pretty alien to me, which is why I do so little TV at this point in my life. Turning forty has given me full-blown permission to sack off any insecurities and worries about how others perceive me and dive headfirst into my own unique weirdness, replete with bags of idiosyncrasies and tendencies that make me tick. If the planets and moon phases are steering me in this direction, I'm all for it. As I said earlier, I would way rather be guided by the mighty planets in the solar system than by a TikTok video (No offence TikTok).

The planets and these huge, beautiful, natural cycles are billions of years old. Who is to argue with that? We humans have been around in the universe for a kitten's sneeze. It's almost embarrassing to think we know more than the natural intelligence at work that's been around for billions of years.

I feel I'm getting a much better perspective on the importance of incorporating this sort of thinking into my everyday to keep on a spiritual path. How could you incorporate the natural cycles into your own life? Could you begin by looking at how you feel during each season and what each change in season could represent in your life? The corner turned from winter to spring giving us all a nod to unfurl our tense, cold arms and to embrace the new life that spring brings. The moment that summer turns orange and the sun starts to dip, could we all take note from the golden leaves falling that nothing ever stays the same and acceptance is our only place of peace?

Look at how the world's, planets' and moon's cycles could impact your own life and what this might reveal about you.

Awareness's Lessons

- Where your attention goes, energy flows. Be aware of where you are putting your energy.

- Look at your blocks in life and they'll probably be your gifts too.

- Watch the natural cycles and honour them. See how you can learn from them and work with them rather than against them.

PART 3

COMMUNICATION

How do you communicate with the world around you? I don't just mean with your family and friends. Nor am I exclusively talking about how you might banter with your local cafe owner or postman. I'm talking about the constant dialogue we all have with the universe. Most of us don't even realise that we are in continual communication with the universe. We assume our thoughts are isolated within the walls of our skull and our words are only caught by those nearby. Yet every thought we have, every word we clumsily utter about how bad we are at dating/organisation/earning money/friendships/looking after ourselves is communicated directly to that something bigger. We are constantly communicating with the world around us with thought, word and expression. Before writing this book I rarely gave this line of communication a thought. I was so busy conversing with people for my job that I felt I had done all the chitchat needed to create a positive and forward-moving experience. How wrong I was.

This part of the book has been a place for me to really look at how I talk with, respect and honour life and the world around me. I hope it is for you too. It's also created new daily habits for me that now feel embedded and important. Having awareness of how and when I'm communicating with the world around me has changed my outlook on everything and also helped me to lift the lid on so many self-limiting thoughts and bad habits I had gotten into. On countless occasions I have exclaimed, 'I can't cope', which of course manifests in me not coping. In those moments I haven't been willing to look at the reasons why I feel I cannot cope. I haven't stopped to make changes that could help me cope better, such as asking someone for help, or settling on the average rather than perfection when it comes to tidiness in the home, work projects and my inbox. Instead, I constantly moan aloud that I cannot cope, so I'm seemingly met with more moments where I feel I cannot. It's a subconscious, ongoing, roundabout of a conversation with life itself which is never-ending as I fail to make any changes. Perhaps if my line of conversation changed to, 'I would love some help, universe', then I might be met with it? We all have multiple subconscious statements we think or speak into reality, much like the law of attraction discussed with Rhonda Byrne earlier.

Within this dialogue, whether conscious or not, we have little respect for life and the world around us. We walk through woodlands without acknowledging the trees that inhabit the land, imbibe beautiful sunsets without humbly thanking the sky for such a spectacle. We take a lot for granted when it comes to nature's perpetual cycles and ever-changing glory. In the Western world we've normalised talking into smartphones yet created an oddity out of talking to trees. How's that for a giant ladleful of disconnection. I have work to do here as I want my relationship with life and the world around me to deepen. I want to understand life better but be equally as intrigued by the answers I might get. I want to feel humbled by the hugeness of life and not dulled by the digital world that I'm indulgently communicating through.

It's time to put down the phone so we can dial up on life and communicate with purpose and intent.

PRAYER

The room is dark and I can hear a fox terrorising my recycling bin below. I must wash out those yogurt pots more thoroughly before putting the bins out. I need sleep but worry is knocking at my door, keeping my eyes open and my heart racing a little too fast. Two friends are having an incredibly tough time at the moment and I feel helpless. Now I know that I'm an Enneagram 2 (the Helper), not being able to help is clearly my worst nightmare. I want to be all action, hugs, biscuits and practical help to others but sometimes problems are too big and too out of my control to help at all. Prayer seems like my only option and, at this time of night, weirdly an intuitive choice.

Why do I only pray in SOS moments? Why isn't it a part of my everyday existence? The first small hurdle I have to get over is how awkward it feels doing it. I prefer to speak the prayer aloud as it feels more impactful and as if I might speak my well-wishes into reality. I'm obviously well versed in speaking out loud but, to hear my own little voice bouncing back at me with no one to catch each syllable, I feel like a bit of a wally. I'm too aware of my own sincerity and, spoken aloud, my prayer starts to sound earnest. I need to seriously get over myself and just remember the meaning behind it.

The other thing holding me back is the worry that I'm a fraud. Prayer has been associated with religion for thousands of years without many of us realising they are not mutually exclusive. I'm not religious as I don't align with one particular methodology, but I am deeply spiritual and want to cultivate my relationship with that entity that is bigger than us. In turn, that desire to develop a more connected relationship with something bigger than myself allows me to solidify a better relationship with myself. The universe is out there but also within me and within you. I know this to be true and understand that prayer could help me really honour this notion in my everyday life.

Ask for Help

I'm not even sure who I am praying to. I don't use a name but I do talk in a strangely relaxed and overly familiar way during my prayers. The prayer might start, 'Hey', as if I were talking to my best mate, or even, 'It's me, Fearne, sorry it's been so long.' I like the free-flowing dialogue that might not traditionally be associated with prayer. After the initial platitudes I ask for help. I ask directly for the support or help needed, in this instance, for my two friends who both have big shit going on. I ask for them to be protected and guided and for them to feel supported and at peace. In this situation I also asked for what might seem impossible. A miracle perhaps? I don't feel limited at all when I'm praying. Once I'm over the initial awkwardness I don't feel judged. I know I can ask with wild abandon and that it will be welcomed if the desire is coming from a good place. Often in life we feel too nervous to ask for what we want. We don't want to seem demanding, expectant, or maybe we have a belief we don't deserve what we really want. Prayer seems to bypass all of this. We are willingly handing over outcomes to something bigger.

We are not burdening anyone or asking for too much, because we all know love is abundant and cannot run out. It's there for everyone – we just might have to ask for it.

When someone I had known for many years died suddenly, I prayed nightly. I let tears stream down my face as I asked, almost begged, for their journey to be peaceful. I asked for their soul to transition without pain or shock and to now be in a state of blissful peace. We can pray for ourselves and for others, even strangers. We can pray for whole countries that are going through awful things. There really are no rules. Well, maybe there is one: you have to believe that your intention and words are going to do something. Belief! That's it! You have to have belief!

Letting Go

Here's the bit about prayer that often gets misunderstood – we think that if the desired outcome doesn't instantly manifest, something has gone wrong. We then feel let down, foolish or maybe even angry. My limited understanding of prayer is that the outcome might not be what we actually asked for. The element of prayer that we find hard to accept is the 'letting go' bit. Prayer is the ultimate surrender as we hand our worries and doubts over to something bigger than us. This 'bigger' might not even live outside of us, or typically, as we would imagine, above us; it might be IN us too.

Letting go means we are accepting that whatever the outcome, it's the one we are supposed to receive. For instance, you might pray that you get the job you just interviewed for, yet the next day get a phone call saying you didn't get the job. The meaning behind your prayer reached beyond your own compre-hension and belief of what is possible. A few months later you get an even better job opportunity which wouldn't have been possible if you had been offered and taken the previous one. I've noticed this happen in my own life on so many occasions. I have expectations, pray, receive a different outcome, feel let down, then later down the line notice the beautiful opportunity that arrived later and in a different guise than I'd imagined. Life tends to only make sense retrospectively, when all the puzzle parts start to join together.

Surrender to That Something Bigger

I have often worried that surrendering means I'm being irresponsible. I fell out with a friend and attempted on several occasions to fix the cracks in our relationship but to no avail. I felt so down and hopeless, and also scared to get hurt again. So I backed away and shut up shop. I hid, but the feelings didn't. On a dreary Tuesday, out of the blue, I would find myself working through sorrow, anger, frustration, heartache as I just couldn't find peace with it. I wrote emails that were never sent, recorded voice notes that are still sat, eight minutes in length, on my phone. I spoke to numerous other friends about it, yet the feeling wouldn't subside. I knew my friend was in a raw state so meeting up wouldn't be OK for me. I knew my mental health at the time wouldn't cope with someone else's blame or anger, face to face. I tend to take responsibility even when it's not fully mine, and I process accusation on a very personal level. I imagined that a meet-up at this point would lead to me self-loathing for a long time afterwards and closing off further. I decided prayer and surrendering might be my only option.

As I asked for peace in this moment for the both of us, for love to be sent in the direction of this friend and for a meeting of minds down the line, I wondered if I was copping out. Was I using prayer as a get-out-of-jail-free card so I didn't have to deal with confrontation? I'm still not sure but I certainly do know that there is no negative outcome to prayer if the intention is good. Handing over the situation freed me up. I didn't feel as heavy carrying the shame, worry and sadness around with me. That alone makes it so worthwhile. When we are lugging a hiking-sized backpack around with us, full to the brim with worries and regret, it'll only make us more reactive to those we love, have less self-compassion and lower our general happiness. If prayer can help us lighten the load, is that so bad? It's not for me to say how you might or should feel about this; I'm just looking forward to learning more and working prayer into my daily life, rather than keeping it in my arsenal for those SOS moments.

It's Deep

Want to meet one of my mates? Course you do. The pandemic was not meant to be a period of time in which I was going to make loads of new friends but weirdly I did. I now have a handful of new mates who I haven't even met yet. One of them is the formidable Donna Lancaster. Over the last five years of my expedition into all things mental health, I kept hearing about this week-long retreat (although we must use the word 'retreat' here in its truest form – please don't imagine pedicures and water aerobics classes, this is not that) called The Bridge. Several friends had claimed it to be life-changing in every way. One friend went on it twice. Donna is the co-founder and director of The Bridge. She no longer runs the retreat as she is concentrating on a beautiful book using her wisdom and knowledge from her years of working with people in a very personal and deep way, but if you want to see exactly what happens at The

Bridge, there is a sublime documentary on Amazon Prime called *Love(d)*. I wept uncontrollably throughout as it's so raw and beautiful. It follows the journey of twelve people as they, led by Donna and her co-founder Gabby, relieve guilt, shame, grief and all other heaviness in an intense six-day course of therapy, ritual and expression. It's DEEP!

Like all good modern-day friendships, I began following Donna on Instagram and introduced myself on direct message, and that started up a flurry of voice notes to each other dissecting life. Since then, we've laughed and cried and enjoyed walks in the park where we share stories and thoughts. Donna's background as a social worker and retreat founder, together with her willingness to share her own stories around pain, is a powerful combination that allows her to work deeply with others to improve their lives. When we chat, we talk about prayer a lot as it's something Donna is extremely passionate about, so it makes perfect sense to let you in on one of our fast-talking conversations.

Friday midday. My stomach is rumbling as I've just done two back-to-back meetings. I need some calm and clarity to get my mind off sandwiches, so am looking forward to whatever happens next. I'm so ready to go deep and talk prayer with my friend Donna.

Me: Donna!!!!!

Donna: Hey, lovely!

Me: First up, why do you think we don't use prayer in everyday life these days?

Donna: I think one reason is because many people only associate prayer with religion. So, if you have any negative associations with religion – for example, if you were forced into it by family or rejected it when you were young – you might then want to stay away from anything you view as 'spiritual'. But I think prayer is for everyone. **You don't need to be religious or to believe in God to pray and that's why I'm on a mission to get people praying again.** Ten or twenty years ago people wouldn't have believed that meditation would be so normalised as it is today. Back then people thought it was just for hippies or religious types, but today pretty much everyone knows the benefits of meditation based on the scientific evidence, so my mission is to separate prayer from religion (unless religion is meaningful for you), and to normalise it.

Me: Yes, we need to get over feeling like a fraud for doing it if we have never set foot in a place of worship. Also, perhaps we need to have a better understanding of the benefits – what do you believe they are?

Donna: There are so many. Prayer is essentially defined as 'an intentional communication with an object of worship'. For some people that will be God, but for me my 'object of worship', if you want to call it that, is life itself. I'm intentionally communicating with life through my prayers. One of the main benefits for me has been to deeply reconnect with life, nature and myself. Through my prayers I have regained faith, true faith. I trust in life now, just like I trust in the seasons and the cycles of the moon as part of life. We forget that we are part of these natural cycles, so what prayer can offer is a deep faith in life again, that everything is as it should be. Prayer helps us remember this and to trust life. Now this doesn't mean our life circumstances are always going to be happy, but it does mean that we do not resist life. Through prayer we learn to surrender to it. This brings with it a real sense of inner peace.

Me: It's such an important point. For many of us there have been big moments where we may have felt we don't trust in life because we've felt let down or experienced pain. Maybe people who have lost something or someone might find it hard to trust in life again. How do we cultivate that trust with prayer?

Donna: It's about having an understanding that, in life, experiencing suffering and loss is just as important as joy and wonder. There will always be periods in our life where we will suffer. This is part of the human condition. Prayer brings you the faith to recognise this and trust in these phases completely. Loss is inevitable; we'll lose others, and even lose parts of ourselves over our lifetime, but this is the natural order of things. Our relationship with life through prayer helps us believe in this.

Me: So, trusting in life isn't trusting it's all going to turn out OK. Trusting in life is about trusting that you'll be OK no matter what happens?

Donna: Yes, it's trusting that underneath everything there is love. You look at a flower, a tree or the sky, it's all manifestations of love. **Prayer gives you the inner resources to lean into the natural cycles of life, with all of their beauty and pain. It allows you to see that love, which is also life, will be holding you no matter what happens and that you will be OK even in your not-OK-ness.**

Me: When we are praying, what do you believe or feel energetically is happening?

Donna: Well, first up it's worth pointing out that all of us are praying without knowing it all of the time. If you say, 'Oh, I really hope so-and-so is OK' or, 'I really hope that this turns out OK', that is a form of prayer. Some people pray with positive hopes and some might pray in a negative way, again unknowingly. You might say, 'Oh, life is just so shit, nothing is going well.' I believe that your thoughts and your words, as well as your actions, are all energy forms. If you pray with respect and humility to the divine, the spirit, life, whatever label suits you, you're sending out light which counterbalances the darkness in the world. That's what prayer does. We need prayer because we need to counterbalance the amount of toxicity and negativity that exists in the world today.

Me: If people haven't intentionally used prayer before, traditionally we might think we are praying to something or someone outside of ourselves, perhaps, in a rather clichéd way, above us. Is it true that the energy or power we believe lives in the exterior is also WITHIN us?

Donna: Absolutely. It's about recognising the interconnected nature of life. What we do to one, we do to all. What exists outside of us also exists within us. Everything is connected. You don't have to give labels to what you're praying to (unless you want to), as I believe it's all kind of the same thing, really. You might call it the divine, the universe, higher consciousness, higher power, but some people also pray to their ancestors' spirits. That's the thing with prayers, there is no wrong or right way to do it. I often pray to trees just because I love them! It feels good to worship trees!

Me: Is the only rule, therefore, that you have to believe it's going to work?

Donna: Prayers help us to believe in prayer! Part of the issue is that because we're such a society of control freaks, we are even trying to control the uncontrollable. We try in our prayers to make things happen because we want them to. Life doesn't work like that, I'm afraid. You could sit in the summer sun praying for snow all you want, and it'll never happen, because it's not the natural order of things. You may even pray for someone you love to be saved but that might not be their life path; better to pray that you can help be supported to ease their suffering. Our prayers must be in alignment with the natural order of things.

Me: Yes, people might not use prayer because they've not witnessed their desired outcome come to fruition, so they don't bother again, like the prayer didn't work. So we're not praying for accurate outcomes but are praying for support. I guess there's a huge element of letting go involved with prayer.

Donna: Yes, we have to trust that the outcome was meant to be, even if it's not what we had hoped or prayed for. Prayer also offers us comfort in the parts of life that we do not understand.

Me: Yes, life is chaos. We're constantly trying to make sense of the nonsensical, aren't we?

Donna: This is another hurdle we have to get over with prayer. Much of it might not make perfect sense to the mind, yet prayer bypasses the mind and goes straight to the soul. This is where you can then work with intuition. Prayer speaks to you via grace. What I mean by that is you might pray then encounter an unexpected event, people turning up in your life at the right time, or clear signs showing you your next step. This is what I call grace but many people don't even notice this or might call it coincidence. Grace is the language of the universe. We have to learn to understand this language and prayer helps us to hear, see, taste, feel and know grace.

Me: How does en masse prayer work?

Donna: There is such power in collective consciousness. It's where great change takes place. If we all focus on an outcome together it moves mountains. In the 1970s the Transcendental Meditation Collective collated data researching en masse prayer. Organised groups of thousands of people collectively meditated with the focus on peace and in the local areas the crime rates lowered. As soon as they stopped this regular en masse meditation the crime rates rose again. Imagine what would be possible if everyone was collectively praying! I adore Deepak Chopra's articulation of the difference between meditation and prayer. He says prayer is for asking the questions and meditation is about listening for the answers. I love that.

Me: So it's a good idea to pray and then meditate directly afterwards?

Donna: Yes. What I do is pray and then I go out for a walking meditation in the woods. So many of my creative ideas and intuitive wisdom arrive post-prayer. Grace speaking to me. Once again prayer bypasses my intellect and goes straight to my soul.

Me: So, really, after you've prayed you need to get quiet and have your ears ready for the answers.

Donna: That's it. We need to get still enough to notice ... Can I tell you about the three different types of prayer?

The first is gratitude where you consciously pray and give heartfelt thanks for the abundance of your life. You might have written a gratitude list before and that in itself is a form of prayer.

The second aspect is wonder, or you might also call it praise or celebration. This is where we take time to acknowledge the wonders of life and celebrate them. This is a very joyful part of prayer.

The third dimension of prayer is request. You can pray for yourself, for others, for people you don't know to be loved and supported. You can ask questions and trust the answers will come.

You can say your prayers out loud, in your head, chant them, or you can even move your body and dance. You can counterbalance the negative energy that we all sometimes feel, through your own prayer dance as you celebrate life and imagine spreading joy. You could put on some joyful music, dance in your living room and imagine a person that you have difficulties with dancing gleefully with you. Spread joy as you're dancing and then welcome in that person with your imagination and dance with them. This might sound odd to some but don't knock it until you've tried it, I say. What you are doing in the form of this prayer dance is intentionally sending love and joy to a person or group that you know might be hurting, broken, lacking love or in pain. It's important to generate your own joy and love first with the dance and music and then you can send your love to those who you are challenged with in life.

Me: Often our go-to is to pray for those we love, or at least like, who are sick, elderly or in need, yet you're saying it is also important to pray for those we find tricky, or are challenged by or don't agree with.

Donna: It's almost more important to pray for those people. Also, in the wider world there are so many people, say world leaders, who are living from the neck up. It's all cerebral without any emotional content, which is the dangerous disconnected stuff of wars. So metaphorically dancing with those people in your prayers and sending them love can help create huge change. Of course, we still need to take action against people who cause others pain, to combat the abuse of their authority or power, but we also need to flood their shadow with light alongside this.

Me: Some might feel they're wasting their love and prayers on awful people.

Donna: But you're actually strategically using your love and prayers to transform others with love while also fighting injustice. It's so powerful. As Martin Luther King himself said: 'Hate cannot drive out hate; only love can do that.'

Me: So action that is driven by just hate and anger will only breed more hate, yet action teamed with love can overthrow the darkness?

Donna: Yes, this is my belief. Often those people we're most angry with on a personal or global level are those who are most in need of our love, otherwise they wouldn't do the shitty things they do. To love them through our prayers is to help them heal.

Me: On a practical level, if you've not knowingly ever prayed, where do we start? Who are we talking to and how do we do it?

Donna: Start where you are at. If you love dancing, then dance your prayers. If you find peace in stillness, close your eyes and ask for guidance, then see what happens. If you feel sceptical, pray on that! Ask to be supported or guided in your prayers so that faith can come. Always start your prayer by saying thank you. A very simple prayer is to think of those suffering in the world and say over and over again for a few minutes, 'May they be safe, may they be well, may they find peace, may they feel loved.'

Just remember, if you haven't knowingly prayed before, prayer will simply help you to cultivate a deeper relationship with life. It will lead you to more love, more joy and more truth as you dare to lean into and trust in life. **A prayer is a wish with wings.**

Me: I love it. Donna, thank you so much.

· · ·

I'm in a slightly negative headspace today so my initial thoughts after talking to Donna turn quickly into worries. How many times have I, unknowingly, negatively prayed? Didn't I, just this morning, curse under my breath as the bin bag split, spilling cat litter all over the kitchen floor, and exclaim, 'TODAY IS SHIT.' I've made so many statements of this nature, my tongue flapping about desperately trying to release the inner tension I feel, without thinking about where those words might end up. I have written off whole days in a single, succinct sentence without even trying to see it from another angle. I've regularly communicated with life in the most negative and untrusting way.

Yet there is also relief in knowing that there are no real rules here and that I can incorporate prayer into parts of my life I hadn't expected. I don't have to get on my knees at the end of my bed like a character from an old movie, nightgown swirling in the breeze; I can do it however and whenever I please.

There are several friends I want to pray for today. One who recently lost her mum, one who has a lot to juggle in life, one who is newly single with an aching heart, one who is feeling scared about job uncertainty. Shall I metaphorically dance with them? My energy is low today so maybe I could work out my own way to send them love and call it prayer. I jump online and pick the brightest, biggest, most beautiful flowers I can find and order them all a bouquet. For my male friend on the list, I find a delicate unisex perfume that evokes a calming sense of being in a forest (apparently). I send each gift off with love and a prayer. A wish with wings that'll carry my love across London to their homes. One mate cried, one told me she didn't believe she deserved them, one said she felt truly loved at a bleak time. So far I'm really enjoying making prayer whatever I want it to be.

Say It Out Loud

Later I text several friends to ask how they view and use prayer. Justine says she often forgets to pray. She tells me she forgets that help is there on tap even though she knows she just has to ask for it. When she does pray, she speaks out loud as she believes she is heard by the universe. Eyes closed, she speaks her wishes to life and instantly feels relieved. Justine adds that she wonders why she only waits until she is on the floor, rock bottom, to pray, as she knows it instantly brings her relief.

Kye says he rarely prays. Only in crisis moments when someone he loves is sick or unsafe. Yet sometimes he finds himself saying aloud, 'Come on, universe, send me something', unsure as to what it is he wants. It seems I'm not the only one who reserves prayer for those SOS moments. Donna's mission to normalise prayer is obviously rather needed.

Grabbing Joy

Praying for myself feels a little self-indulgent. Remember, I'm an Enneagram 2, the Helper, so I know that this is a real stumbling block for me. Asking for help makes my neck turn to stone and my vertebrae crack. My comfort zone is reaching out to help others but then every few months I find myself grey-skinned and dull-eyed, looking in the mirror wondering why I've let myself wear down, paper thin. I'm looking into those dull eyes now. Usually amber bright, today they look jaded and a bit lost. Work has been overwhelming, the juggling act at home relentless, and I've gotten into the habit of just getting through the day rather than seizing moments of joy that are up for grabs. I know all the signs. I've been putting myself last again and the danger button is flashing. I've lost my mojo, my spark, my va-va-voom. I've gotten caught up in the velocity of modern life without taking time to see what the blue sky and trees have to offer me. Burdened by the worry that others will fall without me, or, worse still, blame me down the line for not helping out, I've let life climb on top of me rather than move with me. Yet praying for myself, knowing so many people are truly suffering, well … it feels almost silly and self-indulgent.

I root back to Donna's wise words and the sense of joy behind her thoughts. She talked about prayer like it was a fun game rather than something worthy and serious. This often happens too. I get so serious when I'm tired. I take everything personally and seriously and therefore suffocate fun with a tense, furrowed brow. What I'm learning so far is that leading a spiritual life, or choosing to walk down a spiritual path, requires huge amounts of letting go. As you can probably tell, I'm currently doing the opposite of that. I'm clutching at life's reins with white knuckles, my rings digging into my skin as I squeeze tight. I'm scared to let go as

I'm not sure how much will tumble. Thinking back to Donna, I remember that prayer bypasses the cognitive worries and woes and cuts to the chase. It IS letting go, so what do I have to lose? How much can really fall by loosening my grip on life a little?

Hello There

I wait until the quiet of the evening, both kids snuggled in bed like warm croissants under their duvets. Jesse is still watching TV downstairs so I'm alone and in peace. I rest my head on the pillow and close my eyes. I start, as I always have before, by saying hello. I try to sound less apologetic than I normally do, due to my inconsistency. I begin by stating my thanks, as encouraged by Donna.

'Thank you for my healthy body that moved me through my day. Thank you for my children who teach me big lessons every day. Thank you for the tough bits of life that keep me curious and wide-eyed. Thank you for the warmth of my home, for I know so many out there tonight do not have the luxury, I send them love.' (Gosh, I'm starting to talk like someone who prays all the time; 'for I know', who even am I?). I continue ...

Now for the praise part of the three-layered process. 'Life, I love you, even in all your mess. Today felt like tangled string with no end in sight but I can see the worth in it all. Life, I love you and how miraculous you are. It's so easy for me to forget what a miracle it is to even be alive. The chances are so slim, but here I am. The right combination of timing, people and chemistry and boom, 1981 saw me fly into the world. I am in awe of you, life, and how you are there even when I get caught up in everyday bullshit. Life, I love you.'

So far this is all feeling really nice and comforting and I'm feeling quite sleepy. My brain isn't going off on too many random tangents worrying about tomorrow. I'm focused on this declaration and am enjoying where the words are naturally taking me.

The third part is the ask. For me, this is the tough part. Here goes. 'Please guide me as I feel a little lost. I have been skimming over the surface of life in order to keep on track with work and family life but that's not how I want to live. Please help guide me in the right direction to lose some of the jobs from the pile so I can revel in more free time and idleness. Please give me the strength to ask for help even though it feels excruciating. Maybe help could just show up as a sign that it's the right path for me. Please help me eliminate the stress I often feel in my day and replace it with trust and faith that all will be well. Please help me start really, truly, enjoying life again.'

OK, that was easier than I had imagined. I didn't start berating myself for being self-indulgent and over the top. I let the words flow without too much thought and I feel pretty calm about it all. **It is comforting handing over worries and concerns to something bigger.** I feel lighter not having to carry all of that on my back. And now sleep.

Moving Past Blocks with Prayer

Two days later, my friend calls to say her best mate's sister is looking for work as a PA. Right, I see, it's worked. Even if this friend of a friend's sister isn't the right person for me, even if I can't quite get past my fear that I don't deserve help, surely it's a sign? I make the call and have a friendly chat, which in turn gives me confidence to seek agencies that might have professional help to alleviate how much I have on my plate. We don't have childcare or a PA currently, as I struggle to believe I deserve help, but as Happy Place grows and the projects build up, I regularly feel overwhelmed because I want to make each one as good as I can. I love my job so much and feel so grateful to be creative most days, yet I also know that working after the kids have gone to bed until my eyes sting is probably not always the best option. Again, I refer back to the cultural phenomenon of celebrating busyness, but I know so many magic moments will land in the space I'll create if I find a little help. Coming from a working-class family I'm still feeling uncertain about whether this is the option for me, as I'm used to seeing people around me work long hours and multiple jobs without help. Can I move past this personal block and fear of judgement with prayer? I'm not sure if I'm more scared of you judging me or me judging myself. I think more prayers are needed to help me loosen up and try something new. If I get help and feel stronger and have more time, I'll have more to play with when it comes to helping others or just spreading some happiness to those around me. The sign was there in the form of this out of the blue phone call, so I know I really should follow it. (At this point in time as I edit the book I didn't end up getting a PA. It still feels uncomfortably indulgent, so I clearly have a lot more letting go to do. There is always more to let go of.)

Fear Creating Fear

En masse prayer is something that interests me greatly. Having read so much on how impactful it can be, I wonder why there aren't TV channels telling us all to pray silently at a particular time for all those in need. Why aren't we using our mega-connected media sources to join together for good? Why don't we, say every Friday at 7pm, pray for those sick in hospital? Or pray every morning for less domestic abuse? Surely we're missing a trick here? Never has there been a time when it's so easy to organise en masse events digitally. Imagine the power and impact we could have if we all had the same specific goal in our prayer. It's giving me goose bumps thinking about it. Unfortunately, we are way too used to the absolute opposite: en masse fearmongering. We collectively watch the news, then as a group fear for our lives, subsequently creating, well, more fear.

No Time for Panic

A year ago, a young relative suddenly got very ill. It was a huge shock to all of us but, guided by his incredibly strong and deeply spiritual parents, we all collectively prayed when it was really needed. During a lifesaving operation we all prayed hard. Each family member in different parts of the country gathered every ounce of positivity and energy available and put it into prayer. His parents sat in silence, eyes shut, emitting hope and faith, and we supported that in the very same moment, with our own megawatt wishes. I've never prayed with so much intention, vehemence or power before. There was no other option. There was no time for panic. Prayer was intuitively our collective choice.

There were huge touch-and-go moments but the young relative pulled through and showed us all what strength and tenacity really meant. We cried and professed our love for each other relentlessly over the following weeks and all had a lot more faith in collective prayer. There is real power in it.

Do you have any blocks with praying? Who or what do you want to pray for? How could you incorporate it into your everyday life? How could you pray with others for the same desired goal? These are all questions I'm asking myself daily at the moment and I urge you to do the same. Remember, it's the language of grace, it's our way of communicating with life itself. Get on your knees, lie down, close your eyes, shout it out loud, dance, do what feels good to you, and send out those wishes with wings.

A Prayer by Donna Lancaster

1. Find a quiet, comfortable space to sit where you won't be disturbed. Gently hold your hands out in front of you, palms turned up towards the sky. Feel the energy touching your palms. Close your eyes and breathe slowly and consciously. Imagine breathing in and out through your heart, feeling it soften and expand with every breath. Give thanks for the gift of this precious moment.

2. Turn your attention to your left hand and, with your eyes still closed, imagine this hand is symbolically holding your life as it is today. Contemplate the reality of all you are facing at this time, including any of the struggles and challenges, while also acknowledging the gifts and abundance you are thankful for. See the images and examples of your reality in your mind's eye and try not to judge. Just notice as you look and continue to breathe into your heart. Feel the weight of your life held in this left hand.

3. Turn your attention now to your right hand, still with your eyes closed and breathing into your heart. Imagine in this hand you are symbolically holding life as you pray for there to be life, peace, good health, safety, love, compassion and kindness, perhaps the end to your and others' suffering ... whatever feels true to you today, that you wish to pray for. Once again, feel the weight of your prayers in your right hand.

So you have life as it is in the left hand and life as you
pray for it to be in your right. Give them both your
equal attention. Breathe.

4. Keeping your eyes closed and palms up, notice
   that, in between your two hands holding these two
   experiences of reality and prayers, there is a space.
   Imagine this is a space for your higher power/universe
   or intuitive wisdom to come through. Turn your
   attention to this space and give it your full presence.
   I invite you now to ask for a message from your
   higher power/wisdom to support you in this moment
   of your life. A message to allow you to surrender to
   the reality of your life circumstances alongside praying
   for change. You may receive a message in a word,
   song, image, colour or energy. Trust that whatever
   comes is exactly what you need. Notice …

5. Then slowly turn your palms to face each other and
   very slowly bring them together in prayer hands, as
   you do so absorbing this message into your two
   hands representing reality and your prayers. Hold your
   prayer hands in front of your heart. Bow your head
   with humility and gratitude. Take a deep breath and
   open your eyes.

SIGNS

I've been positively tingling at the thought of writing this section of the book. Is there anything more cosmic and thrilling than getting a sign? I think not. You might not even realise you've been sent signs. You may have missed them or overlooked them, eliminating them with a heavy dose of cynicism. Before I get into the examples I've experienced from my own little life, it would be foolish to dive into the micro without looking at the macro, which we have an even larger, unhealthier disregard for.

Over the last one hundred or so years we, the human race, have seemingly speeded up time. We race through the day, which bleeds into a week then a year, trying to get somewhere. Where are we trying to get to? The mythical land of peace? Away from our own thoughts? I think about this all the time but have so few answers. Why can't I stop? What am I missing by not stopping? Sometimes we are moving at the speed of light driven by our need for 'stuff' and 'things' to feel like we are someone or to paper over the cracks of who we don't want to be. We sprint to the finish line so we don't have to FEEL quite so deeply, dodging pain and discomfort where we can, like a giant game of dodge ball; sometimes squashing happiness with our haste too, just in case it decides to dissipate before we've truly leaned into it. We race, we run, we distract and we miss the signs: not only ones meant for us to make positive change on a personal level but also the big, metaphorical billboards that alert us to our collective wrongs or ignorance. I don't mean for this observation of the modern world, and how we react to it, to lead to any feelings of shame. We are all caught up in this one. The structures and frameworks we live in make it very hard to step off the Ferris wheel.

Big Positive Change

The recent Covid-19 pandemic, with its pain, loss and loneliness, still has ripple effects in motion today. Those who lost the irreplaceable in 2020 will be hard pushed to find the positives, but can we collectively see any fragment of its hugeness as a sign? Or maybe a few signs? In the first lockdown I could certainly see how the slower pace and lack of stimulation allowed me a new clarity I perhaps had ignored previously. I found new, simpler joys in watching the green parrots in our local park and finding slippery newts in the stream with my kids. Do I really need to book pricey tickets to a theme park I actually don't want to be at, to keep my kids happy in the holidays? Do I really need to go to every party I'm invited to, even when they cause sweaty palms and pre-arrival anxiety? I could see my own likes and dislikes with much more certainty and could see the signs present, guiding me down a more authentic and ultimately simpler path.

I know the same luxury of clarity won't have been the outcome for all, but can we collectively see how some elements of the pandemic were signs? Signs that we should give/offer more care and attention to our neighbours rather than strangers on Instagram thousands of miles away? Signs that we should look at how constant global travel and importation/exportation are devastatingly harming our planet? Signs that ceremony and gratitude (through our weekly praise for the NHS) make an almighty impact? I wonder how many of these signs we will keep in mind as we lurch forward with eager minds and wallets out, on the other side. It's, of course, a huge undertaking to completely change our cultural mindset and outlook on life but not impossible. We've already seen how flexible hours at work are now much more understood and accepted for those who benefit from working from home. I, for one, love being able to do my radio show and podcast without setting foot in anxiety-inducing, busy, noisy London. In this instance we have collectively taken a nod from the signs we were shown and have made positive changes to modify the way we work. For some being back in a work place – with people to bounce off and an atmosphere of motivation is better – yet there are now options for how some of us (office workers) want to work.

Can we, going forward, see losing certain species of animals as a sign that we've become too greedy and need to make changes, rather than shrugging with detachment because we weren't aware of 'that species of shrimp' in the first place? Can we see the devastating, wildlife-threatening bushfires in parts of the world as a sign that we need to rethink how we shop, eat and travel? Each time we see an image of an oil-slick bird glued to the ocean's surface, or hear about koalas going up in flames in vast forest fires, we are receiving a sign. I spoke with Jane Goodall on my podcast recently and she said we mustn't let the pandemic distract us from the much bigger threat to human life; the climate crisis and lack of biodiversity is our biggest problem yet. We must take note of the signs. In these big examples it seems the planet is directly communicating with us, although sadly a lot of the time it falls on deaf ears. I hope we collectively take heed of the planet's cry before it's too late. When it comes to our own individual lives, it's more like the universe, or something bigger than us, is communicating from an unknown place. Who, or what, is trying to tell us something and how do we start communicating back?

Herons Striding

Slight gear change but I'm going to waltz away momentarily from the burdening and overwhelming problems we see playing out globally, to my own little life, to offer some light relief and perhaps some examples that might jog your memory as to when you have received signs in life.

In 2011 I was newly single after a broken engagement. I was exhausted, perpetually hungover, ready for newness and still feeling quite lost. Early one spring morning, I stepped into the shower to get ready for work at BBC Radio 1. I was rushing as usual as I had pressed snooze on my alarm one too many times. Hurriedly washing my pits, something caught my attention out of the bathroom window. Something huge. In profile, stood a tall, elegant heron, looking authoritatively over the gardens below. At the time, I lived in central London, away from any open space or greenery. What was a bloody huge heron doing just one roof away from my own house? Seeing a heron a mere metre away in central London is a bit like having a close encounter with a pterodactyl. I was stunned and stood watching without moving. He eventually spread his ginormous wings out wide and flew off into the early morning pink sky. I ran out of the shower and grabbed my phone, googling the meaning of seeing a heron. The first search that popped up was the Native American meaning of a heron visitation. The explanation read that it was a sign of patience and good luck while other meanings I found online alluded to stillness and tranquillity. My shoulders dropped from my ears to where they belonged as I took so much comfort from my little visit. If patience was what was needed, I would take the heron's nod as guidance. If tranquillity was in order, rather than the chaos I was feeling, then I would seek it. If good luck was on the way, I was willing to accept it. Thank you, Mr Heron. It might just have helped me get into the mental space where I was willing to heal, as a couple of months later I met my husband!

The Name Game

Do you mind if I tell one more story? I did warn you I was excited about this subject. Without giving you much time to mull over whether you want to hear it or not, I'm diving in. When I was pregnant with my now eight-year-old son Rex, with my afore-mentioned husband Jesse, we chose not to find out the gender of the baby. I had a boy's name already in place and a couple of girls' names. My husband and I had travelled to France, as I had a job commitment over there, and were discussing baby names again over breakfast in the hotel. Luckily, we both fell in love with the name Rex for a boy from the start but were still unde-cided on the girl options. As we left the restaurant and climbed the stairs to our room, I noticed a large sepia photo on the wall by our room. It was a grand, handsome ship, steadily moving through calm seas, with the big painted letters 'REX' on the hull. From that point onwards I knew we were having a boy. Four or so months later, a leggy, blue-eyed, dreamboat boy came into the world, under a glaring hospital spotlight, after a very long labour. One look into those deep pools of blue on his little crumpled face and I knew he was a Rex. If I look closer there is even more meaning in our nautical sign. My, now even leggier, boy is obsessed with the sea and indeed boats. He makes drink cartons into canoes, sands down small offcuts of wood into toy ferries and has a long-standing fascination with the *Titanic* and its fateful maiden voyage. He is part sea, happier in its sway than anywhere else imaginable.

Just One More

I lied, there is another story I must tell, but it's completely related to the last. Similarly, when I was pregnant with Honey, my now six-year-old flame-haired daughter, I once again chose not to find out the baby's gender. This time we had the girl's name Honey and boy's name River decided before the birth. On arrival at the hospital, already five centimetres dilated, I went to use the loo before I had my first examination. When washing my hands, I saw four bottles of hand soap lined up, all with 'HONEY' written on their labels.

Just a coincidence? Too weird to have been predicted in any fashion by an unassuming photograph on a hotel wall or toiletry bottles aptly scented with bee nectar? I guess it's up to personal interpretation but, for me, finding meaning in these small moments brings me joy and makes me feel connected.

Having Hope

As far as I can tell, signs can turn up in any shape or form. It could be a song that randomly starts playing on your phone which brings you a relevant message, numerical patterns that keep showing up, the right person calling with a message at the right time; it could be found in books, in pictures, in the words overheard. Signs are everywhere if our eyes are open to them, but how do we keep our peepers alert and ready for guidance? I'm not sure if in these moments of receiving I've been particularly vigilant or even aware I'm looking for signs, so I need to dig deeper, for my sake and yours, to find out how we can cultivate a mindset where signs are ubiquitous and helpful. Are they always there yet we just don't see them? Do they pop up randomly at the right time? Do we see them but miss their meaning? I'm determined to find out more, mainly because I find signs so thrilling. As well as seeing signs we need to have faith in them. There is little point in us receiving signs if we have little faith in their validity and power. Surely the faith part of this equation is the pertinent factor that steers us down unknown paths and boosts us with confidence and hope?

Well, luckily for you and me, I know the queen of signs personally, Ms Gabrielle Bernstein. I LOVE Gabby so much. I've gone from fangirl to friend in the last couple of years and have learned so much from Gabby's friendship and wisdom. I first met Gabby when she came on my Happy Place podcast, which was a total dream come true. Prior to this I had read all of her books and used her tapping techniques in times of stress. It was one of those click moments where we just kind of knew we would be mates. We've chatted on the phone across the Atlantic ever since and she has helped guide me, even in the writing of this book.

Gabby needs little introduction but if you haven't read her brilliant books, such as *The Universe Has Your Back* or *Super Attractor*, here's my personal description: she looks like an actual angel yet has a gravelly, commanding voice you take note of. A sort of celestial rock star: Blondie with wings. She's built a community of followers who hang off her every husky word and has guided people from all over the world through chaos and crisis with her wisdom, lived experience and faith. Want to meet her? How could you not!

Me: GABBY!!!

Gabby: I love your sweatshirt.

Me: Hey, thanks, it's from my friend 'Larry Pink the Human' who is a music artist. Look, I'm so excited to talk to you today, Gabs. (I call her Gabs these days ... I know!). Let's start with the absolute basics here: what is a sign? How do you determine a sign?

Gabby: I should start with the concept that we are all able to, at any given time, connect to a spiritual realm. That spiritual realm is the energy and frequency that we have within us but, in our human experience, often block. The more we meditate, relax our nervous system, the more at ease we feel, the more in sync we become with the support systems that are available to us beyond our comprehension. I would refer to those support systems as angels, guides, deceased family members, entities in the spiritual realm. I would also refer to them as 'the universe' or 'spirit', as it's also an energetic force. If you're in the flow, you're in sync with that universal energy. When you're in that flow you notice things become easier, that you are able to think about things and then they come into your life; you have an idea and manifest it into form. You'll start getting messages from all around you. Spirit guides and this universal energy will be primarily guiding us in the pursuit of our spiritual growth and personal development. So, while you can ask the universe for signs, which is all fine and good, the main purpose is to connect with the spiritual realm in the pursuit of developing our faith. First let's nail down the fact that when we are being guided, we are being guided towards what is of the highest good, for our wellbeing and universal wellbeing. It'll be the right direction even if in the moment it feels like it's the wrong one.

Me: Now, this isn't a case of some people getting signs and some people just not getting them, right?

Gabby: Anyone can have a sign.

Me: So, what, we just don't see them?

Gabby: We are always being guided but we are not always receptive to that guidance. In addition to that, it's important to remember that guidance is a conversation. So, for example, if you and I are not WhatsApping frequently we are going to lose contact, right?

Me: I would hate that (a little too desperate?).

Gabby: It doesn't mean that we can't reconnect but we have to remember it's a relationship. So, the more you bring to it, the more you'll get out of it. So you want to be in constant contact with the higher power. That might look like a prayer or asking the universe for a sign. Using signs is a way of communicating, so view the communication back at you as a sign. Sometimes you can just ask for a sign to know if you are being guided, it doesn't have to be something specific.

Me: So, to be really clear, what might that look like? A song? Numbers? A feeling? A person?

Gabby: You could say very specifically, 'Universe, show me a butterfly.' You've set the intention and the sign. But also, if you are in constant communication with the universe, then you will receive signs that you haven't even asked for. That divine intervention steps in. This happened to me recently with my new podcast. The idea wasn't on my radar but so many people kept individually mentioning that I should do one. Sometimes the universe does for you what you can't do for yourself. Those are signs too. When you feel connection to the guidance you are indeed being guided.

Me: What if you ask for a sign and it doesn't show up?

Gabby: That is a sign too. If you're saying you need a sign to reveal you're on the right path for a particular relationship you're in and you don't get a sign, that IS a sign. It's communication. If I call you on the phone and say, 'Call me back if I'm in the right relationship but don't call me back if I'm not', and you don't call, that is the sign.

Me: What happens if you're getting signs and you recognise them as signs but you're choosing to ignore them?

Gabby: If you don't SHOW UP for WHAT'S UP, it'll keep showing up. If you're not listening, then you're going to continue to be presented with the same obstacles in life.

Me: Last week I had so many signs and it felt so magical. I've been laughing a lot at how obvious they are. They were all quite self-explanatory and instant. Yet I know that sometimes signs for me have taken years to really appear and have meaning. Is there a timeframe when it comes to signs?

Gabby: Well, I think that regardless of whether you receive the actual visual or cue, the guidance is connected to you as a sensation. You may not get that quick hit of direction but you may get a sense you're on the right track. You have to trust all forms of guidance. The main message is **the more in tune you are, the more joyful you are, the more positive you are, the more receptive you are, the easier it is to receive messages.** If I'm being an arsehole and keep calling you and asking you, 'Tell me I'm in a good place, tell me I'm in a good place, tell me I'm in a good place', you'll eventually get pissed off and just ignore me, right?

Me: Never, but I get the metaphor.

Gabby: I have to come to you humbly and say, 'I'm willing to hear your guidance.' The humility and surrender are required to really get you in the flow of guidance.

Me: How do you stop this turning into superstition? My understanding is a sign is full of hope and positivity and superstitions are usually based on fear.

Gabby: We've all built up these belief systems which are like a thick wall that separates us from the spiritual realm. If we want to have that connection, to be open to it, we have to be committed to dismantling that wall. Each time you pray, set a positive intention, listen to a positive podcast, read a positive book, you're dismantling the wall, so you can connect with faith. It's a choice. You want it, so keep dismantling the wall, or you think you don't want it and keep the wall in place.

Me: There is a process we can all follow here. We can actively dismantle our blocks to the spiritual world and then start to listen for guidance. The way we can dismantle those blocks is choosing what information we imbibe and how we want to communicate with the world around us. Is that correct?

Gabby: Correct.

Me: Rhonda Byrne said something similar when she came on the Happy Place podcast. She said, when she wanted to stay in a really good place when she was making the first *The Secret* film, she wouldn't even answer the phone when it rang in case it was bad news or someone wanting to offload negatively on to her. She committed to staying feeling great so recognised her own agency over how she might do that.

Gabby: When you start to get in sync with life you are in co-creation with the universal presence. It never left you, it's always been there, you might have just chosen to ignore it. To block it.

Me: Can you ask for signs if you're in a bad place?

Gabby: **It's not about being in a good space, it's about being in a surrendered space.** How much control can you release to let that wisdom and guidance come through? In the absence of resistance, you can receive guidance. For me, I might go for a walk, do yoga, meditate, pray, to surrender and open myself up to those signs that are planted for me. Whatever it takes to get you into a receptive space.

Me: So it's all about communicating with life and the universe. So, for someone out there reading this who has never asked for a sign before, where to start?

Gabby: Write it down, think it in your head, there are no rules. I think you should always start with gratitude, so thank the universe for sending you a sign, even before its conception. Or you can stay committed daily to being open and receptive and watch the signs come at you, BOOM! That's when you're living a guided life. That's the next level.

Me: Errrr, a little white feather has just flown by my window and landed right in front of me. Some weird shit has been happening during the writing of this book. (A white feather has been known to be a sign of a guide or angel nearby. Writing this book is constantly surprising!)

Gabby: Yup, that's a sign. You writing this book means you're in the flow of life and surrendering, so you can get the guidance. More weird shit will just keep happening. You're in tune.

Me: It's the most fun book I've ever written. I'm going to keep surrendering. Gabby, I love you. Thank you so much.

Lion Heart

Prior to my chat with Gabby I had noticed signs in my life and even taken heed of them, but I'm not sure I had ever actively asked for a sign. I wasn't really sure how.

Time to give it a go. First up, I needed to work out what my sign should be. As you now know, I'm a Virgo so need a plan and specifics. I tried not to overthink it. Without too much rumination, a lion pops into my mind. Recently my friend Heidi and I had been talking about what we like to call 'lion energy'. A revered and powerful energy that won't scare anyone off but will be respected and understood. An energy we both feel we need in our respective industries. Heidi is a film director and screen-writer, which in her line of work puts her in the minority as a female. She needs that lion energy to move projects forward and fight for her work to be made. I often have big, scary meet-ings and have to make big decisions that will affect a number of people, so lion energy is needed to hold my confidence in place. So I decide to ask for a lion.

There's a dynamic in my life I have been struggling with. An unresolved issue with someone that leaves me feeling uncom-fortable and stressed out. I regularly worry and wonder if I should reach out or leave the situation as it is. I guess asking for a sign might give me the answer from something much bigger than me and my little worries. When I'm stressed, I walk or run, so it's time for a bit of 'hello running shoes, goodbye stress'. For the first ten minutes I fight off the urge to go home and have a bath, then once in a rhythm I think about what question I really want the answer to. I gathered together the right letters and words like a game of mind Scrabble, and I said out loud, 'If I am to leave this situation alone, send me a lion.'

NOW LISTEN UP TO WHAT HAPPENED! This is mad and I'm still in shock. As the word 'lion' slipped out of my panting mouth a car pulled up alongside me, a mere metre away, with the England badge on the bumper displaying not one, but three lions. I laughed out loud and ran home with the biggest grin. I'm still flabbergasted that the answer came in a heartbeat and decided to honour its message as I remembered Gabby's words that we are being guided for the greater good of our wellbeing and others', as well as the universe's.

One week later I visit the wonderful Wendy Mandy, who you've already met in Part 1 (see pages 19–40). I was eager to tell her the tale of my three lions appearing. As I finished the story, she remained silent and in slow motion pointed to her snug sweater. The word 'LION' was stamped across her chest with an almost obnoxious nod for me to keep listening. In my flustered excitement of retelling the turn of events, I hadn't even noticed. There seem to be lions everywhere.

A Ball of Rage

Gabby made it clear that we have to be aligned to receive these messages, which at first brought on a slick of sweat to my forehead. I worried this would mean I had to feel buoyant and sprightly to receive the guidance I so desperately needed. Yet Gabby mentioned it's not about being in a good space but a surrendered space. What does this mean? I had the perfect opportunity to test this one out as yesterday I woke up with a body itching with rage. If you've read any of my books prior to this one, or listened to my Happy Place podcast, you may know that I can jump to anger quickly. It's there, sat under the surface like a stonefish, camouflaged enough that others can't see it, but deadly if trodden on. Sometimes my anger is so huge that I don't know what to do with it. It's too big to be contained in a human body. I try to talk it out with my husband but end up even more infuriated that he is so calm. (Just to clarify for any journalists reading this, the anger was not caused by my husband. No made-up stories about my marriage are wanted here thank-ing-you.)

In this instance the anger is due to a portion of injustice around me that is affecting some people I love hugely. I can feel the red-hot anger bubbling and pinch the back of my own ear so tightly that it draws blood. It was an accident but bloody hurts and has little power in snapping me out of this rage-induced trance. I instinctively put my trainers on. Sometimes physical exercise is the only way I can squeeze this hot-blooded energy out of me. I need to run the boiling lava out of the soles of my feet – sweat the splintering pain out of every pore. I press play on the Beastie Boys and pound the ground with my size sixes until the anger subsides. I reach the top of a hill near my house where there's a little art gallery with ever-revolving local artists. A huge new poster sat proudly in the window with an image of a fireball which seemed to call to me. It encapsulated in picture form the feeling of my head exploding. In the middle of the scarlet flames were three words which related directly to the situation I was trying to unpick. My lungs heave with relief and I stop pushing my body to release the anger. Instead, it slips away quite easily, taking note of this sign which is quite literally A SIGN. So maybe I don't need to feel tiptop to receive. Alignment seems to be less about ensuring I always feel great, benevolent and courteous and is instead just a willingness to surrender to something bigger than me – a commitment to move with life rather than against it. With even more faith instilled, I jogged home with a lighter step listening to Fleet Foxes to bring the pace and heartbeat down.

The Final Goodbye

Speaking to Gabby has also made me realise that signs don't have to exclusively guide us, they can also just offer comfort. In my early twenties I woke up one morning in the little cottage I lived in at the time. Every stair creaked with age and history as I made my way down to forage coffee from the kitchen. To get to my beloved kitchen-dwelling coffee machine, I had to walk through my living room but on this particular day something stopped me in my tracks. One of my portraits I had painted, which usually sat to the right of the TV on the wall, was instead in the middle of the room on the floor. How the hell did this painting jump two-odd metres off the wall by itself? I lived alone, bar my two moggies, and all the windows were shut without even a hint of a breeze to aid this mysterious manoeuvre.

I slowly hung the picture back up and headed to the kitchen to drink caffeine and get my brain in Sherlock Holmes mode to figure out how this could have happened. I turned my mobile back on while the kettle boiled and my mum rang within seconds. My beloved grandad Phil Savage had passed away over-night. He had been poorly in hospital for some time and, ever since my nan had died a few years prior, had never been quite the same. My brain started to slot everything into place and, amid the tears, I smiled, knowing that my grandad must have moved the picture in the night to show me a sign he was saying goodbye. He was the most incredible artist himself, painting large sailing ships crashing through mountainous waves. He loved that I painted too and was always complimentary about my portraits. I'm not asking you to believe this story, but for me it was pure comfort: a goodbye without words, a last practical joke from the cheeky trickster Phil.

Have you ever experienced the inexplicable in a moment where it really mattered? Count that as a sign!

'90s Freckles

We also can't skim over the fact that we might have missed vital signs due to the dreaded smartphone. How tragic that we might have missed important, potentially life-changing signs because we were too engrossed in our screens. I dread to think how many signs I've missed because I've been too busy laugh-ing at Celeste Barber videos on Instagram or searching 'country, chic, maximalist interiors' on Pinterest. Surely part of our earthly lesson in this section of the book is to start looking up rather than down?

Before mobile phones, same-day deliveries and wifi, I would often go camping with my family in the summer. One year, in France, with freckles splattered across my nose, cycling shorts on, and film camera hanging around my neck on a luminous cord, I would lie in the grass and watch the stars for hours. If I got a shooting star I was buzzing. It felt like it was for me only. A sign, a welcome to make wishes, a nod that I was supported and held by the night sky. I would grab it with both hands, scrunching my eyes in a desperate attempt to pin every dream on to this one star (usually an unrequited boy crush).

I looked up rather than down so often back then. The '90s provided the perfect decade to dream, wish, watch for signs and keep connected. This is the strange thing about technology – we think it's making us more connected yet sometimes it's doing quite the opposite. It's of course a delight to be able to call your mate on the other side of the planet, or FaceTime your nan you haven't seen in six months. I've also loved making new friends purely through communities based on Instagram. Without social media I wouldn't have brilliant people like Bryony Gordon, Elizabeth Day and Annie Price in my life; I also wouldn't get to follow people like Vex King and Brené Brown to get my positivity hit online each day, but how much have we lost along the way? Have we lost a sense of balance and collectively? Have we stopped placing value in the wonders of nature and the universe we live in?

We've created whole new, non-existent universes that live on a screen – a digital universe that seems never-ending. It's there, yet not at all. Ephemeral, with an everlasting sting that keeps us addicted and disconnected.

Rainbow Bridge

As this section of the book draws to a close, one particular story sticks in my head that my mum told me. When I left home aged nineteen, I was shortly thereafter replaced by a dog. A wondrous golden retriever named Wilf. He became my parents' new fluff-baby with his downturned eyes and shiny black nose. My dad took up an unrivalled, peaceful friendship with this dog that used to make me jealous. I longed for a companion so loyal and loving. My mum made copious amounts of new friends while out stomping the green fields of Ruislip. As many of us know, the painful part of having a pet is the knowledge that they will one day leave us. It's heart-wrenching to even think about. The day Wilf was put to sleep was up there with one of the most painful days of my parents' adult life. He was their best bud, their trusty evening hug on the rug and in ways their joint soulmate. As both my folks trudged through this heavy grief, my mum also became witness to some magical moments... some big beautiful signs. One morning when feeling lacklustre and full of sorrow, my mum heard a voice ring in her ears, 'Rainbow Bridge'.

She had no clue what this meant or what to do with this information but went to her desktop and typed in the words to try to gain some clarity. The first search result that popped up was a poem about animals, including a line that referenced the Rainbow Bridge – the crossover for all our beloved furry friends as they leave us and go elsewhere. In this moment my mum felt a peace wash over her knowing that Wilf had made it to wherever he was headed, and was happy and safe. A vital part of moving through grief brought on by an inexplicable voice carrying a beautiful message. Again, perhaps Mum would have missed this voice altogether if she had been too consumed with her phone or computer, too distracted by music or TV. Giving yourself space to pick up these messages is essential when we are looking for hope in those moments where we feel totally out of control.

Whether you're reading this in book form, feeling the pages touch your skin, listening with headphones as you go about your business, or otherwise, I hope that after this chapter you'll spend a little time looking up, not down. After exploring this chapter with glee and enthusiasm, I am even more committed to the idea of having an ongoing dialogue with the universe around me and within me. I want to be all ears, yet not desperate in wanting answers… patiently listening with hope, and vigilant with a sense of curiosity. Universe, once again, I humbly surrender to your voice and guidance and am willing to put down my phone long enough to take heed of all you tell me.

RITUAL AND CEREMONY

In the modern world we seem to have completely swapped ritual and ceremony for same-day-delivery purchases and toast gulped down as we sprint out the door. We place importance on the end result; the 'getting', rather than the doing itself.

Already today, I have fed my kids breakfast, painstakingly got them dressed for school (why is this always so difficult?), done an online workout, filmed an interview on Zoom, slurped down a coffee at lightning speed, fired off twenty or so emails, and it's only 1pm. As usual, I've raced through my day as though time is running out. The clock ticking makes my nervous system go into hyper-drive: a human whirlwind, perpetually chasing her tired tail. I might be ticking things off lists, and keeping on track at work, but what am I missing? I'm so quick, organised and methodical, but at what cost?

I'm sure there must have been moments of ritual in my day, but so rushed was it that they've merged into habit rather than something sacred. My morning coffee, for example. It cannot be missed. Without a cuppa I would collapse, void of personality, into a pile of pyjamas on immediate arrival to the kitchen. It signals the start to my day, a willingness to let sleep go and welcome the unknown of a new sunrise. Yet did I recognise the meaning behind it as I spooned the pungent granules into my favourite mug? I'm more likely to have been running through the list of actions that needed to take place next. Make kids breakfast, find school bags, text back friend I forgot to reply to yesterday… the ceremony of starting my day lost in a sea of future noise.

Closing Bones

I look to other cultures and parts of the world, in awe at the time taken to mark the ripples of life. A dear Chinese friend of mine held a rice-based ceremony in my kitchen after my daughter was born. I watched with peaceful curiosity, as this friend slowed down to an unknown pace to perform such a ritual. Without truly understanding the meaning behind the actions, I felt the sacredness of it entirely: the love, good intention and care taken to converse with the universe in a language I was yet to understand.

I also once took part in a closing-of-the-bones ceremony after the birth of Honey to help bring back my fragmented self. A friend of a friend wrapped my wobbly body in swaths of fabric, binding each lump of flesh to bone, in an effort to stitch me back together. After labour my body felt like it didn't really belong to me any more. Nipples like sandpaper and hips that seemed to point in entirely different directions felt unfamiliar and out of control. The fabric, wound several times round each limb and body part caused a squeezing sensation that was as comforting as it was terrifying. A human mummy, surrendering to the lack of control I had in this moment. More fabric, now wrapped around my face, left only a small area untouched for breathing through my nose and mouth. My eyes closed beneath the reams of cloth total blackout consuming me. I was left, in silence, and asked to call back the parts of me that might have left during pregnancy or labour. I called upon my wants and desires that I had parked to navigate nine months of total sickness. I called upon my everyday movement and pelvic floor. Come back to me, pelvic floor (which, by the way, still is yet to return). As I was released from the tightly bound cloth, I felt like I was experiencing the noise and colour of everyday life for the first time.

These moments stand out because they seem to be rarities in the modern world. Why aren't all new mothers given the time and opportunity to think about what has been gained but also lost during pregnancy and childbirth? Why isn't every new human celebrated with a gentle ceremony to acknowledge their sacredness? I suppose we do have rituals and ceremony in the modern world that celebrate this – baby showers and birth or naming ceremonies – but sometimes they are acted out with familiarity rather than seeking the true meaning of the moment.

The Flickering Flame

There is ritual in the small, ignored moments, such as taking your shoes off when you enter someone's home (excluding my mum, who refuses to take her heels off, anywhere, EVER). It's not just so you don't walk mud on to their cream carpet, it's also a sign of respect that you are leaving the outside world where it belongs as you enter their home. **You might not recognise ritual in the ordinary and everyday but it is woven into our lives if you open your eyes to it.**

Think about the last time you went to a birthday party or gathering. There are the fundamentals that you have to tick off the list to ensure the birthday has been honoured each year. A cake, which might be a Victoria sponge, oozing with cream and jam, is in fact an offering, a gift shared out among those you love, full of joy and gratitude. Then there is the blowing out of the candles with each candle holding a year of your life on Earth. The flame flickering represents the light you carry. We don't think about any of this as we watch our kids huff and spray spittle over the bouncy birthday sponge, but the meaning is in there, embedded beneath the familiar.

I'm pretty old school in a lot of ways and highly cherish manners above all else. If someone gives me a gift or has me stay at their house, I will always send a thank-you note. Not only is there something thrilling about receiving a letter in the post that isn't a bill, it's also got 'ritual' written all over it. That piece of paper, tattooed with biro ink, is full to the brim with gratitude. I'm not only offering up thanks to the person I benefited from in the first place, I'm also putting those words of thanks out into the universe. I'm letting the universe know I am indeed grateful.

Even in non-religious wedding ceremonies there is the throwing of bouquets over shoulders to be caught by gaggles of intoxicated women. The cutting of the cake is not the most exciting of things to watch but is met with rowdy cheers and rapturous applause. There is throwing confetti sky high, to trickle back down like spring-time blossom. These are all very obvious rituals but often still actioned on autopilot rather than being laced with a deeper meaning.

I have been to so many weddings. In the year 2012 I went to nine within the space of eleven months and for six of them I was pregnant, which meant aching feet and a lack of gin-fuelled dancing. I have watched confetti being thrown with glee but have never given a second thought to look at the meaning behind it. Confetti has been thrown since the Middle Ages, with its conception in Italy, where participants in local festivals would throw sweets, eggs (I can see why this one didn't stick around on the wedding scene), coins (ouch) and fruit. In 1875 an Italian businessman started selling paper confetti, which was cheaper than sugar-coated nuts and candies. In Britain, before paper confetti reached our shores, rice would have been thrown at newlyweds, which I'm imagining was slightly painful and irritating. Whatever was being chucked, it was a well-wish of good luck and happiness for the bride and groom – wedding guests quite literally throwing their love and luck to the delicious couple. Next time I'm at a wedding, clutching a handful of coloured paper, I'm going to make sure that, when I throw it, I put some serious love and luck behind it, rather than worrying about how much of it has landed in my hair.

Talking to the World Around Us

At this point in history we find ourselves with depleted oceans, threatened species of wildlife and barren land that would have once been hectares of lush forest. Perhaps our biggest, most detrimental bout of ignorance is our complete disregard for gratitude when it comes to what our planet can offer us. We take, take, take without ever making any effort to communicate with the land and life around us. We cut down trees without a thought, fish the oceans dry on a daily basis, and build on sacred land without asking its permission first. In our own homes we use paper to write on or read from without honouring the tree which allowed us this gift. We eat fruit grown from far-flung trees without thanking the planet for bearing such beauty in the first place. We go on holiday to new pastures and set up camp like we can wander freely without first communicating with the unfamiliar ground beneath our feet. The human condition in the West seems to be one of ignorance and superiority when it comes to the planet we live on. We've gotten so comfortable with it. I'm guilty of all of the afore-mentioned. I don't say thank you for the food I'm eating. I'm usually too busy trying to keep my kids' bottoms on their seats during mealtimes. I didn't ask the land around me for permission before I moved into our family home. I didn't whisper to the undulating sea whether it was OK for me to enjoy its waves when in Dorset.

We have forgotten how to communicate with the planet we live on. I say forgotten because, of course, for many thousands of years humans had the utmost respect for the land they walked on. The elements were something to celebrate but also fear: each strike of lightning, or overwhelming flood, seen as a form of communication from Mother Earth or spirit. Many cultures still today share this sacred language with the land around them. In Bali you will see small offerings called *Banten*, which are parcels of cut leaves and rice paper containing gifts for ancestors and the spirits of the land around them. In Japan thousands of people gather to stare in awe at the cherry blossom trees. Respecting the annual beauty of this bloom is sacred and allows the residents and tourists who visit the Cherry Blossom Festival the chance to honour new life, and nature's fleeting beauty. The elements are not only honoured but viewed as a divine force in ritual in Cambodia, where water blessings take place regularly. We can see ceremony and ritual woven through so many cultures today that celebrate the Earth and its inhabitants: the Masai tribes welcoming guests to their land with their jumping dance, the *Adamu*; the rubbing of noses by the Maori people, who for generations have used this sacred *hongi* as a symbolic gesture of greeting. Australia's indigenous communities have a long-standing custom to welcome non-natives who need safe passage through Aboriginal or Torres Strait lands.

Many of these communities have had their ancestry and traditions threatened by the greed of the Westerners or the fast-paced, ever-changing and moving, digitally progressive world. We might have quick broadband and contactless pay to speed up shopping experiences but the price we've paid spiritually has been huge. So many communities the world over are still fighting for land that their ancestors settled on thousands of years ago and, with that struggle, hold tightly to their customs and traditions. Their resistance to conform to the skyscraper, tarmac-covered, tense and disconnected modern world is met usually with a huge lack of understanding from those wanting to either develop on sacred land or ignore tradition altogether. I watched the most beautiful yet heartbreaking documentary on Disney Plus recently called *Into the Canyon*. Documentary makers Kevin Fedarko and Pete McBride trek the length of the Grand Canyon, meeting and conversing with indigenous people of the canyon to help highlight the threat their land is under. I was shocked and at times fuming watching the developers push harder and harder to get permission to build a tourist spot on the lip of this sacred canyon. The plans for a shopping mall, restaurant and skywalk chiselled into the rust-coloured rock obviously caused the indigenous community huge heartache, stress and fear for their future. It was a clear example of how the modern world, along with its need for more, more, more, has total disregard and zero respect for what has existed and thrived for thousands of years. This is an extreme and devastating illustration of our ignorance when it comes to the land beneath our feet, but surely there is still opportunity for us to honour the earth we walk on in our everyday lives?

Polishing the Ordinary

Ritual and ceremony are a direct way to communicate with the planet we live on and the universe beyond, using offerings, speech and fully encompassing gratitude.

If you are religious and enter a place of worship regularly, it's likely that the whole experience is bound by ritual. Each step through the process of worshipping has meaning and perhaps an action to marry the intent. Because I don't (regularly enter a place of worship), I can clearly see the huge gap in my life that could be filled with so much more meaning. I don't want to just skip through life without looking at who and what I'm taking from, without giving thanks. I don't want to march through big life moments without marking them with gratitude in some way. I don't want to only see the mundane as actions to get through, in an attempt to complete a list. **I think ritual and ceremony might be the polish to shine the ordinary in my life.**

Alex Bedoya, the founder of Be One Again, is a sacred personal development guide. Coaching people to connect and feel oneness through the sacred and ritual is not only her great passion but also her life's work. Originally from Ecuador, with a stint working in the corporate world in the States, she now dwells in a bucolic English countryside setting and has travelled the world, working with and learning from indigenous peoples. The catalyst for Alex's spiritual path was a spell in A&E due to stress while living in New York. Alex acts as a conduit for the messages from the people she has worked with in indigenous communities, with their permission or sometimes at their request. She has lived in certain communities for long periods, to get an understanding of how we can all connect with the sacred, a sacredness that these communities want to share with the masses in an effort to see a more peaceful, less greedy, slower-paced world.

Me: Alex, what exactly is a ritual?

Alex: To me, spirituality is my day-to-day life. It's the gratitude for all the blessings I have. Walking can be a ritual. Anything. After spending time with indigenous tribes and wisdom keepers around the world, I realised that spirituality was quite simple. **It's a daily prayer woven into the fabric of your day-to-day life.** It can be anything you can imagine and is not separate from you. I consider a ritual an honouring of my relationship with the living world around me; it's my connection to spirit, a conversation with nature, an offering, an acknowledgement of the sacred. Even when I'm making breakfast it can become a ritual, honouring the preciousness of the food, my body, slowing down time, entering into gratitude for all that I'm receiving. In a ritual you are recognising the meaning behind everything which otherwise goes unnoticed.

For a while I lived in a community of shamans in Mexico and everything they do is ritualised. It's how they connect with water, fire, soil; it's all about the land and Mother Earth and it's all about giving and receiving. At first it took me by surprise because I could see in my own life that I was really good at giving but, when it came to the receiving side of things, I felt so uncomfortable. That's when I saw the imbalance in myself. We exist right now in the modern world in a state of imbalance, not only in our relationship with nature and with others but also within ourselves.

Me: There is such global imbalance. In the Western world, we see the planet as one big endless resource.

Alex: I have met many indigenous people from different parts of the world and from different communities who received the same message over a number of years through their dreams and prayers. They all understand that now is the time for them to go out of their communities and share the lost wisdom with us. They needed us to know how important it is that we make relationship with Mother Earth and all living beings. They call us 'the younger brothers and sisters'. In order to bring this urgent wisdom to us, many of these indigenous people had to leave their homes. Some have travelled from the Amazon rainforest – to leave their natural environment for a few years to share their knowledge with us has been a painful process for them. Yet they did it so the rest of us can start emanating what they have been carrying forever.

Me: It's such a beautiful message that I just pray we can, en masse, take heed of. Otherwise, it'll be too late. Huge change feels hard to comprehend but on an individual level it's interesting to look at our own inner imbalances. It's also brilliant to hear that anything can be a ritual. A lot of people may assume rituals are not for them because they're esoteric and might require crystals, or something special. You're saying you can make ritual a part of your everyday. Does a ritual always have to have a 'doing' element to it?

Alex: Prayer, meditation, they can both be rituals. It doesn't require special knowledge or paraphernalia. Yet an action can also be ritualised. In moments like buying a house or flat, **rituals allow it to be a rite of passage, a way of honouring the momentousness and entering into the right relationship with what's happening.** When I moved to the countryside, I prepared myself for the move. I went to the waters in the village and announced myself to the waters. I said to the river, 'I want to be a part of this.' You have to ask permission. You wouldn't go to someone else's home without announcing your arrival, and you might also bring a gift with you. You have to do the same with nature. In Mexico, they call the ocean *Haramara*, which means Mother Sea, they see her as a woman. The same in Brazil; it's called *Yemanja*, a powerful sea goddess. You'll find different names in different parts of the world but they all have the same respect for nature and bring offerings to demonstrate that. An offering could be a flower that you lay in the waves of the ocean.

Me: So it's a relationship with the world around us, something we seem to have lost in the modern world. We've got so caught up in the speed of life and have stopped communicating with it. So many indigenous people do this without thinking about it, it's ingrained in them. It's such a shame we've lost that connection in the West. I remember before I climbed Mount Kilimanjaro in my mid-twenties I asked the mountain permission. I had been reading some pretty cool spiritual books around that time so thought it would be a good idea. Standing at its base I felt tiny and knew I needed support from the mountain itself for the climb. I got so sick up the mountain and nearly had to abort the rest of the climb but somehow the mountain gave me the space and time to heal and I made it to the top. I'm so glad that I had that dialogue with the mountain.

Alex: When you meet elders or wisdom keepers, they will tell you that a mountain is one of the most sacred beings. Making an offering is a way of recognising and connecting to the sacredness. Everything is energy.

When I was in the Amazon rainforest in Peru, I also asked the jungle for support and I received exactly what I needed for my healing. It's one of the most important things for us to understand when it comes to our view and relationship with nature: that we are part of this big ecosystem and that it is an honour to be in relationship with Mother Nature. Recognising that it is vaster than us and that it's not about imposing upon the living world but coming to learn from it; it is a dynamic exchange. Can we believe that nature can speak to us? Children seem to understand that.

Me: Can you tell me more about your time in Mexico living with elders and Mexican grandmothers?

Alex: I lived in Mexico for almost a year and, while I was there, I wanted to heal my endometriosis. I ended up living with shamans and elders for nine months, being in ceremony, sitting around the fire and connecting with prayers. I realised I was disconnected from myself and my true essence; I came to see that my illness was a symptom of this disconnect from my emotional body. Can you believe that after those months I was able to heal my body? It was all about restoring trust in my body and going deeper into my own shadow – into those parts of the self that were hard to look at and be with.

Being in nature and in ceremony, sitting around the fire and connecting with the fire, helped me to understand that we are living in heaven on Earth. Children are better able to appreciate this, to live in the present moment and in joy.

During my most recent trip to Mexico, I saw how full of joy the grandmothers – the elders or medicine women – were, always full of grace, laughter and cheekiness. I had always taken my spiritual path so seriously but watching them I saw they were so full of life. They taught me to love myself as well as the world around me. I met a seventy-five-year-old grandmother who was one of the most vital, sensual women I have ever met. She had a daily practice of rubbing a potion made of honey and rose petals on her body. She said that, as a single person, we are always waiting to be touched and that the body expresses this longing. Rubbing the honey on our bodies is a way of giving ourselves the sensuality we long for, a way of falling in love with our skin, with our bodies. The skin absorbs the nutrients and the love. She exuded such trust in the belief that love was coming to her, and she was opening to love through these sensual rituals. I found it so inspiring! She was so clear with me about the importance of connecting with my skin, with my femininity and really owning my womanhood. These women taught me so much about leading from the heart and that this is an embodied practice – it's not just an idea but a way of living. I learned from them that there are two main things we need in life: vitality and joy. Joy can be a ritual.

Me: How do you make joy a ritual then?

Alex: When it comes to joy we need to connect with our inner child. Our inner child always knows what we want. It could be two scoops of ice cream, whatever it is that brings you joy.

Me: In the modern world we get into bad habits of having negative thoughts and rushing about. Do we need to have discipline to incorporate ritual into our day?

Alex: Yes, I think we do. For our physical bodies we might do yoga or running to make us feel good; we need to do the same for our minds. Our mind always wants to live in the past or the future. Ritual can bring us back to the present. I have to meditate every day and have the discipline to do so, but it might be different for you. It could be cooking, or a walk in nature. It needs to be a healthy habit every day. It's not the activity itself that matters but the presence you bring to it. During my last trip to Mexico, I learned a lot about the physical body and using ritual to acknowledge and honour it. Often, we are just in survival mode. When we take the time to care for our bodies and make this special by using a ritual, we are sending energy to our physical body that carries a message: 'My dear body, I love you, we are safe, we are protected.'

Me: I felt so connected to my physical body on a recent trip to Dorset. I swam in the freezing sea every day and allowed my body to adjust naturally without the cerebral part of me getting in the way and sending me into panic. It was liberating.

Alex: Yes, swimming in the sea can be a beautiful ritual. You are allowing the body to feel freedom as you move through the water. You are telling the body, 'I am alive.' Approximately 60 per cent of our body is water, so we are reconnecting with the elements inside and outside of ourselves.

Me: When we look at ceremony, how can we start to put that into everyday life? Not just ceremony that we are used to, like birthdays, but ceremony around the everyday stuff?

Alex: We can always start with intention. Intention is bringing consciousness and awareness to everything we do. **By bringing intention to everyday stuff, the most simple act can become a small ceremony.** What if we slow down during dinner and make it ceremonial? We can bring the intention of gratitude to everything that we receive: gratitude to our bodies for being alive, gratitude to the food and the place it comes from, acknowledgement to the children around us for keeping the magic in our lives. If we invite our children to introduce ceremony, they will create the most wonderful moments. We just need to see the world with the same aliveness again. Indigenous people live their lives in eternal ceremony, connecting with the seasons, with the moon cycles, with the animals around them, with their dead ones, just listening, feeling, being.

Me: How can we add ritual to our relationships with other people?

Alex: The way I start adding rituals to my own relationships is by bringing them into my own meditation and prayers. I always visualise my parents – unfortunately they passed away. Every morning I light a candle for both of them, knowing that they are with me in spirit. This is my way of honouring them and my ancestors, a daily ritual of love and remembrance.

When I cook a meal, I put my prayers into the ingredients; I ask for health and abundance. It's all about the intention, the purposefulness we bring to any moment. For instance, if we choose this meal to be a celebration of our love, every step of the process becomes an expression of our care and attention.

When my loved ones and friends come together, the meal becomes a ritual. We take stock in the moment of what it is we are sharing and we mark the occasion in whatever way we see fit, bringing beauty to the moment. It's a creative act. It doesn't have to be big – the important thing is that it has to be meaningful to you. You have the freedom to make it your own.

Walking in the forest can become a family ritual: give some seeds to the trees as offerings, say your name to the wind, walk in silence and listen to the birds, close your eyes and feel the sun together. Share what you are experiencing.

Would you like to do a ritual with me?

Me: Errr, YES!!! I would like nothing more.

Alex: OK, to begin I'm going to ask you to write two letters. The first is a letter to yourself in which you acknowledge all your self-limiting beliefs. Write down all of the things you know are blocking you in your life. The second is a letter to the universe; introduce yourself and then write down what your intention is for the book. Write about how you plan to open people's hearts with this book. Then, let's meet up next week and I'll tell you what to do next.

* * *

Being a first-class nerd, I've written the two letters within thirty minutes of being instructed to do so. The first letter to myself was easy. I know every self-limiting belief I have intimately. I know them so well because they're constant thoughts that torment me when things are going well or when I have an abundance of love or experience on the horizon. As I've mentioned previously, I often don't believe that I deserve good things. I think I haven't tried enough, worked hard enough or am not a 'good enough' person, whatever that means. This letter flew out of my pen at lightning speed.

Letter two felt gentler. Penning an announcement to the universe felt powerful, to the point where I quietly wondered why I had never done this before. I used to prolifically write a diary, but that was more of a loquacious ramble through life written to myself. Announcing myself to the universe felt completely different and steeped in humbleness. I know what I want my work going forward to achieve: connection. It's so crystal clear to me at this point in my life. I want to feel part of something that is bigger than me and also for that connection to help others. I want to help people discover their own worth and value in this world, as I discover mine. Over the last few years of building my brand Happy Place, I've not only started the ball rolling with that one but have begun the healing process for myself. I'm now approaching a point where I know what I'm here to do and that has brought me confidence and has uncovered my self-worth. My letter to the universe was exciting to write. I even did my best handwriting in an attempt to show my respect. It felt like magic was flowing through every syllable and each neatly performed curve and flick.

My letter to the universe:

Dear Universe,

My name is Fearne and I'm a forty-year-old female willing to learn and keep exploring life as fully as I can.

Firstly, thank you for giving me the space to write this new book. I'm astonished each time a new, wise soul walks into my life willing to share their stories with me. Thank you for sending them my way. I have loved writing this book and as much as it's been a cathartic and game-changing experience for me, I desperately want the same for each person who kindly buys the book. I want each reader to turn the pages and soak in all of this wisdom gifted to us by the extraordinary people in this book and for their lives to change for the better too. I want this book to bring comfort, solace, calm and mostly connection. I want the readers to know that they can let go of old stories and self-limiting beliefs and move forward in life, lighter and brighter, with their hearts beaming forwards and their souls nurtured and cosy.

I want this book to bridge the division between people and their supposed differences. For uniqueness to be celebrated and not used to pull people apart. I want the focus to be love and hope instead of the fear and doom we are so often presented with. I hope this book can be a tonic for those who are struggling, in pain and left in the aftershock of trauma. I've learned so much from this book already and have been able to wade through the last few metres of PTSD sludge to a new, lighter and freer place. I so hope that the readers of the book can experience the same. I hope it helps them to heal, or for them to help others heal who they love. I will keep pouring as much heart and soul into this book as I can and not worry about others' judgements or negative opinions. There can be no room for that here.

Thank you for the time and space.

Yours humbly,

Fearne

I eagerly text Alex to notify her of my nerdiness and set a date for the ceremony.

Burn and Bury

I sit looking at my fake grass, cursing myself for not asking the soil beneath my feet if it was OK that I covered the patchy, barren, real grass with Astroturf a few years back. How could I have been so arrogant to have no concern for the land itself? I wonder if doing a ritual on Astroturf takes some of the beauty out of the occasion? I don't have too long to worry about this as my very first ceremony is about to start. Alex has the most soothing voice you've ever heard. It's featherweight and honey, so feels instantly calming. Alex instructs me to close my eyes and take a deep breath. I am then to announce myself to the universe again, this time out loud. A block of flats overlooks my garden so I speak softly so as not to draw too much attention to this unfolding scene. Next, I am to pick up the first letter that I wrote to myself. Alex asks me to stroke the letter over my head. I'm to wipe away all of these self-limiting beliefs so that they leave my physical body and transmit their energy, instead, into the letter.

I spend time really extracting the thoughts and sentences I often hear on loop, imagining them all seeping into the fibres of the paper. Alex instructs me to go with whatever feels right as I'm to move the letter to any other body parts that might be holding tension or these beliefs. My throat starts to burn; I move the letter to my neck. All of those words I've not said aloud when people have belittled me, confirming my own self-limiting beliefs. A hot ball of fire whirrs as I swallow but starts to dissipate with each swipe of the letter. My neck and right shoulder feel like they've been cast in iron today so there is definitely something lurking in there too. I brush the letter over the surface of my skin, picking up the debris of self-criticising stress.

Next, my tummy. I hold so much emotion in that area; you might too? It's a soft part of my body that feels private and slightly vulnerable. I don't like people touching me there at all so assume this is a fleshy area to concentrate on today. I move the letter over the softness, collecting those old stories as I go. The womb, just below, needs attention too: the divine feminine that carries so much movement and power; the monthly cycle representing the pain, release and continuation of life. This whole-body scan takes maybe twenty minutes or half an hour. Time seems irrelevant at this stage.

A match is struck and within seconds this letter, along with the body's energy attachments to it, are up in flames. Fire feels exciting. It's not often you set something alight. Maybe a nice scented candle, but, with the intention to incinerate forever, it all feels slightly different. I grin as I stare into the amber flicker, careful not to burn my fingers while also catching the ashes below in a small tray. The smell makes me think of bonfires in our old back garden in Eastcote. Dad would pile up old wood from building work he had been doing, with newspaper on top, and we would watch the flames tower above us. The smell makes me feel like I'm about eleven years old. The innocence and excitement of life at that age envelops me. Bye-bye old stories and beliefs, I'm done with you. Alex tells me to find a spot in the garden where there is some soil I can move about. I dig a small hole with my kids' mini gardening spade and tip the ashes from the letter into it. Next, I cover over the hole with fresh soil and tip a small bowl of water on top, as Alex asked.

Now for the offerings. I have four bright purple flowers that I picked from a bunch specially for today. On top of the flowers I sprinkle raw cacao, which Alex says represents the sweetness of life. I'm to know that the ashes, along with their stories, will be absorbed by the soil: the end of a chapter, the marking of something new. I feel lighter already. The next part of the ritual is to be undertaken when I'm next setting out to write this very book. I'm to take my letter full of intentions to the universe and put a white candle on top of it. Each time I set out to write I'm to light the candle so that the light can penetrate my intentions and bring them to life. How beautiful! Why have I only used a strong coffee and biscuits as a writing aid previously? This seems like such a special way to mark the opening and closing of each writing session.

Hello Trees

The next morning, after the whirlwind of the school run, I sit down at the kitchen table and open my laptop. My little white candle sits atop my letter to the universe waiting to conduct the light. I strike a match and say thank you to the universe for the opportunity to write such a book, a book that will hope-fully not only help others but has really healed me in ways I couldn't have imagined. You can do the same with any work or plans you're working on. Like Alex said, set your intention, write it all down, then place your candle on top of your letter to conduct the light.

In fact, these last few days I've observed life and my own scuttling through it with newly open eyes. Tree surgeons arrive at the house with ropes and saws ready to cut back an unruly conifer at the back of our garden. Normally I would make tea, provide the odd biscuit and ensure the tree surgeons were all right, but today my focus is much more on the tree itself. I still made a bloody good cuppa for each of the chaps doing the work, but first of all I asked the tree if it was OK for us to proceed with the work and notified the tree that it was in the name of growth. There was no direct answer and one wasn't really needed; it was more a moment of respect and an attitude of humbleness to nature that I had previously overlooked.

A New Language

When I'm writing I try to get started as soon as the kids are at school and write until my arse numbs. When I can no longer feel the fleshy pads touching the chair I go for a walk. I'm very lucky to live near a big park with green expanses, woodland, green parakeets and lush ferns everywhere. Normally I'll pop headphones on and listen to a podcast or music while I re-en-gage my legs and arse. Today I didn't. I looked around, and I mean properly looked around. I stared up at the trees with wonder and noticed small details on their bark, smiled with glee when a green flash of parakeet swooped above and thanked the earth beneath my feet. Usually, my appreciation would be on a sub-level while my brain mostly engaged with what I was listening to, but today I focused my mind on the beauty around me. I made a point of feeling humbled by the wild, ever-changing scenery and to say thank you out loud.

I've always felt gratitude for the park but I had never articulated this to the universe before. This new dialogue felt so natural and like I had discovered another language overnight. I've noticed it's also stopping me from getting distracted with negative thoughts. Usually when I'm stomping round the park, my mind will wander. It might go back to a point in time I don't want to recall; a regret, a mishap, a missed opportunity. I could waste a whole hour's walk pondering one moment that I have little control over. My walk today felt more like a ritual – one purpose, one intention and a dialogue with the ground beneath my feet. I was in the moment and found happiness in nothing more than what I was seeing and experiencing.

We all know that the feeling of lacking drives us into somewhat dangerous territory. I could easily manoeuvre from recalling an upsetting or regretful time into feeling lacking in wisdom or common sense and then let that spiral into self-loathing. In moments of self-loathing we are much more inclined to react rather than stop and let things be processed. Self-loathing corrodes our outer layer of positivity and hope, so we are more easily triggered by our exterior world. To numb the pain of what we see and feel around us we might eat without thought or enjoyment, buy something we do not need, lash out at another to reduce the inner tension. If we walk with intention and discipline our minds to only focus on gratitude for nature's wild expression around us, there is less room for the negative and for reaction without thought. Today, there was a distinct lack of pointless shopping, eating chocolate and shouting at my husband post-walk. Win-win.

What moments in your day could you make into a ritual? Which ceremony or mindful moment could bring you back to the present moment and stop you from spiralling into self-doubt or -loathing? Get in nature where you can and talk to Mother Earth's beauty and engage in a dialogue that will enrich your soul. **Let ceremony teach you the language of self-love.**

MEDIUMS
AND INTUITION

There is perhaps some cynicism around psychics and clairvoy-
ance but isn't that just because we are so wedded to the idea of
linear time? I'm not professing I have any knowledge of or insight
into how we can expand our minds to see outside of the confines
of time on a clockface; my little pea-brain has not the capacity
for such physics but I do like that thinking outside the box when
it comes to time allows us to tap into our own intuition.

Your initial judgements might lean towards a cartoon character mystic, crystal ball in hand, glimpsing into the future to
warn of potential threat or disaster. Yet maybe you have tales to
tell of inexplicable happenings that are too extreme to merely
be labelled a coincidence. You might call it gut instinct, intuition, or perhaps even psychic activity. Whatever the label and
varying degree, it often feels like something much bigger is at
play. I have no clue as to how this knowing feeling creeps in
and where it is coming from but I'm deeply intrigued and have
my own stories to tell.

River Warning

We've all had those moments where a friend we are thinking about calls out of the blue or a song we were humming comes on the radio in that exact moment. Is that a coincidence or are we picking up on something else? We may have had intuitive dreams which have foretold future events, or had visions that lead us to a potential future opportunity. Sometimes it's simply a feeling without images or sounds yet equally as profound. I had an experience that, still to this day, makes no sense and makes me slightly shudder.

It was a wet spring-time morning and my husband was away on tour. Rex was a red-cheeked toddler and Honey a wee bubba with a shock of flame-coloured hair. Weekends with Jesse away and two small kids usually felt slightly daunting so I always tried to ensure we had things planned or people to see. Getting out of the house early in the day also kept me sane as I could tick 'fresh air' off the list that day. I live not far from the River Thames so thought a stroll by its waters to try to spot some ducks might be an entertaining short excursion. As I neared the riverbank I started to get a really uneasy feeling. It came out of the blue but tightened my neck muscles as I felt anxiety crackle inside my bones. I held Rex's hand tightly and with the other hand gripped the buggy handle like my life depended on it. We carried on down the river in search of mallards and swans but the feeling intensified. I didn't have a visual image in my head or a voice speak to me, but I sensed that someone was about to fall in the river and I hoped to God it wasn't one of us.

As I squeezed the blood out of my hands gripping Rex's tiny, plump fingers, we neared a cafe, which appeared like an oasis. A pit stop was needed to gather myself. Whenever anxiety attacks, I spiral into internally beating myself up somewhat. I curse myself for being so ridiculous and unable to cope with the slightest change or extra responsibility. My head started to throb as the anxiety and thoughts of someone falling in the river grew to a crescendo. As I approached the ramp to push the buggy up the slope to the cafe I heard a wail and a clatter and turned around to watch a slow-motion scene unfold. My eyes tried to catch up with the movement to my left and stalled on a lady in a wheelchair thundering down a steep set of stairs towards the water. Usually a peaceful spot where tourists queue to pick up a river rowboat for the afternoon, these stairs now took on a whole new terrifying shape.

I stood in horror, bottom jaw hanging loosely and eyes bulging wide. I was frozen to the spot, watching her partner run at pace towards her to try to stop the imminent horror. I still feel sick thinking back to this moment. She hit the water but was embraced a nanosecond later by her partner who was now by her side in the deep Thames water. He pulled her to the steps as other passers-by, unencumbered by young children and a buggy, helped pull the chair out of the water and settle the poor lady. Both drenched and in total shock, the woman and her partner now sat on the steps gathering themselves after this out-of-the-blue moment.

I gulped dramatically and blinked in the moment, wondering what the fuck just happened. How on earth had I picked up on this event ten minutes before it had even happened? A freak event demonstrating the uncontrollable anarchy of life. There are too many variables for this random moment to have been a coincidence. I felt completely spooked by the whole thing but so utterly relieved that the couple were OK and had no more than a bit of shock to contend with.

Tune In

As horrific as that episode was to stand witness to, it did give me hope that we can all tune in to events in the future and use it to help guide us to keep growing and learning. There are of course incredible people out there who are completely tuned in and use their skill to help others daily. My husband regularly speaks to a clairvoyant to make contact with his late mother Krissy. Jesse's mum died in a moment of shock and trauma. An accidental drug overdose ended her life without any time to prepare for such a loss. Jesse and his mum were incredibly close, as it was just the two of them in a flat in south-west London; every second spent together, navigating life as a duo. The lack of closure for Jesse has been insurmountable, so having some kind of connection and communication with her has been deeply healing and soothing.

I also have a very lovely and generous friend who loves a bit of 'alternative therapy', so has, on more than one occasion, gifted me a session with a medium he highly recommended. The first time he arranged this little gift I was told to call a number and then keep an open mind. The dull, long-drawn-out phone ring confirmed I was connecting with someone very far away who had no idea who I was. She didn't, at this point, know my name or anything about me as my friend had set it all up anonymously.

The soft American voice told me to say aloud my name, birthdate and place of birth. That was it. After just one tiny sentence she went off on a forty-five-minute escapade into my life with unbelievable accuracy. You might already be rolling your eyes at the craziness of this. Perhaps your pupils are now pointing to the back of the room as you view this as unnecessary and even lavish. It was indeed a treat but these sorts of sessions are only viewed as perhaps extravagant because it's not the norm. It is the norm to go and blow money on booze at the weekend and equally as acceptable to buy bags of cheap clothing you'll only wear once. It's all a matter of perspective, I guess.

Lavish or not, I was having the time of my life. Jotting down notes at high speed and nodding with a Cheshire cat grin plastered over my face, I listened intently as she kept relaying the advice that I had to write books. I didn't inform her that I already had written books as I was intrigued by where she would steer this chat. She also kept mentioning the word 'sunflower', using it to describe how I should see myself in life, face up to the sun, standing tall. What made this particularly strange was that the week before, my son Rex had become obsessed with the Post Malone song 'Sunflower' and had played it relentlessly after school for the previous five days. There were some personal and sensitive issues she touched on which really helped to bring me clarity and perhaps in a few cases some solutions to ongoing problems. Again, I have no idea how she did it and where she was drawing this insight from but I lapped up every minute, like a mystic cat to cream. It was eye-opening, life-affirming, magic-confirming, and made me focus on the expanse of life rather than the minutiae.

Looking Back

The differing nature of intuition seems to span from coincidences that bring a little joy, to having full-blown visions that manifest into reality, and everything in between. No matter how big or small these moments are, they are meaningful and can help us have faith and find comfort. Using intuition isn't exclusively about looking into the future. I recently read and loved the book on near-death experiences called *After*, by Dr Bruce Greyson. A near-death experience (NDE) is something remembered by the individual even though the body and brain were showing no signs of life. This is such a beautiful way for us to have faith in our own souls. If memories can be recalled without the brain's involvement, then we know there is another part of us just as alive and complex as the body and mind.

In this mind-blowing book Dr Greyson collates stories from hundreds of people who have clear memories from a near-death experience. His interest was piqued after a patient he was operating on talked of watching him, even when he was out of the operating theatre, at a time when she was showing no signs of life. She had clear details to share, like a food stain that had been on Dr Greyson's tie that day and what he was doing and where he went when outside of the theatre itself. After some exploration, he discovered countless other stories that matched the inexplicable in this experience.

Dr Greyson, although with a long medical background, is often not taken as seriously by the medical world as there is no scientific explanation for these miraculous moments. He argues, 'At what point does a collation of stories become data?' All research is based on an accumulation of information that is processed as numbers and averages, to then be included within the confines of science. At what point can his huge mass of stories make that crossover? Without total scientific clarity, perhaps this will never happen. The lack of clarity, of course, is due to the fact that we are still not using the full extent of the human brain. We might be able to build computers and send people into space but there's still so much undiscovered potential when it comes to the human brain and how we engage with our senses fully. The tales collected by Dr Greyson are too frequent and too vivid to be ignored. These experiences might not be traditionally classed as intuition or the psychic, but I think it's really important and interesting to include this subject matter in this chapter, especially if we are willing to break down the boundaries of time itself.

A Magical Tale of Art and Music

David Ditchfield has one of the most remarkable near-death experience stories to tell, with tangible results to prove the profound nature of what he saw, felt and heard while technically dead. After a horrific freak accident where his coat got trapped in a train door and he was dragged at speed along the railway tracks, he was rushed to hospital where the most inexplicable situation unfurled. Here David recounts the experience he had and how it has completely reshaped his life.

After the accident, I was taken straight to the hospital Emergency Department. I remember being in agony from the pain and losing a lot of blood from my injuries. The doctors were rushing around, prepping me for emergency surgery and it was at this point, waiting to go into theatre, that I had my NDE. One minute I was looking up at the harsh fluorescent lights on the ceiling, the next minute, I was instantly transported to another world entirely. I didn't have the sensation of floating up and out of my body, which some NDErs (near-death experience-ers) report, I just closed my eyes to cope with the pain and, when I opened them, I found myself in another world.

It was incredible to experience such an instant shift of world like that. All I knew was that I was now somewhere that didn't seem to have boundaries, just dark space all around me, and I became aware of a deep, overwhelming sense that I was being cared for. Beautiful orbs of light appeared, pulsating with colour, going from orange to green to red to yellow. I turned my head to look either side of me and realised I was lying on what appeared to be a large slate rock, like a granite monument or slab. The strange thing was, it was remarkably comfortable to lie on. This is when the thought came to me. I was dead. I had to be. And I felt entirely comfortable with the thought. I didn't fight or resist it at all. It wasn't that I wanted to die; in fact, during the train accident itself, I'd done everything I could to survive it. But this place felt so wonderful, so peaceful and calm, that I just wanted to keep lying there forever.

After a while, and I have no idea how long it was as it felt like each moment was infinite, I felt curious about my injuries so I raised my head to look at my body. Astonishingly, my arm was intact, there was no blood, no bruising, all my injuries had gone. And the creased, bloodied hospital gown had also gone. Now I was naked, except for a silver-blue-coloured cloth that covered the lower half of my body, hanging down over the sides of the grey slab in soft fine folds. The cloth was like nothing I had ever seen before. It had the appearance of fine satin or silk and felt so smooth and light on my skin. It shimmered like rippling liquid when I moved underneath it.

Then, I looked up and saw three large symmetrical, rectangular-shaped light boxes overhead. The light they emitted was intensely bright and somehow healing. It was then I felt the presence of someone close. I lifted my head again and saw a beautiful androgynous Being stood at my feet. The Being wasn't feminine or masculine. It was neither, yet both at the same time. A strange and beautiful Being with white-blond, wavy hair and pale, luminous skin and a simple black cloth worn over its body. And I felt safe, because I felt total trust in its love and compassion. This Being felt like the keeper to my Soul, my higher self or my Guardian

Angel. And for the first time in my life, I felt complete. All my feelings of guilt, shame and anxiety belonged to the other world. Here, I felt closer to the pure essence of who I was in my Soul, with all the layers of baggage I'd carried through my life lifted from me.

Then, two more Beings appeared on either side of me. They were more human-like, more feminine in nature, and both had warm darker skin tones and jet-black hair, with Brazilian or American Indian type features. These two Beings moved their outstretched hands over different areas of my body, as though healing me with some kind of energy that I couldn't see. Not only healing the horrific trauma that my body had just been through but it felt like they were healing my Soul itself, all the emotional wounds I'd had over the years.

As I lay back and allowed this energy of pure uncondi-tional love to heal me, I began to think about my family back in the hospital who had been gathered around my bedside earlier. Now that I believed I was dead, I wondered how they were coping back in the other world. I felt no sense of urgency or distress about their grief, because I now knew there was life after death and they'd all get to experience this wonderful place one day too. But I wanted to check they were okay, so I leaned over the side of the granite slab as though this new world was above the hospital and, somehow, I'd be able to look down through the hospital ceiling and see them all below. What I saw instead was the most awesome sight, a huge waterfall of stars, the size of Niagara Falls, but instead of water, millions of sparkling stars cascading down into multiple dimensions. And when I looked down into the middle of the vortex waterfall, I found myself looking from one galaxy into another as if gazing into infinity. This was *when it hit me. I wasn't in a small darkened space at all, I was in the Universe itself.*

What happened next was the most profound moment of my NDE. An infinite tunnel of white Light appeared. This Light was the most powerful of all the Light sources I'd seen, with dramatic flames slowly circling round and round its brilliant white centre. It got closer and closer and the healing energy of love it radiated was so powerful that it felt as though every single molecule of my body was vibrating with love. Somehow, I knew I was witnessing the source of all creation. To me, this was God. Not the image of God that I'd always imagined, some old male figure with a long white beard, like Michelangelo's depiction on the ceiling of the Sistine Chapel in the Vatican. This Light was the energy of pure unconditional Love and it was the Source of all. At this profound moment of realisation, I came crashing back into my body in the hospital. Just as suddenly as I'd arrived in that wonderful world, I was brought back to this one. The contrast was shocking. All the pain came flooding back into my body, the fluorescent overhead light was too hard and stark to look at and the frantic noise of the hospital so loud and overbearing. But as they wheeled me into theatre, I was full of awe and wonder at what had just happened and felt a sense of indescribable joy at experiencing such unconditional love.

Straight after my NDE, I was literally rushed into the operating theatre for an eight-hour operation to save my arm and deal with the other injuries I sustained. Sometime around 2am, I woke up from the anaesthetic, hospital equipment beeping and whirring all around me. I was unable to move. The surgeons took skin grafts from both legs to rebuild my debrided arm so every part of my body hurt. In the dark, I tried to process what had just happened. A horrific, shocking train accident and a profound NDE. The two experiences couldn't be more opposite in the realm of human experience. Part of my mind kept reliving the terrible frightening moments of my accident, the moment when I was pulled underneath the train, but a deeper part of me felt an incredible feeling of joy and peace from the impact of the NDE. Going through a spiritual experience like this is quite literally mind-blowing. So, despite the pain and accident flashbacks, the ultra-vivid NDE and its impact on my understanding of life was over-whelming. As the night progressed, the question of why I'd been 'sent back' began to consume me. To be honest, it was so beautiful in that other world, I didn't want to come back. But it felt like I'd been sent back for a reason and, as the night wore on, the insight came to me that, like other NDErs, I'd been sent back to offer a message of comfort to those that need it. The message that there is life after death and we are more than our physical bodies. People sometimes ask me if my NDE was simply an effect of the medication they gave me in hospital, or some kind of post-accident hallucination. But, as I explain to them, the narratives of dreams and drug-induced halluci-nations are generally chaotic, random and fade over time. In contrast, I've never forgotten a single moment of my NDE. I can recall it all even years later, every ultra-vivid moment of it, as though it happened yesterday.

The idea to start painting came to me that very first night when I was lying in the hospital bed. I was consumed by a feeling that I had to somehow capture, in painting form, what I'd seen in that other world, show people what an Afterlife experience looked like. We so often read NDE accounts, but very rarely see a visual portrayal of what the NDEr saw. The biggest challenge I faced wasn't remembering the details, I've never forgotten a single moment of my NDE, the challenge *was in capturing the beautiful colours weaving and flowing through the darkness, the incredible Beings of light, the shimmering blue cloth and stone altar I was lying on, the dimensions of galaxies and entire universes all around me and the incredible quality of love emanating from the tunnel of light. It wasn't easy and it took a long time, but once I started painting, I knew I was being helped. Over time, I realised I was channelling ideas and inspiration and, with this help, I ended up creating a series of NDE paintings that represented my experience, as best as I could.*

My school was rough, a large inner-city comprehensive. I really struggled with the academic side of things due to my dyslexia, so spent most of my school days gazing out of the window at the back of the class. I liked drawing as a child, mostly on the back of my school books, and I'd do the odd sketch here and there for mates, cartoons or pop stars' faces, that kind of thing. But it wasn't exactly painting the Sistine Chapel. I left school with hardly any qualifications, so the only choice for someone like me was a course in extended education, which was a kind of vocational training in how to draw letters for adverts, not a great career choice for someone profoundly dyslexic. After being sacked from my one and only proper job, which was stencilling letters on badges and T-shirt designs, I moved to London. I taught myself how to thrash out three chords on an electric guitar and played in various punk and pop bands for a while. The NDE changed everything for me and inspired me to reach for a level of creativity that I had never been capable of achieving before. Right from the very first night in hospital, I had really strong visions of what I wanted to paint in my head, but no training in how to produce the quality of fine art painting needed to realise these visions on canvas. Eventually, I sensed I was being guided by Spirit and if I allowed this help to come through into my work, the paintings would happen, regardless of my lack of training.

The music came later. This was even more of a surprise as I've never received any formal training in classical music and, to this day, I still can't read or write musical notation. But just like the visions of my paintings, I felt compelled to compose and, with the help of some computer software which translates music played on a synthesiser (even one-fingered playing like mine) into classical sheet music, I composed my debut symphony. It was called 'The Divine Light' and was inspired by my NDE. I was lucky enough to have it premiered at a sell-out orchestral performance to a standing ovation.

Since then, I have been commissioned to write further classical works which have also been premiered at sell-out performances and I've completed more than thirty paintings and a number of commissioned artworks. As with my paintings, I realised early on that I was getting help with my composing from a Higher Source. This was evident, as even the most accomplished classical musicians I've met have told me that they would never attempt to compose a symphony. So even though I played guitar in pop and punk bands, it was no help whatsoever when it came to composing this type of music. That's why I know I am being guided by Spirit when I'm creating my art and music.

My NDE changed my whole perspective on life in several key ways. First, it taught me that death is just a transition. So now I have no fear of it. None whatsoever. And this insight has also helped me in dealing with the inevitable passing of loved ones. I still deeply grieve the loss of their presence in the physical world but, on a deeper level, I also feel comforted in the knowledge that death is only the end of the physical self.

Second, the NDE revealed to me that I was constantly living in my head, rushing through life, often consumed by negative thoughts and self-doubt with no awareness of how these thoughts were driving unhealthy behaviours. And I'd lost touch with the real me, or my authentic self as I call it. But the moment-by-moment awareness of my NDE was life-changing for me. In that world, time did not exist. There was no past or future, no thoughts, no worries. All I experienced was being in some kind of eternal presence and I've never forgotten the incredible sense of peace that came with it. I felt part of some greater energy force or Being, I now refer to as the Universe. This intense experience of timelessness still inspires me in my daily life. I meditate every day and do my best to become aware of my thoughts and feelings without judgement, especially if they are anxious or negative thoughts. Being in the present moment is not easy and I don't always manage it, but the knowledge that there is a much more peaceful way of being in life remains a great inspiration.

Finally, the other key thing my NDE taught me is that all life has meaning and purpose. If we allow our authentic self to emerge and trust in the Universe, we create the space for synchronicity and opportunity to manifest and point the way ahead. Life is an incredible journey, full of challenges but also full of opportunities to learn and grow.

I am blown away by David's story and feel peaceful knowing that I can take some of the power away from my mind and its propensity to ruin my day with negative thought. What a bamboozling and profound experience with miraculous aftershocks. Do go and check out David's paintings online as they are remarkable and have captured the divine light and power that he felt during his NDE. Likewise, his symphonies carry a harmony and grace that envelop you in peace. There are countless stories of NDEs if you go and search for them, each one giving us hope, peace and an opportunity to understand our soul that bit better.

. . .

There is someone else I would love for you to meet in this chapter. Yvonne Williams is another incredible healer I was tipped off about by a mate many years ago. She is a psychic medium who helps people connect with those who have crossed over, and also with guidance in life. Yvonne is naturally predisposed to intuition as it's in her maternal lineage. She had her first vision aged nine and due to her family's understanding of intuition she learned to use it to benefit others around her. I have had a few sessions with Yvonne over the years and have found her soft demeanour and insight into psychic guidance so helpful. I have so much more to learn on this subject matter, so let's get cracking.

Me: Hey, Yvonne.

Yvonne: Hey, lovely.

Me: When you're working with clients and are using your psychic skill set, how do you channel it?

Yvonne: If I'm working with a client I am opened up as an instrument. I'm a natural psychic medium so instantaneously move into my tool set, clairaudient, clairvoyant and clairsentient. Clairaudient means clearly hearing, clairvoyant means clearly seeing, clairsentient means clearly sensing. Those are my primary tools. They allow me to connect into the frequency and vibration of the person I'm working with. I engage with their guides and spiritual family, my guides at the same time too. I cognitively collate language and format in a way that allows the client to understand what has been downloaded into me and delivered for their greatest good. It's not my opinion or my judgement, it's just coming through.

Me: When you talk about those three ways in which you can pick up that information, do all three always align to bring the message? Or at times do you just hear something without sensing or seeing it?

Yvonne: For me it's always all three together.

Me: You are the conduit for this information but where do you believe this information is coming from?

Yvonne: It's coming from source. That is amalgamated with the frequencies and vibrations that I'm being permitted to pick up, that emit through my client, which is hugely influenced by their ancestors and guides. Depending on what's most prevalent and healing, I will pick up what is needed for that individual on their pathway.

Me: This is a hereditary skill in your family but do you think we've all got the potential to be intuitive?

Yvonne: Yes. It's all untapped potential. Because we are solution-focused as humans, we're not always paying attention to the internal supervisors and voices. We have such manic lives. Everything is so fast-paced so we don't pay attention. It's a shift in focus.

Me: We are so bombarded with outside noise that I guess we are missing a lot of other stuff going on around us and inside of us. How can we cultivate our intuition?

Yvonne: It's like developing the strength of a muscle. Showing a discipline of willingness to develop and hone one's own skills is the best place to start. When I hold a teaching circle, I'm encouraging fledglings to have faith and listen to what they are being influenced by, to then grow into strong, confident instruments.

Me: A willingness seems to be imperative; having faith and a positive outlook on the ability to pick up on frequencies around us.

Yvonne: Yes, to help serve others in a positive way. Inviting in spiritual help that allows us to be better tuned in to all that there is around us to assist and serve others. You have to invite it in.

Me: How much of life do you believe is destined by fate versus how much of it is steered by our own autonomy in day-to-day life?

Yvonne: I believe we come into the world and have multiple pathways waiting for us that determine the growth of our soul. The lessons that we gain through the experiences we have are given before we come into human form.

Me: Is that down to karma?

Yvonne: Yes, or some might say dharma, your purpose. The life you are supposed to be living to grow and learn. **The purpose of life is to go through challenging experiences and to pull**

the wisdom from them as we ascend out of them. Then we are to utilise that wisdom to help others and keep growing. In the middle of difficulty comes the opportunity to ascend and accelerate our innate wisdom.

Me: So, we can use intuition to look for the wisdom within the tough times? We can ask for guidance to understand the 'why' in life's challenges?

Yvonne: That's where me being a trained therapist, as well as a psychic medium, is an interesting blend, because we can find the tools to psychologically navigate challenges but when we look more deeply we can ask, 'What is this experience really asking me to understand more deeply and ascend through?' We might have experienced the same problem two or three times before and we didn't get the lesson and the wisdom, so we experience it again.

Me: I know that one! Ha! I guess our fastest route out of a problem is to always look at the big picture.

Yvonne: If that can be mastered it's wonderful. It's a gentle and simple method but it's so healing and levelling to project forward rather than staying stuck in the anger, angst, anxiety of the problem. Use your own intuition to help you look for the wisdom.

Me: I think in the last year I've attempted to do this as some of the baggage I was carrying around was too heavy. I want the bigger picture now. I want to ascend, Yvonne.

Yvonne: One more thing I really want to point out is that no one should feel scared of intuition or psychic ability. Mediums have been on the Earth for centuries. It's a very beautiful accompaniment to have on your journey through life.

Me: I think some people might not want to have any insight in case something bad pops up as a future prediction.

Yvonne: With an authentic channel, a medium would never deliver bad news, or anything incriminating. An authentic medium only works with love and light and the power of healing. When you're working with intuition only invite the light and the healing in Have boundaries about what you let in.

Me: Yvonne, thank you so much. I look forward to practising this willingness.

My Compulsive Mind

Yvonne has helped me banish superstition and any fear around the subject entirely. Much like in my everyday life, I'm bad with boundaries. I am bad at saying no and often walk around with arms splayed wide inviting all of it in, good, bad and ugly. I'm currently trying to practise changing my ways with that but now need to consider how I boundary my intuition too. A few months ago I was super-anxious about life. I was overwhelmed and felt bombarded by the constant little mental challenges offered. This led to a patch of insomnia and my old friend 'the night-time panic attack' spurred by what I thought were premonitions of a very negative and unruly nature. I spoke about this with Stacey Solomon on my podcast recently as she has experienced exactly the same. I started to believe these awful thoughts and panic that I was having a vision that would, down the line, come to fruition. I was lucky enough to work with a therapist to unpick this attack of my own compulsive mind and get to the bottom of it. It seems an anxiety about messing up at work and being unable to support my family led to this weird compulsive thought that almost became obsessive. With a little more understanding I was able to see the root of the problem and how my mind had cruelly wrapped this negative idea up into the faux form of a premonition. We can wipe out fear and concern about using intuition by only inviting in the good stuff. We have the power and autonomy to do this.

Life's Lessons

Hearing Yvonne speak, combined with David's insight into a life after death experience, I feel I have a little more control over my anarchic mind. At times thoughts grow like weeds and I get so bogged down with the minutiae of what I've done well or badly during my day, but this conversation, like many in this book, has brought me back to a place of hope. **I am hopeful that I can stay willing and open to listen a little better to my own 'inner supervisor' (love this term from Yvonne's chat) and look at the future as expansive and a place to learn rather than something to fear.** I had huge swaths of life stolen by fear after my episode of depression. Life didn't feel hopeful at all. It was shrouded in shadows and beset by bitten-down nails. The past was grim and the future grimmer. I was trapped in a stagnant present and was so terrified of the future I refused to see the lessons that were staring me in the face. Each lesson is now so blindingly obvious but perhaps that's come with time and hindsight. The challenge now is to not lose time when next faced with a problem. Next time, I want to attempt to intuitively pick up the lesson that will help me to ascend and tap into that innate wisdom we all have access to.

Old Stories

Although, for the most part, this book has been a game-changing and positive, joyful experience, I have of course had moments where I've slipped back into old behavioural patterns, habitual traits that are so familiar and comfortable it's like putting my favourite slippers on. It takes no time to transition into these old, negative traits. One tiny trigger can see me acting on autopilot with an old narrative taking hold, rather than having a willingness to sit and listen to my own inner supervisor. Last weekend I sank into self-loathing and comparison. I'm only just resurfacing from it now. A whole week swallowed by the thought that I was useless and unlovable. It's such an old story for me that I'm utterly bored of it, yet that didn't stop me from drowning in its gloom. A vapid, obvious story of a woman too exposed to the reflection of outside opinion, for way too many years, without personal boundaries in place, led to a low self-esteem and a lack of self-worth. I slid back into those shoes so easily. I may as well have been twenty-three again last weekend. Nothing my husband could say helped. His words skimmed off my shoulders like they were slick with oil. I sank deeper and deeper without looking at the numerous times I had felt like this before. So, this is one of those repeated lessons Yvonne spoke about. How many more times will I have to trudge through this shit to intuitively pick up the bigger lesson? I have no excuses. Today is the day.

Sitting, Listening

I sit quietly. The kids are at school and Jesse is in town. A bumble bee the size of a small ball of wool flits in and out of the kitchen and the cats bask in the sunshine outdoors. There is silence, bar a light rumbling of cars in a nearby street. I'm listening in. Hello, inner supervisor, where are you? What can you tell me? I have a pure and undiluted willingness to hear the answers so I can learn this lesson and ascend. At first nothing. I can hear nearby kids playing in a neighbour's garden. I inhale, exhale, listen more carefully, opening myself up to sense, hear or maybe even see the answer. Then I hear words. Not hear, in the sense that a sound was made and heard, but a voice within was spoken and I understood it entirely. 'Get out of the stories.'

Not the most eloquent or beautifully structured sentence from within but one that made sense instantaneously. I know I need to stop swimming through these stories I've created thinking I'm bound to them. I don't need to worry or concern myself with who did what, who wants what, who believes what. Underneath these old stories I can see a bigger, deeper love on the horizon. Looking at these stories with a little more detachment I can diminish their strength. I can even question them. Are they still valid? Are they helping me or anyone else? Doubt it. That doesn't mean I'm elevating myself above these stories to be superior or irresponsible when it comes to accountability, yet I can dilute their potency by dismantling them.

I have a feeling that I am safe without these stories. Disliking others, making them the enemy or placing myself in a moral hierarchy will not save me. **Seeing these stories as nothing but simple, made-up tales is my root to proper, full-bodied safety. A safety where I cannot be harmed or cancelled by others who I have believed are better than me, smarter, more charismatic, or more skilled.** Those kinds of thoughts are merely stories. It's all subjective. I need to quite literally ascend out of this tale I've built my self-esteem on and see the much, much bigger picture.

Can you do the same? Instead of using intuition to work out who your future partner might be or whether you'll get your dream job, can you tap into it to help you see the lessons in life that have been laid before us? Can you see the bigger picture?

Communication's Lessons

- Speak to the world around you. The land, the trees, the sea, the air. Thank it and feel humbled by its beauty.

- Pray even if it's new to you. It's simply a wish with wings.

- Tune in to your own intuition by actively carving out moments of stillness. Differentiate feelings from thoughts conjured by the brain and move to what feels right.

PART 4

SOMETHING BIGGER EVERY DAY

I hope that throughout this book you have gained a little insight into how we can connect with the world and universe around us, from the incredible experts and teachers I've spoken with and the tasks they've set us. I imagine that you've also realised how many spiritual experiences you've already had or have daily, yet perhaps you just hadn't seen them in that light before. We can connect to life and something bigger every day in multiple ways. It's up to you how you do it.

CONNECTION

Last night I was curled up on the sofa, bra off and fluffy socks on, watching my hero, Dave Grohl, in his new documentary *What Drives Us*. I would literally watch Dave stripping paint off walls, so it was a given I was going to watch this the day it was released. It's a stunning look at how rock bands start out in vans and have done since the conception of twanging basslines and deafening drums. He interviews the likes of Ringo Starr from The Beatles, Slash from Guns N' Roses and new bands like the phenomenal Radkey. The interview with Flea from the Red Hot Chili Peppers made me want to stand up on my sofa and jump about like I was on a bouncy castle. He talked about his calling to be on stage and make music, like he had no control over it whatsoever. He went from feeling like a nerdy, jazz-loving, skinny freak, to someone who could let loose and connect with something bigger than himself and his experience of life.

This is how I have always felt about music. I cannot play bass, or the piano or sing like Adele, but I love music to my very core. I have been a music obsessor since the day I discovered my parents' record player. 'Bohemian Rhapsody' clung to my ears and made my heart race and my feet prance. From that second I was hooked and have since woven music into the big and small moments of life. It's one of the easiest ways to connect with something bigger than us.

High Vibes

Musicians (good ones) have the ability to command and connect with a room of people they've never met. I've interviewed enough artists to know that often something else entirely takes over in these moments. A synergy is viscerally felt by all. I've attended some gigs where the vibe has been so potent, I wouldn't have been surprised if the roof had blown off the arena. Watching Led Zeppelin live has to be my best-ever gig. I was Mary Poppins flying so high, face contorted in an uncontrollable grin. The reason it's at the top of my personal gig chart is due to that deep connection the whole room shared. We all knew it was a once-in-a-lifetime opportunity. We were all full to the brim with love and gratitude. We were all singing lyrics, like prayers, back to the band. To me, that is spiritual, a true celebration of life. There was an energy that breezed round the entirety of the arena, with yelps and loud singing raising the vibration further.

It's the same offstage; pure magic is channelled during the songwriting process. I remember Chris Martin telling me that he would stay up late and catch songs while everyone else was snoozing; describing a separation between himself and the song as if it just arrives from somewhere else. Where is that some-where? Again, is it perhaps a combination of the macro and micro, the magic that is everywhere and bigger than us yet also the magic within all of us at all times? I can't play an instrument; I actually failed my Grade 2 violin at school and used to mime my way through orchestra in secondary school, bow hovering two centimetres above the strings. My singing voice is an exclusively shower-related experience, but I know that while listening to music I've had some of the most profoundly beautiful and connective moments. Just walking by the river last week – the Fleet Foxes album *Shore* playing in my headphones, the sun sparkling on the water's surface like tiny diamonds, a heron sat looking out at the canal boats skimming through the waves – it was pure bliss. I felt a connection to all of it, the magic coursing through me, carried along by the sounds of this heavenly music.

Draw in the Light

Art is our way of seeing and hearing the spiritual in life. It brings the ethereal to the forefront and often makes beauty accessible to all. Have you ever stared in awe at a painting in an art gallery or book? I know I have let my eyes sink into canvases over the years in an attempt to understand life a little better. A modern-day example would be the work of Charlie Mackesy. The first time I set eyes on his *Girl and Angel* in charcoal, depicting an angel leaning down to kiss the head of a body curled up tightly on the floor, a tear slid down my cheek. It's not just because Charlie is incredibly technically skilled that his work moves us, it's because he has channelled something that represents the bigness of life.

With each great artist we've marvelled at during school art excursions, in books and on online, we've managed to tap into something that helps us to feel connected. It's often hard to articulate because that connection lies more in a feeling than in words.

I am a keen painter myself and know that, when I'm in the flow, time ceases to exist and I feel a calm and comfort I find hard to access elsewhere. I always hope to capture some truth and feeling in my pieces as I know how majestic it is for an observer when you get it right. Gazing at my friend Jonathan

Yeo's portraits makes my head spin as he seems to reveal the true person behind the picture. It's as though I'm able to connect with that individual, often famous people I've never met, in a way I might not be able to with a photograph. As a huge ballet fan, I also adore getting lost in Degas' works of elegant dancers *en pointe*. I can sense the movement and feel the light, ethereal energy of his subjects.

Art can take us away from the moment and our busy head of ideas and worries and connect us with something deeper and truer. The same goes for poetry. I rarely cry reading books but poetry gets me. Good poetry hits my heart and gives way to a huge exhale. My friend Sarah Merry (best name, I know!) recently gifted me a poetry book by Donna Ashworth which resonated in so many ways. The poem 'Remember Her?', an ode to connecting with our inner child who wants us to take risks and have fun, made me softer, kinder to myself, and gave me permission to relax for a minute. It opened me up and allowed me to look at who I had become and why. It brought up questions and regrets but mostly a connection with all other humans living life and trying to make sense of it all.

Towering Tulips

Another obvious way to tap into that something that is bigger is through nature – the pure beauty and power of nature, which we often overlook as we race through Netflix, or leisurely scroll through Instagram. Our ignorance of the beauty around us is at times extreme. We've been led to believe that humans create everything without noticing the tiny seeds that are naturally scattered by plants, flowers and birds each year. We put all focus and importance on the latest model of smartphone and celebrate its arrival while forgetting to applaud the trees and flowers that create brand-new beauty each season without thanks. Our belief system praises humans for their innovation without honouring what came before us: Nature. Yet each spring daffodils explode in canary yellow, their orange crowns reaching for the sun. Did you, or I, use our brains to think these flowers out of the ground? Nope. Their own unique cycle determined their yearly arrival back into our parks and back gardens without fuss. Is nature powered by the internet? No. If anything, humans are single-handedly destroying what should be naturally evolving each year.

During the writing of this book, I have been keen to tune in to the ever-present beauty of nature rather than staying glued to my phone. Last week, on a spring afternoon, I took a stroll through my nearby park where the amazing local gardeners had planted the most sensational, vibrant flowers in patterned rows in neat beds. The park was teeming with families; ice creams dribbling down kids' hands and parents basking in the afternoon sun, chatting to friends close by. Nobody seemed to be paying attention to the flowers. I walked past one circular bed of white tulips (and this is where it gets weird) and I felt them. This feeling had little cognitive resonance; it was an entirely visceral experience that is hard to articulate. In that second I knew that those tulips, lit up by the sun, were beaming love and light and that somehow they felt very proud about it. They glowed like dimly lit lightbulbs, gently swaying in the breeze. They weren't bothered at all that the nearby humans were just scurrying around them, more intently focused on their hot coffees and conversation; they were so happy to be standing tall in their flowerbeds, petals held out like arms reaching up to the sun. It's difficult to explain this feeling but I knew with all my heart that they felt proud and so happy to be delivering so much beauty even if we were missing it in the rush of everyday life.

I carried on and walked past another flowerbed; this time, red tulips. The same... their velvety petals held aloft with such dignity, offering up miraculous beauty with love and energy. I felt the life within them and the pride they held in just simply being. My heart swelled and I felt a little teary. This whole experience blew me away. I wished in that moment that everyone in the park could feel this too. Now it's all there for the taking whenever we want it, but we do need to ensure we look after it so it's still there for us to enjoy and respect in the future.

Biggest Love Affair

Kitten Grayson runs a London- and Somerset-based floral studio and has a profound love of flowers and plants. From a very young age she was drawn to nature. When she was a small child she would hear the sounds of the plants and trees around her and see colours around leaves. Still to this day Kitten can clearly see such vibrant colours and light when she looks at plants and trees. All throughout school she struggled and spent lessons looking out of the windows watching the trees sway in the breeze, totally captivated. Every day after school Kitten would spend her time exploring the farmland she grew up on. Building dens near the brooks and wandering with her siblings, she found great peace whenever she was out in nature. She knows that the line of work she is in was the only path for her in life.

Kitten also speaks of times when nature has healed her in tough situations. In times where she's felt like she didn't fit in, nature has always brought her back to feeling OK, she says, describing her relationship with nature as her biggest love affair, a deep love that helps her every day. Getting to work with nature every day brings her so much joy as she takes time to work with nature's intelligence. She asks the plants and flowers and landscapes she works with what they need from her. Kitten says that having a relationship with nature is essential to her wellbeing. Working with nature and planting flowers and sowing the seeds gives Kitten a direct connection to life and energy. She goes into a place of pure happiness and unrivalled bliss when working with nature and says it's her addiction. Having a dialogue with nature is key to feeling a deep sense of happiness and calm. She says: 'It's an ever-growing, ever-evolving relationship that can help us learn to care for our planet and learn to care for each other.'

I love how Kitten describes her ongoing conversation with nature and feel deeply inspired to nurture my own dialogue with the plants and flowers in my home. I'm no Charlie Dimmock but I do have the odd house plant that I like to care for. Just the other day I noticed my indoor fig tree had leaves covered in dust, so I gently wiped them clean and spoke to the tree as I did so. **There are so many lessons we can learn from nature every single day,** which help us find meaning and connection in life and help to enrich our soul.

The Big Disconnect

The stark reality is often ignored but painfully obvious. We have lost nearly all connection with nature. Of course, many cultures and collectives the world over still prioritise their relationship with the Earth and environment around them above all else, but in the modern world I fear that not many give it even a second's thought. We see the planet as one big resource and not as something to respect and honour for every gift served up. We assume we will always have supermarkets full of food and oceans full of fish, even if we batter the natural cycles currently in place. I have made valid attempts to rectify my own sorrow around this fact, having a plant-based lifestyle and recycling and using recycled products where I can, but it's still an unsustainable lifestyle and I know it's not enough. These efforts are tiny and insignificant when looking at the much bigger picture. We know how much we are polluting and damaging our planet from all the stats, documentaries and reports on climate change, over-fished seas and the plastic crisis, but what can we do? At times we feel hopeless and overwhelmed as the problems seem insurmountable, with governments not doing enough.

I held the school of thought that action should come exclusively from the top, until I spoke with David Katz who runs the amazing organisation, Plastic Bank. His global banks, which are based in countries where deprivation is rampant, allow individuals living under the poverty line to collect and hand in ocean or littered plastic in exchange for an income, often schooling too. He offered up two game-changing gems for me. The first that until we fix the problem of poverty, we cannot fix the environmental issues we see around us; and, second, that the change has to come from the individual. We can vote with our money. So, if we stop buying drinks in plastic bottles, the companies have no other choice but to change the way they distribute their products. If we question large supermarket chains in our local high street and ask why they don't sell fruit in packaging that is recyclable or, better still, excluding plastic, then they'll be forced into making positive changes.

I felt empowered speaking to David about these terrifying issues and have made a few more environmentally friendly and economically pleasing changes. I have discovered websites like My Green Pod where you can find many products that are helping to create this change. My new best friend is my surface spray bottle-for-life, for which I buy refills that come in little recycled-paper sachets. I pour in the refill, top it up with water and then I can spritz my kitchen worktop until my heart is content.

I will never have to buy another large plastic bottle of surface cleaner ever again and it's working out much more cost-effective too. Often, better choices for the environment seem to be exclusively for those who can afford them, but if you look around you'll see many companies wanting to create accessible, fairly priced, positive change. I don't believe I can have an integrated spiritual connection to the earth around me if I'm simultaneously making decisions that harm it. I'm by no means perfect: I've had several new phones over the years that I use a lot for work and leisure; I order things online that need delivering and there is food waste in my house, to name but a few things I know are not helping, but I'm enjoying looking about for small swaps I can make to ensure I'm respecting the relationship I have with the planet we live on. We cannot let the guilt we might feel for our current lifestyles stop us looking for new solutions.

Laughter Out Loud

One of the easiest ways for us to channel and feel the joy and connectedness of life is to laugh. Think back to the last time you clutched your sides and silently gasped for air due to rolls of laughter. It's the best feeling. After having two kids it's also usually tinged with worry that I'll piss myself, but do not concern yourself with that now. Maybe, thinking back to Donna's section of the book, laughter could even be classed as a prayer. When you are genuinely laughing it's almost impossible to think of anything else or tense your physical body. You go limp like a wet chip and can't hold your own weight. Bliss! Better than any massage.

Yesterday my husband had to film himself for an audition tape so I was assigned the role of cameraperson and instructed not to laugh. Well, we all know what happened there. Jesse had to manoeuvre around our furniture and then pretend he had bumped into an identical twin with a look of surprise and glee slapped on his face. I was poised, ready, taking my role very seriously. I even did a countdown backwards from five, using my hands to notify him when to start. Such a pro. We made it to about eight seconds of the first take before we were both lying on the sofa crying tears of laughter. Pure joy. All troubles removed from brain. All comparison and self-loathing obsolete. We both became channels for total joy in that silly moment.

You'll hear most wise people, sages, thought leaders and spiritual types say that we are not to take life too seriously and I know it's something I need to address. Too often I get caught up in the most serious perception of life and ignore the potential for laughter. Looking for humour in our days is surely a short cut to not taking ourselves or life too seriously. Now, I'm all for that.

Liberation

Living a spiritual life can be whatever you want it to be. You can connect and have a relationship with life in whatever way you choose, but hopefully the wise souls in this book have given you some new ideas too. As I said right at the start of this exploration, writing this book has changed my life. Although fastidiously interested in spirituality since my childhood, this process has acted as a catalyst to look at life from a totally different angle. It's given me the opportunity to dig deeper and peel back more layers to help dismantle my self-limiting thoughts and to have a clearer relationship with my own ego. One big change in this department has been to slowly eradicate the belief that I'm undeserving of good stuff, or that positive outcomes aren't possible without a struggle. I'm still halfway up the curve on this one, learning, surrendering and aiming for liberation, but I'm in no massive rush. It just feels liberating to be on that path rather than stuck where I was before, in a system of beliefs that were holding me back and ruining dynamics and relationships. **What self-limiting beliefs have you been able to let go of, or maybe just take a closer look at, while reading this book?**

I've incorporated so many of the practices, from the wise folk in this book, daily. I do Donna's three-part prayer every night before I drift off. I watch my negative thoughts like a hungry hawk, as advised by Rhonda. I'm constantly in awe of nature and its cycles thanks to Paula and Kitten, and am willing to meet my ego daily as prescribed by Jambo. None of this is easy, but it's essential. Every step requires some discipline and a willingness to let go of the parts of our story we are comfy with, even when painful. Staying stagnant and trapped, as awful as that is, is easy. It's so much harder to make changes. Sometimes it feels too hard to change our behaviour or thought processes. We are so used to feeling a certain way that we forget there are other options. There is no pressure on my part with this one; make changes or choose not to, it's up to us how deep we go in this one beautiful life.

This relates to another lesson I've learned during the writing of this book – there is no right or wrong, or one person more spiritual than the other. There is no scorecard for benevolence and compliance when walking down this path. If we want to nurture our souls and feel a deep connection with life, we can't be constantly expecting gifts from the universe or the outcomes that we've specifically asked for. It's not a game of reward for good behaviour from a mythical being in the sky. This is about a true connection with life; **a willingness to show up and keep trying**; to see difficulties and pain as a chance to grow and gain wisdom, and to not be scared of more lessons in the future. Aligning with spirituality is not about becoming pure or perfect, it's about embracing the chaotic, messy, flawed parts of human life and learning from it all. I know that in the future I'll make mistakes, do regrettable things, act foolishly, have road rage, feel impatient when my kids won't put their shoes on and so on. Committing to this life doesn't mean I can eradicate my fallible parts; it just means I won't berate myself quite so much for being fallible in the first place.

Stay Mystic

My hope for this book wasn't to try to demystify the mystic. Even the most spiritually soaked, tuned in, wise mind will struggle to explain the secrets and mysteries of the universe and life, and that's what makes it all so delicious. I wasn't hoping to give you solid answers on how the magic of life and the universe operate, because that would take the fun out of it. The beauty is in the mystery.

If you started out as a Cynical Cyril at the beginning of this book, I hope you realise that talking about spirituality does not mean you have to consult a crystal ball before choosing your dinner, or use a rose quartz tampon to enlighten yourself, it's simply about *connection*. When we are disconnected, we feel bleak, hopeless, helpless and dull. **Connection is where all the meaning lives.** We can experience things in life yet be totally disconnected, but when we engage with life and the universe around us fully, that's where we'll be able to access the missing puzzle piece – meaning.

I most definitely want a life with meaning. One where I can examine my own mistakes and see the point of them. One where I can break apart pain to see the wisdom inside. One where I can see pure beauty and bliss in the simple, everyday stuff. One where I know I'm nurturing my soul as well as my mind and body. For that I need to put my attention on all that is bigger than me – that beautiful, mystical, at times inexplicable something that is bigger. So big that our minds cannot compute its size. So big that its abundance isn't always obvious to us. So big that it doesn't need to shout or scare us, even when we forget to feel humble and give it respect. So big that we take it for granted and miss the everyday magic happening all around. So big yet also within our human body. The love, energy and abundance of it all, outside of us and within. It doesn't matter what lexicon we adhere to, meaning and connection are available to us all.

As we've discovered, connection can be felt with love, awareness and communication, and can be found in the ordinary, every day. Spirituality is a promise to love. To love ourselves and the planet. It's a promise to be aware. To be aware of ourselves, others and the planet. It's a promise to communicate. To communicate with ourselves, others, the planet and with that something that is bigger than us. It's a promise I'm willing to stick to.

GOING DEEPER

Further reading and information

Part 1: LOVE
Shamans
Wendy Mandy, wendymandy.uk
Gerad Kite, geradkite.com
@geradkite dear friend, practices five element acupuncture
'Under The Skin', Russell Brand, Luminary Podcasts;
Revelation, Connecting with the Sacred in Everyday Life,
    Russell Brand, Audible Originals
@russellbrand
Let It Go, Rebecca Dennis, Happy Place Books
@breathing.tree
First, We Make the Beast Beautiful, Sarah Wilson, Corgi Books
@_sarahwilson_
You Can Heal Your Life; *The Power Within You*; *Heal Your Body*,
    Louise Hay, Hay House
@louise_hay_affirmations

Meditation and yoga
Headspace.com @headspace
Jambo Truong, Jambodragon.com
@jambodragon
'Daily Breath with Deepak Chopra', Deepak Chopra
@deepakchopra
The Power of Now, A Spiritual Guide to Enlightenment,
     Eckhart Tolle, Yellow Kite
A New Earth, Eckhart Tolle, Penguin
@eckharttolle
A Monk's Guide to Happiness, Meditation in the 21st Century,
     Gelong Thubten, Yellow Kite
@gelongthubten
Emeraldandtiger.com, Jasmin Harsono
@emeraldandtiger and @breathe__love

The Law of Attraction
The Secret; The Greatest Secret, Rhonda Byrne, Simon &
     Schuster
@rhondabyrne_thesecret
F**k It Therapy: The Profane Way to Profound Happiness,
     John C. Parkin, Hay House
The Little Book of Hygge; *The Little Book of Lykke* ; *The Art of
     Making Memories*, Meik Wiking, Penguin Life
@meikwiking

Part 2: AWARENESS
Energy
Giselle La Pompe-Moore, gisellelpm.com
@gisellelpm
The Reiki Association, reikiassociation.net
*Speak Your Truth, Connecting with your Inner Truth and Learning
     to Find Your Voice*, Fearne Cotton, Orion Spring

Becoming Supernatural, How Common People are Doing the
Uncommon, Dr Joe Dispenza, Hay House
@drjoedispenza
Craig David craigdavid.com
@craigdavid
Kim Eng, presencethroughmovement.com
The Divine Matrix by Gregg Braden

Enneagrams
To Shake the Sleeping Self: A Quest for a Life with No Regret,
Jedidiah Jenkins, Rider
Spirit Junkie; The Universe Has You Back; Super Attractor; Happy
Days: The Guided Path from Trauma to Profound Freedom and
Inner Peace, Gabrielle Bernstein, Hay House
@gabbybernstein
Robert Holden, robertholden.com
@drrobert_holden

Astrology and Planetary Movement
Paula Shaw, soulfulguiding.com
@soulfulguiding
Lunar Living, Working with the Magic of the Moon Cycles,
Kirsty Gallagher, Yellow Kite
@kirsty_gallagher_

Part 3: COMMUNICATION
Prayer
Donna Lancaster, deepeningintolife.com and
thebridgeretreat.com
'Love(d)', Pinstripe Films, Amazon Prime
@donnalancs

Signs

Jane Goodall, janegoodall.org

@drjanegoodallinst

Celeste Barber

@celestebarber

Bryony Gordon

@bryonygordon and @mentalhealthmates

How to Fail: Everything I've Learned from Things Going Wrong,
Elizabeth Day, Fourth Estate

'How to Fail' podcast

@elizabday

Annie Price

'Out of the Ashes', BBC Three

@anniejprice and @wellwomanclub

Good Vibes, Good Life; Healing is the New High, Vex King,
Hay House

@vexking

Rising Strong; Braving The Wilderness; Daring Greatly, Brené
Brown, Vermilion and Penguin Life

@brenebrown

Alex Bedoya, beoneagain.com

@ayebedoya

Mediums and Intuition

*After: A Doctor Explores What Near-Death Experiences reveal
About Life and Beyond,* Dr Bruce Greyson, Bantam Press

Shine On, David Ditchfield, O-Books

shineonthestory.com

@david_ditchfield

Yvonne Williams, yvonne-williams.com

Part 4: SOMETHING BIGGER EVERY DAY
'What Drives Us', Dave Grohl, Roswell Films and Therapy
    Studios, Amazon Prime
'Shore', Fleet Foxes, Anti Records
The Boy, The Mole, The Fox and The Horse, Charlie Mackesy,
    Ebury Press
@charliemackesy
Jonathan Yeo, jonathanyeo.com
@jonathanyeo
'Remember Her?', *The Right Words*, Donna Ashworth,
    Published by Author
@donnaashworthwords and donnaashworth.com
Kitten Grayson, kittygrayson.com
@kittygraysonflowers

A few more good books

*Radical Compassion: Learning to Love Yourself and Your World
    with the Practice of RAIN*, Tara Brach, Rider
Inward, Yung Pueblo, Andrews McMeel Publishing
The Monk Who Sold His Ferrari, Robin Sharma, HarperThorsons
The Little Guide Book: Bringing the Spirit into the Body, Bonny
    Kinloch, CreateSpace Independent Publishing
*Everyday Grace: Having Hope, Finding Forgiveness and Making
    Miracles*, Marianne Williamson, Bantam Books
Rebirthing: Freedom from your Past, Deike Begg, North Atlantic
    Books

THANK YOUS

I have so much to be grateful for at this point. At the end of this mystic adventure I'm floored with gratitude that I've had the time, space and opportunity to write this book.

First up I would like to thank all at Ebury for going with my slightly out-of-the-box idea. Lizzy, Anna, Ellie, Joel and Laura, thank you for letting me freely explore this subject and move my writing into a completely new and exciting area. I felt as free as a bird throughout the process and surely nothing tastes as good as freedom. Thank you to Lorraine, Belinda and Jennifer for your editorial attention to detail. Thank you to Heike Schüssler for designing such a beautifully ethereal cover that very much alludes to that something bigger. It's stunning and shiny and makes me feel calm just looking at it. Thank you to Loulou and Serena at Ebury and Jonathan at Seagull Design for turning the words and design into a beautiful printed book.

Amanda Harris, book agent of dreams, what would I do without you? An ever-present force pushing me to write in the right direction. I'm also incredibly proud of what we are building with Happy Place Books where we get to celebrate other voices and stories.

Holly Bott at YMU Group, thank you for always returning my stupidly long voice notes and entertaining my worries; there are always worries. Sarah White at YMU Group, thank you for organising my working life so I can stick to being creative and mess around doing rituals in my garden. Mary Bekhait at YMU Group, thank you for always understanding the Happy Place mission and for spotting opportunities for us to reach new audiences and try new things. Holly, Sarah and Mary, I'm so lucky to have you three ladies helping me move forward and grow in my Happy Place mission.

Thank you so much to each of the wise souls who were willing to participate in this book. Some who I have known for years and others who turned up like a spiritual bus at the right time. I have learned from you, basked in your wisdom and feel very happy to know you. Without you, this book would just be weird stories about me spotting white feathers and buying chunks of jade.

Thank you so much to Mumma Cotton for getting me on to this stuff in the first place. Without your unrivalled passion for looking at the hugeness of life and all its possibilities, I wouldn't be writing this book today. Dad, thanks to your no-nonsense, potentially eye-rolling wit; I have approached this project with dutiful caution at times (saying that you are one hell of a psychic guy – remember that time you guessed I was going to call my first-born Rex!). Thank you brother Jamie for your succinct one-liners that you're able to recite verbatim from Mr Tolle when the going gets tough.

Thank you to my husband Jesse – who luckily shares the same interest and intrigue when it comes to spirituality – for doing the school run when I had writing and edits to do and for always sounding excited when I was working on a juicy section of the book.

Rex, Honey, Arthur and Lola, thanks for just being you. Watching you all grow up is one of life's biggest treats and provides enough lessons (sometimes in exhausting, frustrating forms) for me to keep digging deeper, with my heart out front.

Thank YOU for picking up this book. I SOOO hope this book has helped in some way. Maybe you've had epiphanies, maybe you feel you know yourself better, or are able to let go a little more, but more than anything I hope you've experienced some magic. It's out there, everywhere, you just have to be open to it.

Lastly thank you to that something that is Bigger Than Us. Thank you for the words that sometimes poured out of me from somewhere else entirely. Thank you for the signs to keep going with this project and the signs that keep me hopeful in life. This book has cemented my belief in something bigger which has led to my feeling even more excited about life and all its mystery. This book is one long love letter to that something bigger that we can all tap into. **My thanks is as big as it gets.**